Civil Society, Civil Religion

B

Civil Society, Civil Religion

Andrew Shanks

BLACKWELL
Oxford UK & Cambridge USA

Copyright © Andrew Shanks 1995

The right of Andrew Shanks to be identified as author of this work has been asserted in accordance with the Copyright, Designs and Patents Act 1988.

First published 1995

2 4 6 8 10 9 7 5 3 1

Blackwell Publishers Ltd
108 Cowley Road
Oxford OX4 1JF
UK

Blackwell Publishers Inc.
238 Main Street
Cambridge, Massachusetts 02142
USA

British Library Cataloguing in Publication Data

A CIP catalogue record for this book is available from the British Library.

Library of Congress Cataloging-in-Publication Data
Shanks, Andrew.
    Civil society, civil religion / Andrew Shanks.
        p.   cm.
    Includes index.
    ISBN 0–631–19758–3 (alk. paper). – ISBN 0–631–19759–1 (pbk.: alk. paper)
    1. Christianity and politics.   2. Liberation theology.   3. Theology—
    Methodology.   I. Title.
BR115.P7S396 1995   94–45126
261.7–dc20   CIP

Typeset in 10/12 pt Bembo
by Pure Tech Corporation, Pondicherry, India
Printed in Great Britain by Hartnolls Ltd, Bodmin, Cornwall

This book is printed on acid-free paper.

For Liam

Völker der Erde
. . . die ihr in die Sprachverwirrung steigt
wie in Bienenkörbe,
um im Süßen zu stechen
und gestochen zu werden –

Völker der Erde,
zerstöret nicht das Weltall der Worte,
zerschneidet nicht mit dem Messern des Hasses
den Laut, der mit dem Atem zugleich geboren wurde.

Völker der Erde,
O daß nicht Einer Tod meine, wenn er Leben sagt –
und nicht Einer Blut, wenn er Wiege spricht –

Völker der Erde,
lasset die Worte an ihrer Quelle,
denn sie sind es, die die Horizonte
in die wahren Himmel rücken können . . .

Nelly Sachs, *Sternverdunkelung*, 1949

Contents

viii   *Contents*

Preface

I present the following as a memorial to the toil of innumerable laundresses. They helped make it possible.

Or, more particularly, it was the starch they used for cotton items; and the cheap little muslin 'dolly bags' of blue fabric whitener, with wooden handles, to be dipped into the rinsing water. Reckitts' laundry products were not only completely dominant market-leaders in Britain during the Victorian era, they were also a major British export. (In 1851 the Hull-based manufacturers were able to boast that they supplied, amongst others, the Imperial Laundries of their Majesties the Emperor of France and the Emperor of All the Russias.) Maurice Reckitt, born in 1888, was the great-grandson of the firm's founder and, as a result, inherited a fortune. Towards the end of his life, in 1971, he put a large part of that fortune into the Christendom Trust, which he founded for the general purpose of stimulating Christian reflection on issues of social ethics. And over the past three years I have been one of the beneficiaries, as M. B. Reckitt Teaching Fellow in the Department of Religious Studies at Lancaster University.

'My objection to our leisured classes', Reckitt once wrote, 'is that they make so poor a study – and therefore a use – of that in which they are presumed to specialize', namely their leisure. He himself was always a gentleman of leisure, and in many ways an exemplary one. He was, for instance, a great devotee of ballroom dancing and of amateur dramatics. Throughout the 1920s he combined his summer holidays with producing a popular 'ragtime' review, with scripts largely written by himself, at the Palace Theatre in the Swiss resort of Villars-sur-Ollon. He was a passionate croquet player (national champion in 1935, representing England in Test Matches against Australia in 1937 and again in 1956, president of the

Croquet Association 1967–75). His books on the subject are, I gather, major contributions to croquet literature.

The rest of his life he devoted to the cause of what he liked to call 'Christian sociology', by which he meant the theoretical articulation of a non-partisan form of socialism: one embedded in the life of the church rather than in that of any political party, and very directly grounded in Christian faith.

He was perhaps, in certain respects, a somewhat dilettante visionary. 'The trouble with you, Maurice,' a friend remarked, 'is that you always look on life through the steam-heated windows of a wagon-lit.' But he was a visionary, nevertheless. A prolific writer, he also became the chief moving spirit behind the Christendom Group and its journal. We find here an off-shoot of that admirable tradition of Anglo-Catholic social concern which stems from F. D. Maurice; decisively shaped by the successive influences, first of the English 'guild socialist' tradition (represented by such figures as A. R. Orage, S. G. Hobson and G. D. H. Cole), and then of Major C. H. Douglas's 'social credit' doctrine. The Group's title also captures its romantic, Chestertonian nostalgia for certain aspects of the European Middle Ages: in particular the church-centredness of the culture of that period, and its relative freedom from capitalist 'plutocracy'.

In so far as it is still possible in the 1990s, my immediate predecessor here at Lancaster, John Milbank, is I think a genuine Christendom-ite. I am afraid to say that I am rather less so: as will at once become apparent.

Nevertheless, I certainly am grateful to have been given the opportunity of working, alongside such good colleagues, in such a stimulatingly *un*-theological Department as this. The original Christendom Group was once described, I do not know with how much justice, as 'the rudest group in the Church of England'. The present Christendom Trustees are animated by an altogether kinder spirit. They have indeed been very generous to me.

Long may they flourish!

ANDREW SHANKS
Hornby

Introduction

This is – primarily – a work of civil theology. A sketch. It can only be a sketch, because it is an attempt to outline the broad scope of a discipline of thought which, I think, remains sadly underdeveloped.

Civil theology has to do with the interplay between politics and religion. So does 'political theology' or 'liberation theology'. These, however, are generally names for a particular form of confessionally Christian theology. ('Confessional' is often used as a term for denominational theology within Christendom. Here I simply mean: theology whose chief aim is to affirm what is distinctive about Christianity – or indeed any other faith – in whatever denominational form.) 'Civil theology' is something else. It is a type of thinking which, in a Christian culture, emerges out of the history of Christian confessional theology; which still very largely has to do with a reflection on that history; and which, to be sure, by no means precludes a continuing Christian faith – but which, in its pure form, is nevertheless no longer premissed on such faith.

Thus, civil theology and confessional theology represent two radically contrasting attitudes to history. All theology (as I use the term) is essentially constituted as a strategy for the interpretation of history: this is how it differs from mythic thinking on the one hand, and unhistoric philosophy of religion on the other. It is the interpretation of revelation: by which I mean, *any* historical event, of whatever sort, which is seen to compel a critical re-evaluation of hitherto received notions of God. Both civil theology and confessional theology have this much in common. The difference lies simply in the angle of vision. It is not so much a question of what the ultimate court of appeal is: confessional theology is no less confessional when it takes on an 'apologetic' form, appealing to criteria of 'natural' reason, than when it makes a more dogmatic appeal to the data of authoritative tradition (Thomas Aquinas is just as much a confessional theologian as Karl Barth, say.) But, rather, it is a question of what ultimate loyalties govern the argument. Confessional theology is governed, above all, by the theologian's loyalty to his or her own faith community. Civil theology is not.

One might perhaps define civil theology as the theory proper to the practice of civil religion. I should immediately insist, though, that when I use this term, 'civil religion', I do not mean by it what Rousseau meant, who first coined the term: as Rousseau describes it in the concluding chapter of *The Social Contract*, 'civil religion' appears as a minimal deistic cult, exclusively devoted to upholding the sacredness of the legitimate political order. That is not the point at all. And neither am I using the term in quite the same sense as Robert Bellah and those who have followed him, when they speak in particular of 'American civil religion'. Instead, I am trying to imagine a possibility that has never yet been fully actualized. 'Civil religion' is not so much a distinct religion in itself as an aspect of religious practice; not necessarily in competition with confessional traditions, but infusing them, and overlapping their boundaries. Civil theology, in the sense that I intend here, does not preclude loyalty to one's confessional tradition, to one's church or whatever. But, as I have said, it is *governed* by another loyalty – one which is both broader and narrower – cutting across the confessional sort: in effect, a loyalty to whatever makes for genuine openness within the surrounding political culture.

And this then leads to a differing narrative content. All religion is about the definition of social identity – but which identity? The difference is that confessional religion (i.e. religion shaped by confessional theology) takes shape as a meditation on the identity deriving from the worshippers' membership within the worshipping community itself. And its narratives, therefore, are the narratives of that community: the tale of its foundation, the history of its development, the biographies of its leaders and saints. Whereas, by contrast, civil religion is a meditation – within the context of otherwise confessional worship – on the worshippers' other identity as *citizens*. In a religiously homogeneous political culture the distinction may not be all that marked. But civil religion flourishes in a pluralistic world, where citizenship has been most widely extended. There too, of course, one's confessional identity contributes to one's identity as a citizen; but the latter identity is altogether more complex. And the stories that make up the narrative content of civil religion are those that are judged most urgently relevant to the formation of that more complex identity, in each of its various facets. It is, in principle, a discipline of coming to terms not only with one's confessional identity, but also with one's class identity, one's national identity, one's racial identity; with the whole historical burden of those identities, all that they morally imply, how they have to do with God.

What interests me, in other words, is the potential for religion to operate as a means of appropriating the past – generally. It is obvious how destructive unhealed communal memories are. That is: when past injustices are remembered only by the victims, not by the perpetrators; and are therefore remembered with all the more bitterness. Or when memories of guilt, unbalanced by any genuine source of pride, become intolerable. Such haunting recollections are perhaps the chief source of political violence, and of war. And, plainly, religious worship does at least provide a certain framework for the sort of conscientious commemoration that is called for in this regard: the potential context for a community to work through its most traumatic memories in a participative way, *sub specie aeternitatis* – and hence with a degree of calm objectivity, clearing the way to reconciliation. That is what would constitute a truly *critical* practice of civil religion: its narrative focus would be determined, not so much by the requirement of the confessional institutions to maintain their legitimacy, but far rather by the need for just such healing.

In actual practice, of course, the churches commemorate liturgically a whole array of events belonging to the remote past of cultures (ancient Israel, the Roman Empire) to which, outside that liturgical context, their members no longer relate in any real sense at all; whilst other, often far more immediately thought-provoking memories scarcely figure. How much time, for instance, do the churches in Britain, particularly, set aside each year to commemorate the Caribbean slave trade, and ponder its implications in the sight of God? None, or almost none. But (as the Rastafarians, who have abandoned the 'white' Christian God of their parents for that very reason, would remind us) this is a part of British history whose long-term moral consequences are by no means all finished and done with. And the same goes for the legacy of British imperialism in all its other forms too. Or when do they formally commemorate before God the various struggles that brought the British people their present civil liberties, such as these are? When do the churches commemorate the Highland Clearances and other similar experiences of cultural loss; or the history that produced the phenomenon of 'inner city' decay? There is in contemporary Britain just one major civil religious festival: namely, Remembrance Sunday. But Remembrance Sunday is a development out of Armistice Day, which began after the First World War at least in part as a celebration of what George Mosse has called the 'Myth of the War Experience': an attempt to revindicate the militaristic ethos that had helped lead to war, by transfiguring and heroizing the memory of the resultant carnage.[1] In the years following the Second World War this aspect of it has, thank God, to a considerable extent been modified. Even so, it still tends to remain quite a limited commemoration: dealing with the most terrible events of the twentieth century only as they appear from a single perspective, that of our victorious armies. In so far as it is indeed purged of every last remnant of the 'Myth', it clearly can have a vital therapeutic significance. And yet its very isolation from other, complementary modes of commemoration, reviewing the same events from other angles, I think inevitably distorts it. If the following argument has any practical implications, these must first and foremost include the desirability of a drastic revision of the liturgical calendar – to make room for what is missing here.

Civil religion of this sort would be a discipline for the healing of divisive memories, so as to render possible the forging of new bonds of solidarity. But the resulting solidarity, which civil religion both helps bring about and celebrates, is one that transcends the division between believer and non-believer, or theist and atheist. And at once, therefore, the obvious question arises: what then are the proper criteria for it? Inasmuch as it is not a solidarity on the basis of shared faith, they cannot actually, in the first instance, be theological criteria at all. Thus, civil theology also differs from confessional theology in the way it pushes back towards *pre*-theology. Or another name for what it pushes back towards might be '*hiero-logy*': a study of the properly sacred, in which questions of theology would for the time being remain bracketed; a mode of debate equally open to the adherents of all religious (or supposedly anti-'religious') traditions alike. Civil theology, one might say, is a form of thinking situated half way between confessional theology and 'civil hierology' – if such a thing could be imagined. This is primarily a work of civil theology. But, as a result, partly also a foray into the domain of civil hierology.

Civil theology is not, on the other hand, *necessarily* in any conflict with confessional theology. Obviously, there is a conflict to the extent that the latter claims exclusive access to the truth. Or again, to the extent that the demands of loyal membership in the community of confessional faith might be interpreted as tending to produce bad citizens. But these are not necessary conflicts. For confessional theology does not have to make such claims, nor does confessional faith have to have such effects.

And my basic argument here will be that there is a revelatory quality to certain aspects of twentieth-century experience which – if properly attended to – ought to compel confessional theology to drop its defences in this regard. If ever God has spoken, historically, this must be one of the clearest cases. Yet, far from reinforcing the importance of confessional orthodoxy, of any sort, the revelation in question tends on the contrary to relativize its pretensions.

Let me reiterate, straight away, that in advocating the virtues of a certain form of 'civil religion' I do not just mean what Bellah and others describe in the United States of America – even if it does have certain elements in common, sufficient (I hope) to justify the usage of the same term. Bellah is, indeed, probably the most significant pure civil theologian of recent times. But his 'civil religion' is only incidentally about the healing of memories. Like Rousseau's, it is first and foremost about conferring legitimacy on an enlightened system of *rule*. Bellah is a Durkheimian, concerned about the sacralization of good social order.

Thus, he begins his seminal article on the subject, first published in 1967, with an analysis of President Kennedy's Inaugural Address.[2] For it is in his Inaugural Address that the American president appears most clearly in his ritual role as high-priest. The patron saint of Bellah's civil theology is a president, Abraham Lincoln – himself, as Bellah puts it, America's 'greatest civil theologian': a man who, although he held aloof from any particular denominational loyalty, 'in the Second Inaugural Address . . . incorporated biblical symbolism more centrally into the civil religion than had ever been done before or would ever be done again in his great somber tragic vision of an unfaithful nation in need above all of charity and justice'.[3] And then, behind Lincoln, there stand the Founding Fathers of the republic: none of them, perhaps, great theologians; but respecters, at any rate, of moderate and enlightened religion, who also bear authoritative witness to a remarkable experience of civil creativity – within the ruling elite. In some of his later writings Bellah restates his argument as a defence of the 'republican' element in American political culture, against its 'liberalism'.[4] Once again, this is in the first instance a statement about what is ideally to expected from the government: genuine moral leadership, as opposed to a merely prudential strategy of mediating between freely competing pressure groups.

Bellah is no nationalist. Right from the outset he was invoking the values enshrined in American civil religion against the war in Vietnam. From the perspective of his 'republicanism' with a small 'r', the sort of nationalistic piety that pervaded the official rhetoric of the Nixon and Reagan administrations is paradoxically, surely, just 'liberalism' again, in ugly illiberal disguise. And what makes him such a stimulating advocate of the ultimate potential of American civil religion is just his increasingly sharp critique of how it actually operates. This is what differentiates him from his most notable immediate predecessor, Sidney Mead, whose critique is directed far more at the persistence of 'sectarianism' within the denominational churches, and who is relatively unconcerned with the actuality corresponding to his ideal deistic 'religion of the Republic', at the ritual level. In the spirit of Lincoln, Bellah writes of America as having betrayed its civil religious vocation. The vocation is real enough: it has progressively taken shape through what he calls 'three times of trial'. The first was the struggle for independence. The second was the civil war, and the ensuing struggle for 'the full institutionalization of democracy' in the country; the trauma which gave rise to what is potentially the most profound festival of the civil religion, Memorial Day. (Lloyd Warner's classic analysis of Memorial Day in a Massachusetts community, in the immediate post-war years, is a colourful evocation of just how rich an experience of civil solidarity this observance, with all its weeks and months of preparation, has at times become.[5]) The third time of trial began with the USA's emergence as a global superpower after 1945. And the essential issue in this third time of trial, Bellah argues, is precisely whether or not the American civil religion can, once and for all, emancipate itself from the idolatry of nationalism; so that it may develop to become the harbinger of, in his phrase, a genuine '*world* civil religion'.[6]

But (to say the least) in the light of recent experience the prospects for this do not look very bright. And even while he holds fast to the ideal, Bellah is driven to acknowledge that in reality 'the American civil religion is an empty and broken shell'.[7] The covenant has been broken.

He is not unconcerned with the healing of memories. It certainly matters to him that the historic sufferings of the Native Americans should be accorded all due respect in the story-telling of the civil religion. And he is anxious that it should so far as possible accommodate the African American perspective, as well. Notwithstanding Martin Luther King's tactical use of civil religious rhetoric as a means of communication with White America, however, the fact remains that this seems seldom to have been how it works in practice. Nor is it at all easy to see it developing that way. For there are two great obstacles – the actual difficulty of which, it seems to me, Bellah fails in the end fully to acknowledge. In the first place, there is the way in which this particular civil religion remains tied to its origins, as the spiritual pilgrimage of a supposedly 'chosen' people.[8] It came to birth in the years following the Great Awakening, the 1750s and 1760s, with the emergence then, within each of the various Protestant denominations, of a new sense of providential destiny embracing all the American colonies together, as a single people.[9] But that, of course, was just a generalization of the way in which the original Puritan colonists had seen themselves, as emigrants from the 'Egypt' of the Old World. As a crystallization of historic memory this sense of 'chosen-ness' is, effectively, restricted to those who are able in some more or less direct way to feel themselves to be the spiritual heirs of those first settlers.

And, secondly, there is a deep ambivalence attaching to the high-priestly role of the president, inasmuch as the president is not only the symbolic representative of the people as a whole – but also represents the ruling class.

In the case of a Confucian sage-ruler in ancient China – that is, in a culturally far more homogeneous world, without the modern vulgarities of rule-by-propaganda – this might not have mattered so much. But in modern conditions I think that a civil religion essentially orientated towards the healing of memories would look very different. It would not at all be about legitimating the power of those who run the state. Far rather, it would be an affirmation of the proper independence, from the state, of 'civil society'.

The revolutions of 1989 in Central Europe, and the collapse of the Soviet Empire, are often described as a triumph and a liberation of 'civil society'. This concept in fact re-entered political discourse in the late 1970s, as a term for that whole sphere of economic, cultural or political self-organization, independent of the state, which totalitarianism – or (to use Václav Havel's phrase for the stagnant system into which totalitarianism had by then declined) 'post-totalitarianism'[10] – by definition represses; but creative new elements of which were just beginning in that period to reappear, here and there in the communist bloc.

It is, however, a somewhat problematic term, due to the variety of different connotations with which it has been used historically.[11] Let us therefore briefly rehearse this history. When the revolutions of 1989 are described as a triumph of 'civil society' the term is being used in much the same sense as it was earlier used in the Marxist theory of Antonio Gramsci, involved as he was in the struggle against Fascist totalitarianism. That is the closest precedent – although for Gramsci the state to which civil society is potentially opposed is specifically identified with capitalism, and he shares the orthodox Marxist ideal of an eventual disappearance of the distinction between the two realms. Originally, on the other hand, through most of the eighteenth century 'civil society' was just a synonym for 'the state'. And this is also the sense in which Ferdinand Tönnies for instance at the end of the nineteenth century speaks of (civil) 'society', when he opposes it to 'community': for Tönnies, 'the state is itself society' – or, more exactly, it is 'the social reason which is implied in the concept of a reasonable thinking agent of society'.[12] Yet the dissident 'civil society' of totalitarian Central and Eastern Europe might precisely be described as a movement for the restoration of what Tönnies calls 'community'-spiritedness to public life. The second and contrary meaning of 'civil society', as designating an entity distinct from, and generally in tension with, 'the state', dates back to the later eighteenth century and the anti-statist polemic of people such as Thomas Paine, for whom it represents that realm of 'natural' harmony which excessive state intervention serves only to disrupt.[13] Alexis de Tocqueville, then, goes on to draw a three-fold distinction between 'civil society', 'political society' and 'the state', where 'civil society' refers simply to the realm of domestic and economic life, governed by private rather than public concerns. And Hegel distinguishes between the two realms of 'the family' and 'civil society' (corporate economic life and the legal system) – subordinating both of these ethically to 'the state', as that which includes but also transcends them. Hegel, however, simply does not discuss the sort of *civic* initiatives which belong to de Tocqueville's 'political society' or anti-totalitarian 'civil society'.

Let us distinguish between self-conscious and un-self-conscious civil society. It is the former which is explicitly anti-totalitarian in essence: the natural habitat for the conscientious intellectual as such – whereas in the latter intellectuality is valued only in the form of professional expertise, and tends to be policed by a system of patronage. Late twentieth-century self-conscious civil society has grown up in the space which for Hegel is occupied, primarily, just by corporations and churches; but has of course acquired a degree of organizational creativity that he, in his world, could not even dream of. It is, in general, what provides a space for politics independent both of the state and of political parties: the politics, that is, of groups which do not aspire to any direct share in state power, but which are as a result set free to raise the sort of awkward and unpopular questions it is in the interest of political parties, seeking votes, to avoid. This is by no means to deny that civil society is always also open to the ugliest, most unthinking expressions of intolerant prejudice. Yet its basic virtue at least arguably remains: that it is the environment in which these may most rationally be combated.

The 1980s witnessed an experiment in what is really a quite new form of politics in Europe: an attempt to build up a new internationalism 'from below'; a cultivation of international bonds of solidarity between groups, explicitly on the basis of their common participation in 'civil society' so defined, even where the most pressing issues for each of them are quite different. This began in the form of the movement for 'European Nuclear Disarmament' (END), as a coming together of peace movement people from the West with human-rights campaigners from the Soviet bloc. (After 1989 essentially the same project has been further taken up by the Helsinki Citizens Assembly, with a broader range of participants and a, naturally, much extended agenda.) END represented a direct bid to counter and unscramble the insidious logic of the Cold War; its programme was the bringing together of two groups whom the dynamics of the Cold War actually tended to set against each other: two groups with very different priorities, very different perspectives, and every reason – on the principle that 'my enemy's enemy is my friend' – for mutual mistrust. Herein, I think, lies its particular abiding historical significance. In a situation where the propaganda of the Warsaw Pact always made great play with the rhetoric of 'peace', just as the propaganda of NATO made great play with the propaganda of 'freedom' and 'human rights', here was an attempt to uphold the indissolubility in principle of both causes, in such a way as systematically to undercut the propaganda on either side. As the original END Appeal expressed it:

We must commence to act as if a united, neutral and pacific Europe already exists. We must learn to be loyal, not to 'East' or 'West', but to each other . . .

'we' in this case being, essentially, the citizen-activists of civil society, both 'East' and 'West'.

The movement in general (and Edward Thompson, as its most prominent representative, in particular) were of course denounced by the apologists of both establishments: just as the – in Thompson's phrase – 'only-two-sidesmen' of the Warsaw Pact accused END of being a front for the CIA, so the 'only-two-sidesmen' of NATO insinuated on the contrary that it was 'orchestrated' from Moscow, like the Western peace movement in general.[14] However, the obstacles which it faced were not only external. In 1985 Václav Havel wrote an essay which he entitled 'An Anatomy of Reticence': the 'reticence' in question being that of 'dissidents' in the Soviet bloc, in their encounters with representatives of the Western peace movement. Havel himself was by no means hostile to the peace movement. On the contrary, in one of his prison letters he writes,

If I were a West German . . . I would probably be involved at this time [February 1982] amongst many other things, in preventing the construction of the new runway at Frankfurt, in collecting signatures against the siting of Pershing II and Cruise missiles, and in voting for the

Green Party. I feel deep down inside that the long-haired young people who do this and whom I am able to see almost every day on television are my brothers and sisters.[15]

But in this essay he spells out what he sees as the main problems preventing an immediate straightforward alliance here: in the first place, the endless 'peace'-propaganda of the Warsaw Pact countries tended to induce a total allergy among those subjected to it. 'A citizen of our country simply starts to yawn whenever he hears the word "peace".'[16] Secondly, the way in which the official news media presented news of the Western peace demonstrations, as if they expressed a yearning for Soviet-style 'revolution', was also off-putting: 'In such circumstances, what do you expect the average citizen thinks? Simply that those Western peace fighters should get their wish – let them be punished for their naivety and their inability to learn!'.[17] Thirdly, in so far as as the 'dissidents' looked to the West for practical support, they were naturally very suspicious of anything that might smack of 'appeasement' towards Moscow (and Havel refers in this connection to Czech memories of 1938). Fourthly, in a country such as Czechoslovakia there was of course just no scope for 'unofficial' peace-campaigning. The primacy of human rights as an issue was imposed by the simple fact that, without them, no action on any other sort of issue was possible at all; so that, even when the independence of the Western peace movement from Soviet interests was in fact recognized, it still tended to appear to the upholders of Charter 77 or the activists of Solidarnosc very much as an enviable luxury, only available to the spoilt children of freedom. And, finally, the very idealism of the peace movement was suspect:

People in the West are, for various reasons, more afraid of war than we are. They are also significantly more free, they live more freely, and their opposition to armaments has no unacceptably serious consequences for them. Perhaps all of this makes the peace fighters on the other side seem, at least from here, a bit too earnest, perhaps even somewhat pathetic.[18]

Such reactions, Havel suggests, were further reinforced by a typically 'central European' spirit of anti-Utopian scepticism, self-deprecating irony, black humour – old traditions which the bitter experience of radical powerlessness had heavily accentuated.

Yet, notwithstanding all these difficulties, all these manifold possibilities for mutual misunderstanding, a real dialogue *was* begun; the dialogue to which Havel's essay itself belongs. It was a dialogue grounded on an underlying – I think one has to use the word – '*spiritual*' affinity between individuals, who basically lacked any other basis for solidarity. And this, then, raises the question: how the spirit dramatically illustrated, for example, here – the true spirit of a healthy civil society, clearly aware of its vocation as such – might best be preserved, nurtured, put to work, in the very different political circumstances of the future?

As Hegel so famously says, 'When philosophy paints its grey in grey, then has a shape of life grown old . . . The owl of Minerva spreads its wings only with the falling of the dusk.'[19] The grey in grey of this present text originates out of a retrospective meditation on that dialogue, now that its time is over. And what I want to argue is that – if civil society is to have the spiritual underpinning it requires, long-term – one of the things it calls for is, precisely, the contribution of a new form of civil religious culture.

Indeed, it seems to me that in a certain sense, today, the practice of prayer has acquired a whole new purpose. Namely: to operate as a *medicine against propaganda*. On both sides of the dialogue of the more critical elements of European civil society in the 1980s there was a group of people engaged in a struggle with established forces that were overwhelmingly better resourced to make propaganda; and hence, to a large extent, in a struggle against propaganda as such – with all its distortion and suppression of corporate memory. This is what Havel, for instance, meant when he opposed 'living in the truth' to 'living in a lie'. In the context of a culture of propaganda the role of religion must surely be transformed. And yet those with public responsibility for the conduct of religious life have, for the most part, not yet even begun to think about what this implies. The problem is that, inasmuch as we lack any proper practice of civil religion, the churches (and other religious bodies) leave the public shaping of our identity as citizens to the propagandists of the political parties, without really staking out the appropriate space to respond directly in another critical idiom of their own. To some extent they flirt with propaganda themselves. Or else their critical response remains altogether indirect.

By 'propaganda' I mean: the systematically co-ordinated use of all the available resources of the modern mass media to reinforce a single message or ideology, with the intention of reaching the widest possible audience. In this strict sense, therefore, propaganda did not exist before the nineteenth century; although, of course, there have always been its moral equivalents – mostly in religious form. Nevertheless, the problem it poses is, in a number of respects, essentially new. Obviously propaganda can serve some very desirable goals: raising funds for charity, say, or promoting health education. Not only does the commercial propaganda of the advertising industry, by stimulating appropriate consumer demand, help facilitate the continual self-adjustment of a growing market economy, but equally, if in the future ecological pressures force us to accept considerable restrictions on the way we are accustomed to behave as consumers, that too will presumably require the widespread use of propaganda techniques as a means of public education. And as for the uglier sorts of propaganda – the propaganda of racism and other forms of intolerance, the propaganda of militarism, or the propaganda which is the stock in trade of the pornography industry – do not these also need to be met by counter-propaganda? No doubt. But even so, however noble may be the aims towards which propaganda is directed, the fundamental problem remains.

In the first place, propaganda aims at shifting, directly, the behaviour of large masses of people – their behaviour, rather than their thinking. And this can only be done by latching on to, and trying to exploit, already existing assumptions and prejudices. The propagandist cannot hope to make people more thoughtful, or to call in question already crystallized opinions. Propaganda can superficially appear quite harmless, therefore, since of course we are not 'persuaded' by it; no one ever changes their mind as a result of it. Of course not. But it functions, instead, by means of the artful manipulation of stereotypes, which it thereby also tends to confirm. So it helps to *inhibit* people from ever changing their mind.

And secondly, political propaganda in particular – designed as it is to galvanize rather than to persuade – is most immediately effective the more it is able to approximate, in its world-view, to paranoia, whilst retaining a necessary modicum of credibility. In so far as the simple dictates of propaganda effectiveness are allowed to determine policy, the natural outcome is therefore fascism. That, one might say, is just what fascism is. In the religious domain, it is also what that peculiarly modern phenomenon, 'fundamentalism', is: a form of religious faith whose whole content has, in effect, come to be determined by the perceived need to maximize its propaganda impact. 'At least', Goebbels complacently noted in his diary on the evening of *Kristallnacht*, as the Jewish shops lay smashed and the synagogues were burning, 'no one can call us boring'. Effective propaganda needs to be exciting, and it certainly benefits by being kitsch: bartering heart-warming consolation for unquestioning loyalty, and projecting all evil on to some external source. Propaganda owes much, or most, of whatever dynamism it may possess to a collusion between propagandist and propagandee, systematically moulding reality into a set of convenient and simplifying semi-fictions; adapting reality so as not to have to adapt oneself. It may play upon feelings of guilt and shame, but only at the level where guilt is an internalizing of society's reproach against the individual, to the extent that the individual has in some way failed to live up to conventional expectations. For the purposes of propaganda, *corporate* sin by contrast is always what others have committed. To try and grasp the nature of sin at a deeper level – sin as (to quote Dorothee Sölle) 'collaboration and apathy',[20] collaboration in and apathy towards the corporate failings of one's own community, which one nevertheless still loves and to which one still remains loyal – is, at once, to step outside the world of propaganda and call it all in question. Christ, according to the gospel, 'bore our sins'. And one might propose it as a fundamental criterion for the spiritual health of any religious congregation, that one ask to what extent it too is ready to own, and so to 'bear', the sins of the various wider social categories of which it is part. Which is not just to say: 'We are all guilty' – for it is clear that that in itself is nothing more than a placatory gesture, tending to de-sensitize us to the responsibility proper to each individual. But rather: 'We will obstinately continue to love, and to own, this corrupt tradition, even whilst resolutely refusing to gloss over its corruption.' (Cultural traditions, like individuals, are not only to be loved when they are good.) That, in the first instance, is what it would take for a religion to have the sort of healing power which is required here. It would have to become a much more active medium than is usual for that most difficult and paradoxical thing: the anti-'political' politics of communal repentance and atonement, proper commemoration in that sense.

This would, pre-eminently, be a matter of good civil religion: where one deliberately drops one's defences against the critical voice of the outsider. In the un-civil world such voices are shut out by propaganda on the one hand, and by official secrecy on the other. And even when a whole system of evil for some reason collapses, so that the propaganda and the secrecy are abruptly swept away, and the whole reality of what has been going on is shockingly exposed for all to see, whether they wish to or not – as was the case in Germany after the collapse of the Third Reich, or as in Central and Eastern Europe following the downfall of communism – even then, old habits die hard. At once new forms of propaganda spring up, incorporating and exploiting the sense of horror people feel at the past; not, as regards those most directly responsible, in the spirit of 'there but for the grace of God go I'; but instead demonizing them, in order to attack others by association.[21] Good civil religion would surely represent the most direct antithesis to that.

Or again, let us return to the phenomenon of nuclear 'weapons': this is a still more difficult type of reality, in moral terms, to take to heart; in fact the most difficult of all, the issue in relation to which the inevitable mismatch between propaganda and reality is generally at its most extreme and grotesque. For, the experience of Hiroshima and Nagasaki notwithstanding, it remains so altogether beyond the grasp of our imagination; and they were in any case such small-scale affairs by comparison with what is threatened now.

Indeed, I put the word 'weapons' in inverted commas as a reminder that the very language in which the issue is usually discussed is itself problematic: already, it helps to gloss over the sheer enormity of what is involved. The gas ovens of the Nazi 'final solution' were not weapons, they were instruments of genocide. And in so far as nuclear deterrence deters, it does so by threatening not war but genocide. Weapons are designed as instruments of war; which, however atrocious it may be, is still not the same as indiscriminate massacre. But nuclear 'war' is also a misnomer, at any rate for most of the scenarios it is supposed to designate: it is most unlikely that the use of such so-called 'weapons' could be confined within the limits of that more familiar hell we call 'war'. We speak of 'the Bomb'; but in so doing we turn aside from the basic *qualitative* difference between nuclear 'warheads' and every other sort of implement of destruction we call a 'bomb', namely, the radioactivity they spread, the lingering poison in soil and air, the incalculable genetic after-effects on future generations. 'The unleashed power of the atom has changed everything except our modes of thinking, and we thus drift towards unparalleled catastrophes.'[22] Up to a point the same might be said of of all the new technologies of mass destruction: nuclear, chemical, biological and 'conventional' too. Language lags behind reality, and this is so even before one comes across the more deliberate use of cosy euphemism by the designers, the salesmen, the bureaucratic administrators of the nightmare. Even the language of anti-nuclear peace campaigners tends to fall into the same trap. This is not to prejudge what the proper answer may be to any of the complex short-term questions relating to government policy on disarmament. It is a criticism only of the manner, or the atmosphere, in which such questions are publicly debated. The problem with purely secular political discourse is that it tends to proceed on the assumption that we all know, or at least could know if we had sufficient information, what we are talking about. But in this case we do not; no matter how much information we may have, we cannot. We need – more urgently here, it seems to me, than in the face of any other worldly reality, just because of the unique difficulty of the matter – the extra potential linguistic/imaginative resources of a religious discipline, so that we may at least perhaps begin to apprehend what is actually involved; so that we may, in other words, at least begin to link what we know in our heads to an appropriate response of the heart. The threat is so unimaginable, we can not truly grasp what is at stake. We do not know what we say when we speak of these things – any more than we know what we say when we speak of 'God'. We are faced here with a 'mystery', with a blasphemous counter-mystery, as it were, to that of God, needing to be dealt with on the same level: that is to say, meditatively, liturgically, as well as politically – for the politics' sake.

I am by no means denying the propaganda quality of a good deal of the publicity put out by the anti-nuclear peace movement. But what concerns me is how the debate can be moved on from that level, on both sides. The propaganda battle over the question of nuclear disarmament, which raged so fiercely in the early 1980s, has been a battle fought out in terms of competing fears: fears of enemy aggression, fears of nuclear 'war' itself. Always, the argument is: 'we' are threatened – by 'them', by 'it'. The deeper moral issues – which are the issues raised by the way we threaten others – can scarcely be addressed at the level of propaganda (or only in passing, as part of an argument about the reasons why 'they' might feel compelled to threaten us in response). But, whilst the perfectly justifiable fear of destruction may be the beginning of peace-making, it would surely take a good deal more than fear alone, however intense it might become, to build the sort of genuinely new 'new world order' required, in order so far as possible to contain and to defuse the continuing danger of nuclear proliferation. The building of a truly peace-able 'new world order' clearly also depends on a fundamental re-evaluation of all the traditional ethical assumptions about loyalty and treason by which the old order has hitherto been upheld. Again, this would not mean disowning one's people: unlike certain forms of peace movement propaganda, it would not just be a matter of identifying one's cause with that of humanity in the abstract. On the contrary, the moral issues relating to the new technologies of mass destruction are, I think, only seriously addressable by the citizen of a state which possesses them in so far as one speaks from a position of the strongest possible identification with the 'we' which that state professes to represent. However, it obviously does mean a very different sort of identification from one which would glory in this 'weaponry' as a symbol of national status in the world. For the citizen of such a state, it must rather entail a sense of solidarity in sin. In the long run, if it is to do more than merely ride the tides of political fashion, the peace movement surely needs to be more than a movement grounded in enlightened fear; at the same time it also needs to be grounded in this sense of sin. And is not peace-making, on that moral basis, a job for the churches, and the other religious communities? I am not saying that it is only for them. But after all, like it or not, they still remain the most widely respected and authoritative institutions in our culture, when it comes to the public interpretation of what calls for repentance.

Yet in order for churches and other religious bodies to fulfil this role, they would first have to establish their right to do so by acknowledging, in the frankest of terms, their own historic failures. It is true – if one simply confines oneself, for example, to the part the churches played in relation to the peace movement of the 1980s – that the record is not entirely dishonourable: the various official church reports and pastoral letters on the issue that were published in that period, or at least some of them (such as the Pastoral Letter of the American Catholic bishops, or the Church of England's report, *The Church and the Bomb*[23]) undoubtedly did make a distinctive contribution to the debate, in the attempt they made to rise above the propaganda level. Church-related peace groups did do useful work in helping to raise awareness of the problem; in the Netherlands, especially, the Inter-Church Peace Council (IKV) provided much of the overall co-ordination for the movement; in West Germany the 1981 *Kirchentag* in Hamburg was a key event in the launching of the movement, and again the 1983 *Kirchentag* in Hanover was another major event in its development.

Even so, it is still, I think, disturbing how marginal to the general debate the properly ethical dimension of the matter was allowed to remain; how easily it was all reduced, time and again, to the level of party-political posturing and point-scoring; and how ineffectual the churches on the whole were in criticizing this. The extent to which the debate within the churches – when it got beyond the older, more general issue of absolute pacifism – tended in effect merely to reproduce that secular debate, with perhaps the fig leaf of a few scripture texts apologetically appended, is disturbing; disturbing, too, how little discussion there had been beforehand in the churches, and how swiftly the whole issue could then lapse from their collective consciousness again just as soon as the immediate crisis eased.

Why was this? We have here an issue belonging so completely to the present day, so alien in every way to the world that confessional Christian tradition looks back to. There could not, I think, be any clearer illustration of the need for the infusion of a far more vigorous and critical 'civil' element into the very innermost life of these churches: an urgently prioritized commemoration of the events that have brought us to this pass – as having all the subversive significance of the most primary sort of 'revelation'.

The problem, however, is that the Christian tradition in particular has always tended to harbour a deep-seated mistrust of civil religion; a mistrust often reinforced (as Bellah complains[24]) by looking only on its worst distortions, and contrasting these, not with the actual reality, but rather with the very highest ideals, of Christian particularism. So civil religion is sometimes spoken of as if it could *only* be an adjunct of government; or even tarred by association with that entirely different phenomenon, the sort of tribal religion whose most spectacular twentieth-century manifestation was the 'faith movement' of the Nazi 'German Christians' in the Third Reich.

This visceral hostility is, to be sure, quite understandable. For did not the church begin its life in bitter conflict with an established civil religion linked to a tyranny, that of imperial Rome? It is not only individuals whose minds may be enduringly scarred by a traumatic infancy or an unhappy childhood. The same may be equally true of the collective mind of a religious culture; and Christianity is perhaps the clearest of all examples.

The painful circumstances in which it came to birth have on the one hand left Christianity – centred as it is on the image of a crucified dissident – with a uniquely rich potential to articulate a critical vision for 'civil society'. Crucifixion was, after all, the ultimate instrument of the state for the repression of its critics. And yet, on the other hand, is it not precisely the still uneradicated imprint of those self-same circumstances which does most to prevent Christianity from fulfilling that potential? The pagan empire persecuted the early church in a somewhat absent-minded or sportive manner, cruelly but only sporadically, and therefore ineffectually. Such persecution did little to hinder the church's growth; it may even, by virtue of the inspirational heroism it evoked among its victims, have positively contributed to that growth. But the fact that it was ineffective at that level does not mean that it made no long-term difference to the church. On the contrary, it is clear that the persecution did leave a deep impression on the church's sense of its own identity, in the decisive formative period of its history. Three hundred years of being persecuted is not a good beginning for a community supposedly dedicated to the free-spirited pursuit of truth. Nietzsche makes this point in his characteristically unbuttoned way:

> That *martyrs* prove anything about the truth of a cause is so little true I would be disposed to deny that a martyr has ever had anything whatever to do with truth. In the tone with which a martyr throws his opinion at the world's head there is already expressed so low a degree of intellectual integrity, such *obtuseness* to the question of 'truth', that one never needs to refute a martyr . . .[25]

At all events, it is clear that a good deal of the distinctive character of traditional Christianity derives from the ferocity of its initial struggle for survival.

Thus, in order to survive and prosper, a community under continual threat needs two things. First, it has to be preoccupied with maintaining its unity. It has to have a clear structure of leadership, and it has to have a clear sense of its boundaries, of who is in and who is out, and of what is required of all its members, so that its enemies cannot play one group of them off against another. There were those within the early Christian communities, the Gnostics, who resisted the development of a (respectably patriarchal) clerical hierarchy for the church, grounded on the doctrine of apostolic succession; and who resisted the imposition of a clearly defined church orthodoxy, framed in universal creeds, based on a strictly limited canon of sacred scripture, expressed in a uniform liturgy, and entailing the excommunication of heretics. The orthodox church, despite all persecution, thrived. Gnosticism by contrast hardly needed to be persecuted; unpersecuted, it just faded away.

And then secondly, a persecuted community flourishes by being self-obsessed. It must glorify its martyrs – again, the Gnostics showed no interest in martyrdom as a vocation. It must also insist upon its own radical unique-ness, as early mainstream Christianity did in proclaiming so emphatically, '*extra ecclesiam nulla salus*'. It must turn its members' attention away from the concerns they share with their unbelieving neighbours; it must throw open a whole other world to them, more fascinating than the common one. But, obviously, both these instincts – both the preoccupation with unity and the other-worldly self-obsession – in so far as they persist, will militate power-fully against any form of civil religion, even the most friendly. For civil religion is intrinsically affirmative of pluralism, both among the various communities of a faith-tradition, in response to each one's different political setting, and also within them, as it promotes citizenly discussion. And its very essence is this-worldly.

The great villain of early church history for a political theologian like Jürgen Moltmann is Eusebius, the first great church historian – Constantine's ideologist – with his semi-Arian stress on the monarchical authority of God the Father as a heavenly model for the earthly authority of the Christian Emperor. What Eusebius records as the goal of divine providence at work in history, the conversion of the sovereign, was in reality, it is suggested, the great catastrophe from which the church has still not fully recovered, its seduction by worldly power; which it is the whole vocation of an authentic political theology to analyse and to combat.[26] But from the point of view of a critical civil theology the underlying problem runs far deeper than that. It is not so much a matter of the compromise here, simply as such; as if, in other words, it would have been better somehow to have clung to the more heroic spirit of earlier times; but, rather, it has to do with these neurotic defence mechanisms of the church. Which – far from being abandoned when, as a result of its rise to power, they had ceased to be necessary for sheer survival – instead just shifted in function, to serve the interests of imperial power; as providing a tightly organized potential agency of universal pacification. From this point of view there was no golden age. Long before they are systematically enshrined in the dualistic scheme of Augustine's two 'cities', the defence mechanisms can already be observed in operation, at least to some extent, right back in the New Testament church itself, the church of the first Pentecost.

I say that they were, and are, 'neurotic' – I mean that they became neurotic: a rigorous clinging to the early church tradition in all its particularism may well continue to be appropriate enough in circumstances where Christianity is again persecuted. In our situation, though – where the churches are not persecuted, and where indeed there is very little immediate danger of it, since they are so patently harmless – might not the inheritors of Christendom at least begin to reconsider whether they really need to be quite so attached to the consequences of that original defensiveness?

Indeed, there are I think excellent confessional-theological reasons for such a reconsideration. That is: if one wants to take seriously the universal-representative role of Christ as the crucified dissident – or the way in which the original symbolic significance of crucifixion in general, as a Roman institution with deterrent purposes, helps to determine the antithetical symbolic significance of the resurrection of the crucified. For the defence mechanisms clearly do get in the way here. A church institution on the defensive will gladly celebrate its own collective dissent, in so far as it has not yet attained cultural hegemony; yet it will never be so inclined to celebrate the courage of the conscientious individual dissident, simply for civil liberty's sake. And – as I have also argued, at greater length, elsewhere[27] – this reluctance surely does tend to result in a distinct moral impoverishment of its christology.

But the confessional theology of a non-defensive church would then, of itself, open out into the more inclusive solidarity-building debates of civil theology. (Themselves, in turn, opening out into the yet more inclusive ones of civil hierology, and so on.)

Conceived as a systematic attempt to explore what that might involve, the argument of this book therefore proceeds as follows:

(a) Chapter 1 traces a certain way in to civil theology, as a meditation on the 'revelatory' qualities of twentieth-century experience. It has chiefly to do with the most traumatic of all historical memories in the contemporary European context, that of the Nazi genocide; and begins from the basic question of how such a thing was possible – not just in terms of the most immediate causes, but with regard to the deeper structural weaknesses it highlights in the European cultural tradition as a whole, and its Christian religious component in particular. To this end, I consider two specific analyses: those of Hannah Arendt and of Simone Weil. Arendt's argument becomes the basis for a further elaboration of the concept of 'civil society' (even though this is not a term she herself uses). And the contrast between the two also serves, in a somewhat dramatic way, to highlight the issues at stake in the invocation of a religious absolute, in relation to politics.

(b) Then, having as it were finally entered into the domain of civil theology, in chapter 2 we pause to survey the surroundings. This chapter deals with two things: first, the contrast between the civil theological critique of modernity adumbrated in chapter 1 and the strictly confessional theological critique developed, perhaps most notably, by Kierkegaard and Barth; which I set alongside the tentative movement of Bonhoeffer's thought, under the direct pressure of events, away from Barthian confessionalism towards a more 'civil' approach. And secondly, the historical emergence of at any rate some more or less remote anticipations of civil theology, as such, within Christendom (from Machiavelli to Hegel).

(c) From there it next becomes a matter of stepping back: to try and define the scope of that broader discipline – what I have called civil hierology – which an authentically critical civil theology, so to speak, 'discovers' in the background to its historical analysis of revelation. On the one hand, this sort of civil theology is the theological articulation of a certain mode of solidarity within civil society, transcending traditional 'onto-theological' divisions: that is the topic of chapter 3, a discussion in particular of Jan Patočka's notion of 'the solidarity of the shaken'. On the other hand, it gives theological expression to a certain set of theology-transcendent virtues. And chapter 4 is an attempt to define these – with primary reference to the conflicting philosophies of Hegel, Nietzsche and Levinas.

(d) Finally, chapter 5 is a brief, modestly Utopian résumé of what I would see as the *ideal* inter-relationship of civil religion, civil society and the state.

1 *Negative Revelation*

It is revelation which supplies the criteria for theology – but by what criteria does one recognize revelation?

For confessional theology this is not a problem: such thinking presupposes a particular given, well-defined revelation, as its focus. It does, however, become a basic problem for pure civil theology. (That it raises the issue so naggingly is, I think, one of civil theology's major virtues.) Clearly, one cannot predetermine what revelation's theological content must include, for if one already knew the content there would be no revelation. Yet a revelation that did not carry conviction would also not be revelation. It has to have at least some measure of compelling force, for its deliverances to be more than just a matter of arbitrary collective opinion.

And so, what then *ought* to compel us?

On the one hand, at the pre-theological level, one can surely determine at any rate certain basic virtues necessary for the discernment of revelation – against which no authentic revelation would offend. (This will be my theme in chapter 4.) On the other hand, more positively, it is clear that any authentic revelation will be characterized by its transformative power, and hence its shock quality. It is where everything that was hitherto taken for granted is more or less abruptly called into question that one may talk of 'revelation'. That is: where it becomes apparent that the old ways can no longer *honestly* be upheld without a comprehensive rethinking of their rationale.

The general concept of 'revelation' arises out of Greek reflection on Semitic faith, with its concomitant sacralization of historical consciousness. (In chapter 3 I shall be discussing the intrinsic value of a heightening of such consciousness.) *Apokalupsis* may come in sundry different shapes. It may occur directly in the inspired utterance of the prophet, from Amos to Muhammad and beyond. Or it may be transmitted indirectly, through thought-provoking stories of human moral struggle. And such stories, in turn, may be of various kinds: they may consist, initially, of small-scale provincial drama, as in the gospels. They may have the form of a national epic, as in the case of the exodus from Egypt. Or – why not? – they may represent developments on an altogether more global scale.

Here, my concern is with the revelatory shock-stimulus to theological reflection inherent in the global twentieth-century phenomenon of totalitarianism. That is to say: the twin catastrophes of totalitarian rule and totalitarian (high-tech genocidal) 'warfare'. There are, indeed, other aspects of twentieth-century experience which might also be regarded as 'revelatory', according to the broad definition given above. Contemporary feminist theology might very well be presented as a response to new 'revelation', for instance, in view of the profoundly patriarchal character of all the dominant religious traditions of modernity. So too, in the context of Christendom, might ecological theology perhaps. However, it is the experience of totalitarianism which, I would argue, most dramatically highlights the need for civil, not just confessional, theology. For totalitarianism represents, precisely, the total destruction of citizenship. And we learn what things we should hold sacred perhaps most vividly through the experience of their absence; most of all, when that absence is the outcome of their sacredness being explicitly denied, their being deliberately neglected or suppressed. To borrow a concept from Emil Fackenheim, one might term this: 'negative' revelation.[1] Negative revelation is what passes through the darkness of 'My God, my God, why hast thou forsaken me?' – which the experience of totalitarian genocide globalizes.

There are of course other ways of interpreting this experience, theologically, besides the 'civil' approach. And in chapter 2 I shall be considering the Barthian confessional response, in particular, for comparison. In this chapter, however, I begin by juxtaposing the reflections of two other witnesses to the catastrophe: first Hannah Arendt – to whose monumental study of the origins of 'totalitarianism' we largely owe the word itself, in its current meaning – and then Simone Weil. Two Jews; close contemporaries (Arendt, born in 1906, was just three years the older); both ending up as refugees from Hitler's Europe; both obsessed with the need to make sense of the horror, and grasp its full scope: it seems to me that they represent two intriguingly different – in some ways altogether opposite, although in the final analysis perhaps also complementary – interpretations of its ultimate revelatory implications.

The differences between Arendt and Weil are certainly striking. Both set out to analyse the underlying material preconditions for the possibility of totalitarianism, as a cultural phenomenon, in the distinctive life processes of a modern industrial economy: that is, in the imprint left by those processes on the collective soul of the labouring masses. Yet whereas Arendt is concerned above all to criticize the incursion of the ethos of, as she puts it, 'the *animal laborans*' into public affairs – that is, the priority generally given, both in liberal mass democracies and by totalitarian regimes, to the ruthless maximizing of economic production and consumption – and therefore advocates giving *non*-economic concerns priority instead, Weil by contrast is preoccupied with the humanizing of labour, and sees *that* sort of economic issue as the highest priority: as it were, tackling the ethos of 'the *animal laborans*' at source. And still more radically: whereas Weil's response to the spectacular evil of totalitarianism is to turn aside from every merely 'relative' good to that which is 'absolute', Arendt on the contrary regards 'absolute goodness' as being just as inimical as 'absolute evil' to the kind of healthy political culture needed in order to resist the pressures of mass society.

Weil's death in 1943 preceded by some years the publication of Arendt's first major properly philosophical work, *The Human Condition*, in 1958. And, so far as I am aware, there is no evidence that Arendt ever read any of Weil's more notable theological writings.[2] But this chapter is an attempt to set up a debate between them, as a way of opening up the theological issue.

Hannah Arendt

Let us begin with Arendt. Considered as a whole, her work may be said to provide an essentially three-fold analysis of the revelatory challenge posed by the totalitarian experience to the European cultural tradition in general. So, from an Arendtian point of view, that experience compels us to re-assess

1 the nature of freedom, as a potential attribute of the *vita activa*;
2 the value of authority, as a bulwark against violence; and
3 the moral significance inherent in 'the life of the mind'.

To be sure, in speaking here of 'revelation' we are immediately going well beyond her own frame of reference. Although she touches on certain aspects of religious history from a political perspective, she does not anywhere write either as a believer, or as a non-believer in revelation; she is, quite deliberately, not a theologian; and there are moreover clear indications that her instinct would have been to recoil from the sort of enterprise here being attempted.[3] But, of course, a great deal of the creative impulse behind, in particular, Christian theology has always come from its critical encounter with that which is radically 'other' to it, and the problem of sorting out what it may absorb from what it must reject: in the Patristic period in relation to Platonism; in the Middle Ages in relation to Aristotle; in recent years perhaps most notably in relation to Marxism. Latin American 'liberation theology' is only the best-known example of this latter development, but one might equally refer to the influence of Ernst Bloch's Marxist philosophy on contemporary German 'political theology' (Jürgen Moltmann, Johann-Baptist Metz, Dorothee Sölle); or, indeed, to the half-concealed role of Marxism in the background to Karl Barth's thought.[4] And it seems to me in fact that the – profoundly un-Marxist – Arendtian reading of modern history could, if properly attended to, prove to be a yet more fruitful stimulus to theology than the Marxist one.

This is especially the case with the first of the three issues distinguished above.

Isonomy

Clearly, no matter how broad one's usage of the word, a 'revelatory' insight must be more than one which lends itself to incorporation in a mass-market-able ideology – even the most liberating such ideology. Totalitarianism abolishes all forms of freedom, other than freedom from responsibility. But, so far as the 'liberal' freedoms go – freedom of enterprise, freedom of movement, freedom of speech – it scarcely required the experience of total-itarianism to reveal to us the value of these: they are the birthright of modernity, in many places already well established long before the emer-gence of the totalitarian alternative. Far rather, surely, if there is any element of revelation here, it lies in the perception of that which totalitarian society has in common with the society of liberal mass democracy: in that aspect of the matter to which, for example, in the 1980s Václav Havel was drawing attention; the apprehension that, as he put it,

> the totalitarian systems warn of something far more serious than West-ern rationalism is willing to admit. They are, most of all, a convex mirror of the inevitable consequences of rationalism, a grotesquely magnified image of its own deep tendencies, an extremist offshoot of its own development and an ominous product of its own expansion. They are a deeply informative reflection of its own crisis.[5]

Nor does this cease to be the case, even when totalitarianism is on the retreat.

For what made totalitarianism possible in the first place? The question can be answered at various different levels. In the first place, there is the sort of answer which Arendt attempts (with primary reference to Nazism) in *The Origins of Totalitarianism*: an interpretation in terms of the immediate historical preconditions for the appeal of totalitarian ideology: the terrible dislocations resulting from rapid industrialization and imperialist expansion, opening up the intoxicating sense that nothing was fixed, everything was possible, just so long as one allied oneself shrewdly enough with the great impersonal forces of History; the associated weakening of the more rooted forms of nationalistic sentiment, and their displacement by racist ideology; the dangerous plight of the Jews, as political outsiders; and so forth.

But at another, more general, level, one might also argue that such a thing could never have come about were it not for the intrinsic weakness of the preceding political culture – *as a culture*; that is to say, the lack of any sufficiently widespread pre-existing understanding of, and attachment to the possibility of, spontaneous political action, at every level. Thus, if one distinguishes as Arendt does, sharply, between 'politics' and 'ruling', there is a certain sense in which totalitarianism arises, essentially, from a desire for the total abolition of politics, the total replacement of politics by administration, secret intrigue and violence.

And yet liberal mass democracy does not exactly maximize the scope for politics, in this sense, either. Havel speaks of totalitarianism as a convex mirror held up to 'Western rationalism'; and what he evidently has in mind is the technological rationality characteristic of any form of modern bureaucracy. Arendt, for her part, describes bureaucracy as 'the most *social* form of government'.[6] In her analysis, the primary specifically modern obstacle to good politics is the emergence of 'society' to be the dominant element in the public realm. This opposition which she develops between 'politics' and 'society' is, to be sure, somewhat idiosyncratic – and will certainly require reformulation, in order to distinguish the latter from 'civil society', with which (in the way that term has now largely come to be used) it obviously has nothing in common whatsoever. But let us first try and clarify what she means.

Arendt's notion of 'society' is in fact quite confusing, because of the way she uses it to conflate two quite different sets of historical data. On the one hand, in those places where she associates it above all with bureaucracy she is responding, in particular, to Karl Marx's understanding of historical causality, as being grounded at its deepest level on the evolution of what he calls 'the productive forces of society'. From this point of view, Arendt defines society as: 'the public organization of the life process itself'.[7] And she tells the following story.

Once upon a time, the story begins, there was actually no such thing as society, so defined. Instead, there were two very sharply differentiated domains: the public world of politics and the private realm of the household. That is how it was in ancient Athens, for example. But, there, public debate was never concerned with 'the organization of the life process'; it was never about economics. *Oikonomia*, the Greek word from which 'economics' derives, meant 'housekeeping': economics was strictly a matter for the household, and not the *polis*. The *polis* was the space of freedom, where citizens met as equals to share opinions; it was a culture of radical pluralism, 'the most individualistic and least conformable body politic' ever known.[8] The household was the opposite: it was where humdrum necessity ruled, the inglorious business, simply, of providing for the most basic requirements of life; and where, for efficiency's sake, absolute monarchical power was vested in the head of the family – a place, therefore, of imposed uniformity. 'Privacy' originally had connotations of deprivation, which have now faded away: it was the sphere of those deprived of freedom, the place of women and slaves; hidden away; the *megaron*, the dark interior out of which the citizen emerged into the bright sunlight of public affairs. The freedom of the public domain was paid for, and guaranteed, by its strictly preserved otherness from the private in every respect.

Modernity however, as Arendt interprets it, is essentially founded upon the abandonment of this clear-cut classical distinction. For that which is social is neither public nor private. Already, the feudal order represents a drastic shrinkage in public space, which is preserved (at any rate in the purest form of feudalism) only tenuously in the other-worldly context of the church; but 'in the modern world', by contrast, 'the two realms constantly flow into each other like waves in the never resting stream of the life process itself'.[9] Here economics has invaded politics; and this means that the same narrowly defined uniformity of interest that was once supposed to distinguish the private household is now projected on to the public realm: 'The collective of families economically organized into the facsimile of one super-human family is what we call "society", and its political form of organization is called "nation".'[10]

What is most decisively new in the modern nation-state, she argues, is the way its *raison d'être* is increasingly defined in terms of public housekeeping; the way it comes to be perceived, first and foremost, as an agency for the promotion of ever-greater economic productivity. Initially, the nation-state was moreover also structured on the model of the antique patriarchal household, that is, in the form of absolute monarchy; only later, as the sheer complexity of its business outgrew the capacity of that model, did it develop into the 'no-man rule', as she puts it, of bureaucracy.

And then bureaucracy brings with it a whole new academic culture as well. In the eighteenth century Adam Smith invented the new science of 'political economy'; the nineteenth century saw the development of sociology: both of them, in the first instance, disciplines for the study of human behaviour *en masse*, the raw material of bureaucratic calculation; behaviour not action; predictable, anonymous, statistically measurable. But 'statistical uniformity', Arendt writes,

> is by no means a harmless scientific ideal; it is the no longer secret political ideal of a society which, entirely submerged in the routine of everyday living, is at peace with the scientific outlook inherent in its very existence.[11]

This, in short, is one meaning of 'society' in her thought: it is what finally prevails when politics is reduced to an endless preoccupation with public opinion polls, and the relentless bandying back and forth of statistics, the special property of the bureaucratic expert.

Yet, on the other hand, she also uses the word in a sense deriving from the very different notion of 'good', or 'polite' society. Here too we are dealing, as she sees it, with a specifically modern phenomenon (about as old perhaps as these terms themselves); and what she has in mind, in this case, is – it seems – the tyranny of fashion.

Of course, there always has been fashion. But what is peculiarly characteristic of modernity is the way in which fashionable society begins to evoke a new sort of resistance: the emergence of the essentially new figure of the lonely individual in rebellion, self-consciously as an 'individual', against 'society' in general. This rebellion appears in a wide range of philosophical expressions.[12] One example she cites is that of John Stuart Mill; and the sentiments of his essay *On Liberty* are indeed scarcely conceivable prior to modernity. Another is Jean-Jacques Rousseau, 'the first articulate explorer and to an extent even theorist of intimacy': publicizing his own privacy in order to defend privacy, as a subjective principle, against the social prejudices of the fashionable Parisian salons. She refers to the Romantic movement as a whole; one might equally point to Kierkegaard, and to twentieth-century Existentialism.

More generally, she suggests that the history of society might be seen as coeval with the history of the novel – which she characterizes as 'the only entirely social art form'. For is not the novel pre-eminently designed as an exploration of intimacy, and of the conflicts between individual and society? (Rousseau, of course, was also a pioneering novelist.) She traces the origins of 'good society' back to the royal courts of the early modern absolute monarchs, such as Louis XIV's Versailles; which is where we find the first direct forerunner of the novel, in the *Mémoires* of Saint-Simon. And there she already finds the first seeds of twentieth-century 'mass' culture:

> All the traits which crowd psychology has meanwhile discovered in mass man: his loneliness – and loneliness is neither isolation nor solitude – regardless of his adaptability; his excitability and lack of standards; his capacity for consumption, accompanied by inability to judge, or even to distinguish; above all, his egocentricity and that fateful alienation from the world which since Rousseau is mistaken for self-alienation – all these traits first appeared in good society, when there was no question of masses, numerically speaking.[13]

But the history of society, from that starting point, is fundamentally a story of rapidly accelerating expansion, as the demands of fashion came to impinge upon ever wider sections of the population; culminating at last in the final absorption of everyone without exception into the truly 'mass' society of today.

This is obviously a rather different story from the first one, which began in ancient Athens and culminated in the rise of the modern academic disciplines of economics and sociology. And the difference is further highlighted, for instance, when one considers Arendt's account of the French Revolution: for if Robespierre's Reign of Terror was a war against hypocrisy, 'war upon hypocrisy was war declared upon society'[14] – hypocrisy, after all, is the most social of vices, if one thinks of society in terms of the rule of fashion. Yet, from her other perspective, she also sees the Terror precisely as issuing from a disastrous eclipse of the political by the social: as the original, authentically political gains of the Revolution were extinguished in the pursuit of a chimerical economic goal, the abolition of poverty.[15] So it was at the same time both a war against 'society', and a triumph of 'society', depending on which sense of the word one is using. Or, again, consider her account of the revolutionary role played by the labour movement from the mid-nineteenth to the mid-twentieth century:[16] she sees this movement as having 'written one of the most glorious and probably the most promising chapter of recent history' from a political point of view – even though its whole identity was primarily defined in relation to economic issues. She herself acknowledges 'the apparently flagrant discrepancy' in this, and explains it on the grounds that the admission of the working classes into the public realm, their political emancipation, preceded their incorporation into society (*qua* the realm of fashion); so that 'the very pathos of the labour movement in its early stages . . . stemmed from its fight against society as a whole'. Which may be true – but nevertheless does not remove the fact that (as she also admits) the distinction between the political and the economic really is very hard to maintain in this context.

But does that mean that her argument is therefore simply incoherent? In these particular instances it is certainly confusing. However, the fact of course is that in the particular sort of political environment where she is writing, and which she is intent on criticizing, namely, modern party political democracy, the two stories she tells – distinct though they are – clearly do converge.[17] They converge for the simple reason that economic growth has tended to become a dominant criterion for governmental success or failure within that world; whilst growth in productivity is, of course, largely dependent on the constant manipulation of fashion, in the shape of consumer demand. In a modern/'post-modern' mass culture the artificially defined common interests of fashion have almost entirely come to coincide with the, so to speak, continual expansion; they have come to form a single concerted pressure to conform. And that coincidence, then, is what Arendt, quite consistently, calls 'society'.

However, it is clear that this is not 'civil society', in the sense defined above.

To mark the difference, let us call it 'society *qua* enterprise'. For it is society as shaped by the monistic enterprise of economic growth, or by the monistic enterprise of fashion. 'Civil society', by contrast, is precisely what Arendt terms the domain of 'politics', as opposed to the domain of 'rule' (the state).

But now compare this distinction to the one Michael Oakeshott makes between the two opposing views of the state which he analyses in *On Human Conduct*: the state as 'civil association' and as 'enterprise association'. In these terms, 'civil society' is what the state allows to flourish independently, in so far as the state sees itself as a 'civil association'; 'society *qua* enterprise' would be what the state, viewed as an 'enterprise association', seeks to represent and to shape, or that body of opinion which actively demands that the state behave as an 'enterprise association'.

Oakeshott is also a thinker centrally concerned with the pathology of totalitarianism. Yet his analysis is not Arendt's. For him, the basic moral of the story is that we should beware of *any* notion of the state as an enterprise association – in this they are at one. However, Oakeshottian civil association is very far from being equivalent to Arendtian 'politics'.

Another way in which he formulates his argument is with reference to the contrast – originally to be found in Roman private law, and then taken up into mediaeval political thinking – between *societas* and *universitas*. A *universitas* was an association which might be treated as a single corporate 'person' in law. A *societas* was not: rather than representing any single substantive common interest, a *societas* was understood, simply, as a place of regulated encounter and co-operation between individuals of differing interests. (Arendtian 'society' is in spirit clearly much more like a large-scale *universitas* than a *societas*!) And for Oakeshott the critical issue is the relationship of government to law. The highest priority for a state conceived as a *societas*, or 'civil association', must be the maintenance, so far as possible, of stability; that is, the upholding of the rule of law – the substance and application of which will, of course, always need to be adapted in response to changing circumstance, but only in order to conserve its generally recognized authority. Oakeshott is an admirer of Hobbes: the great original exponent of the view that governmental authority should be based solely on the citizens' will that there should be order rather than chaos; as opposed to any supposedly 'natural', or revealed, *telos* for humanity, which might dictate additional goals for the state as a *universitas*; goals to which the value of stability would be subordinated. Yet he is not – as Arendt is – at all concerned with the positive virtues of citizenly participation in politics. That is the critical difference.

Certainly, it is vital in his view that the citizen should actively assent to the authority of the state; he also wants to go decisively beyond Hobbes in this respect, in the direction indicated by Rousseau and, still more, Hegel: towards a more sophisticated account of the proper grounds for that assent. Hobbes, with his exclusive reliance on the motivation inherent in an enlightened fear of chaos, lacks, as Oakeshott puts it, 'a satisfactory or coherent theory of volition',[18] he is so intent on arguing against the folly of religious fanaticism that he fails to give due attention to other, more reputable motives which might on occasion come into conflict with the simple love of peace. Oakeshott prefers the Hegelian legitimation of the state (to which we shall return) as an expression of 'Rational Will', or *Geist*.[19] But he stops at assent; he is by no means a positive advocate of politics as a character-building way of life, the Classical vision which Arendt is seeking to revive.

In one of her more sweeping formulations, speaking of the Greek view of the *polis*, Arendt writes, 'Under no circumstances could politics be only a means to protect society';[20] and then goes on to give a series of different examples of politics reduced to such a protective role. Thus, the state may be regarded as the protector of 'a society of producers, as in Marx, or a society of jobholders, as in our own society, or a society of labourers, as in socialist and communist countries' – all of these are quite straightforward examples of society *qua* enterprise. But also: 'a society of the faithful, as in the Middle Ages, or a society of property-owners, as in Locke, or a society relentlessly engaged in a process of acquisition, as in Hobbes' – these, by contrast, are not; or at least, not necessarily so. Faith may no doubt become an 'enterprise': the crusades would be an example of that (as would anything meta-phorically referred to as a 'crusade'); but in so far as it is a matter of inwardness, to do with the salvation of the individual soul, it is not. The parties to the social contract, as Locke or Hobbes conceive it, may or may not be enterprising; but it is not their enterprises that they seek protection for, in the first instance: the contract guarantees the same basic protection for all, the enterprising and the not so enterprising alike. Indeed, it is basically a protection against the 'relentlessly acquisitive' and aggressive enterprises of others. It would seem, therefore, that Arendt's notion of 'society' is after all somewhat broader than was suggested above. Besides 'civil society' and 'society *qua* enterprise', perhaps we need yet a third category to capture this something extra, the sort of 'society' that Hobbes and Locke, for instance, were championing; and which Oakeshott also champions. Let us call it 'society *qua* order'.

But is not this three-fold categorization of society *qua* enterprise/society *qua* order/civil society also directly reminiscent of the distinction she develops in *The Human Condition*, between the three basic constituent elements of the *vita activa*: labour, work and action?

The whole point of this scheme obviously lies in its relationship to her political polemic.[21] Each element represents a type of experience which, in so far as it determines one's frame of mind, translates into a particular view of the proper business of politics. There are no clear boundaries: in many activities an element of 'work' overlaps with both 'labour' and 'action'. But 'work' differs from 'labour' in that, rather than simply serving the basic needs of life or the immediate consumer-appetites of luxury, it is what shapes and furnishes the world long-term; producing distinctive artefacts, designed to last; or, in general, a stable context for life; the essential stability of which then also differentiates it from 'action' – in that 'action' is what, on the contrary, disturbs and initiates.

The point is that to each of these three categories there corresponds a distinct problematic. The dominant secular ideologies-of-enterprise, focused on issues relating to the production and distribution of wealth in the sense of consumer goods and their benefits, are obviously direct expressions of the ethos of labour. As are their religious equivalents: equally removed from anything enduring upon earth, but focused on the rewards of the after-life, they are essentially a projection of ecstatic release from the drudgery of labour. By contrast, the conservative notion of politics as a quest for stable order is chiefly inspired by the analogy of work. Hobbes again provides the classic example of this: when, in the Introduction to *Leviathan*, he speaks of the 'making' of a state, like making 'an artificial animal', or an 'automaton that moves by springs and wheels as doth a watch'[22]; as reliable as a good watch. If society *qua* enterprise is the natural domain of the *animal laborans*, then society *qua* order is the artificial construct of *homo faber*.

What Arendt, on the other hand, seeks to oppose to both of these is a political theory focused instead on the altogether deeper problematic of 'action'. The question she is intent on posing is, thus, how best to harness the energy of action – in order to multiply the possibilities for future action?[23] Or, how best to create open spaces for the future proliferation of political creativity? Totalitarian politics is of course also, initially, a mode of action; this, though, is action not opening up the space for further action, but on the contrary aiming to promote the very opposite of action, that is, pure 'behaviour'. It is in the very nature of enterprise ideology, even at its most liberal, to measure success in behavioural terms. As a radical openness to new beginnings, however (the expression of, as she puts it, human 'natality'), the ethos of authentic action is equally inimical to conservative ideology. And the natural arena for such action is either a participatively pluralistic state, or else – *civil* society.

Oakeshott defines the difference between 'enterprise association'/*universitas* and 'civil association'/*societas* in terms of the different sorts of purposes they serve: the former is dedicated to some '*substantive*' purpose; but the type of purpose the latter serves can only be formulated either far too abstractly – as 'happiness', 'human excellence', *eudaimonia* – to determine any concrete decision; or else – if it is said to be 'peace' or 'security' – by reference to the successful maintenance of the association's own purely formal structure.[24] But what about the Arendtian ideal? There is nothing 'substantive' here either.

Moreover, from the Arendtian perspective, Oakeshott's position, for all its critique of enterprise-politics, fails in the end to provide for a sufficiently vigorous counter-culture. Oakeshott is a political philosopher. However, Arendt, I think very convincingly, argues that there is an intrinsic contradiction in that role: philosophy is the love of wisdom, as a phenomenon not of the *vita activa* but rather of the *vita contemplativa*; a solitary pursuit, fundamentally withdrawn from any immediate concern with political action, the very spirit of which it is therefore unable, in the last analysis, to comprehend. Her (un-philosophical) political thought, on the contrary, is premissed upon *amor mundi*, love of the world, meaning the world of action. As opposed to enterprise-politics or the politics of conservatism, the type of politics she celebrates might therefore be called 'worldly' politics. It is sometimes also referred to as 'republicanism'; republicanism, however, is a term which has come to have all sorts of other somewhat unfortunate connotations by virtue of its adoption by 'Republican' political parties. Another, and perhaps more useful, designation might be 'isonomy', from the Greek *isonomia*, originally meaning 'equality maintained through law'. Or, as she herself puts it, 'no-rule': thus,

> [the] outstanding characteristic [of isonomy] among the forms of government, as the ancients had enumerated them, was that the notion of rule (the 'archy' from *archein* in monarchy and oligarchy, or the 'cracy' from *kratein* in democracy) was entirely absent from it. The [Athenian] *polis* was supposed to be an isonomy, not a democracy. The word 'democracy', expressing even then majority rule, the rule of the many, was originally coined by those who were opposed to isonomy and who meant to say: What you say is 'no-rule' is in fact only another kind of rulership; it is the worst form of government, rule by the demos.[25]

What she looks to, in short, is the maximum practicable expansion of the worldly space, guaranteed by law, for 'no-rule'. *Genuine* isonomy.

Political philosophy, on the other hand (and Oakeshott is no exception), naturally tends to be concerned not so much with the expansion of *no*-rule, as it were from below – but rather with the issue of what constitutes *good* or *legitimate* rule. For political philosophy is the philosopher's view of politics. More specifically (so Arendt suggests), it originates in the Platonic interpretation of the death of Socrates: as a symbol of the supposed intrinsic conflict between philosophy and the *polis*, which Plato concludes can only be resolved by putting the philosophers in charge. But this in fact entails a drastic suppression of worldly politics. Although Plato is no advocate of society *qua* enterprise – and at least in that sense not a proto-totalitarian thinker – in proposing the abolition of private households for the *polis* elite, he is nevertheless envisaging their conversion into a single household, that is, the most all-encompassing form of rule possible. And, moreover, the legitimacy of this entirely un-worldly Platonic regime is also based on a radical devaluation of 'opinion', the essential currency of political life – now seen as that which the philosopher's 'truth' does away with.[26] Here political wisdom has already become not so much a matter of judicious action – since the possibility of spontaneity in action has virtually been abolished – but, rather, the making and preserving of an ideal order. The philosopher appears as *homo faber*, in the figure of the original legislator: fabricating his state, to use Plato's own analogy, like a sculptor chiselling a statue;[27] a role which Plato himself takes on in his final work.

Obviously, Plato represents the anti-worldly aggression of philosophy at its most repressive extreme. And yet, from the Arendtian point of view, what has most importantly been lost to sight in this approach to politics largely remains lost thereafter. Aristotle may abandon the notion of the philosopher-king, but he still assumes the superiority of the theoretical life (*bios theôretikos*) over the life devoted to human affairs (*bios politikos*).[28] Like Plato, he too relates the task of the theoretician far more closely to the craftsmanship of the legislator than to the action of statesman, ranking the science of fabrication (*epistémé poiétiké*) above practical insight (*dianoia*) and political science (*epistémé praktiké*);[29] he too is centrally concerned with justifying the existence of rulers – for which (unlike Plato) he appeals to the evidence of 'nature'.[30] And, she complains, 'the political philosophies of Plato and Aristotle have dominated all subsequent political thought'; even when their concepts have been 'superimposed' upon very different political experiences.[31] In its character as an attempt to step right outside the framework of philosophy as traditionally conceived – by uncovering that which, by virtue of its most basic presuppositions, philosophy has forgotten – Arendt's thought is comparable to that of Heidegger or of Levinas. The radicalism of her claims is of the same order as theirs. (I shall come back to both Heidegger and Levinas later.[32])

However, that is only the beginning of the problem. And this is where we begin to re-enter the explicitly theological domain: for these tendencies have also been further compounded by the influence of Christianity, in at least two major respects.

In the first place, Christianity has added a whole new dimension to the philosophical notion of legitimate rule, by introducing the concept of freedom as an attribute of the problematically sovereign will. Arendt actually puts a great deal of emphasis on the originality, in particular, first of the apostle Paul, and then of Augustine, when it comes to the understanding of 'freedom', in relation to the will.[33] In fact, she observes, the concept of 'the will' – as opposed to desire or intention – first comes to prominence in the Stoic doctrine of Epictetus, a contemporary of Paul's; but for Epictetus it was not the sovereignty of the will that was problematic. The will, in his thought, is sovereign by definition; the one who wills is one whose triumph is assured, since the will's activity is simply to accept things as they are; such acceptance is always possible, and wisdom lies in 'willing' that which is, rather than desiring that which is not. The real problem of the sovereignty of the will, by contrast, only arises when there is a perceived conflict between 'I will' and 'I can', the conflict which Paul 'discovers' in Romans 7:15, when he writes: 'I do not understand my own actions. For I do not do what I want, but I do the very thing I hate.' What Paul and Epictetus have in common is simply the radical inwardness of the liberation they aspire to, its complete independence of exterior circumstance. But Paul's 'discovery' lies in the perception that it is not only – as the pagans assumed[34] – 'base' souls who may find themselves in a state of internal conflict. For the internal conflict into which he finds himself plunged is due, rather, to the infinite exorbitance of the demands of Christian discipleship: so that, the more he takes these to heart, the greater the natural resistance they inevitably evoke – a conflict which only grace can resolve. And so in Augustine's thought, where this Pauline experience first becomes a theme of properly philosophical reflection, in an extended meditation on the problematic nature of 'the will', the proper business of the will is no longer understood as *amor fati*, but instead as the choice of the 'heavenly city' over the 'earthly' one; the heavenly city being defined as the society in which the will to charity is sovereign, as it is in each saved soul. Herein Arendt finds the original source – by virtue of the analogy (borrowed by Augustine from Plato) between the soul and the state – of the widespread preoccupation in modern political philosophy with the rationalization of sovereignty also in secular terms. This then comes to paradigmatic expression precisely in those developments to which Oakeshott attaches so much significance: Rousseau's notion of the 'general *will*', Hegel's notion of the 'rational *will*'; a type of concept quite alien to ancient Greek or Roman political thinking.

What, in short, she sees as having happened here is that the worldly-political notion of freedom as an attribute of action has been supplanted by the – initially quite unpolitical – notion of freedom as an attribute of the will. And this has then been projected back on to the political realm, with the effect of providing a new rhetoric for, and so further reinforcing, the philosophers' concern with the rationalization of rulership, as opposed to the defence of isonomy. For isonomous freedom does not at all belong on the same level as freedom *qua* the sovereignty of reason. The former is a creative phenomenon, involving compromise and co-operation among numerous agents who are in this context quite unsovereign. The latter is a disciplinarian affair involving an inner drama of struggle, for sovereignty within each soul, between the good will, whose aim is to serve the perceived best interests of the community as a whole, and the desires that arise out of the individual's own particular interests. A political theory focused on this is naturally bound to be preoccupied with the institutionalization of assent, the public reinforcement of the good will. But that then tends to issue in a very different set of priorities from those of isonomy. What really counts in this case is the salvation of the individual soul, rather than the best, in the sense of the most open, possible public debate. And the means of salvation tends to be identified with the self-mortification involved in costly obedience – which is all too easily interpreted as cutting short debate.

Secondly, she observes, Christianity also successfully accomplished what Plato desired: the popularization of heaven and hell.[35] Plato's myths about the after-life – in *The Republic*, in the *Phaedo* and in the *Gorgias* – are of course quite openly part of a strategy of rule. His thinking on this subject begins with a turning away from the traditional Greek aspiration to a share in the immortality of the gods and the cosmos, through one's partipation in, and contribution to, the immortal *polis*. Thus, as she puts it, in the perception of pre-Platonic Greece,

> Men are 'the mortals', the only mortal things in existence, because unlike animals they do not exist only as members of a species whose immortal life is guaranteed through procreation . . . The task and potential greatness of mortals lie in their ability to produce things – works and deeds and words – which would deserve to be and, at least to a degree, are at home in everlastingness, so that through them mortals could find their place in a cosmos where everything is immortal except themselves. By their capacity for the immortal deed, by their ability to leave imperishable traces behind, men, their individual mortality notwithstanding, attain an immortality of their own and prove themselves to be of a 'divine' nature.[36]

This is an immortality obtained through action. But Plato, in exalting the contemplative vocation of the philosopher over all else, promotes the alternative aspiration to participate in eternity instead: the opposite of immortality; to which one gains access only in the experience of solitary thought. This is actually quite incompatible with his myths, which speak of the after-life in temporal terms, and which tell of the corporeal pains of the damned, even though he still teaches the mortality of the flesh. Hence his manner of introducing them – in effect, as convenient fictions. However, since he also wants to establish the rule of the contemplative few over the non-contemplative many, the myths are designed above all to help justify that rule to those who lack the necessary rationality to recognize its necessity on grounds of pure logic alone. They provide additional sanctions. Nothing could be more cynical than Plato's 'theology'; a word which he himself was, as it happens, seemingly the first to invent, and which he associates directly with the art of founding cities, the skilful subordination of the many to the few. And so, one might say, in his philosophy Plato displaces immortality with eternity; whilst in his myths he displaces worldly immortality with other-worldly immortality.

Christianity, however, not only preserves the philosophical orientation towards eternity but also, by virtue of the doctrine of the resurrection of the flesh, is able to invest the notion of other-worldly immortality with far greater weight than Plato had. Arendt differentiates sharply in this connection, between two stages in the evolution of Christian thought. At first, she suggests, the primary emphasis was on Christ's descent into hell, his defeat of Satan and liberation of the previously imprisoned dead; much less on hell as an enduring threat to the wicked. But she identifies the decisive turning point as occurring in the fifth century, when for instance the doctrines of Origen were officially condemned: Origen's charitable anticipation that eventually even Satan himself might be redeemed, along with all other sinners, and his rationalistic interpretation of the pains of hell in terms of an inner agony of repentance, rather than the cruder but perhaps more effective deterrent of actual fire. It is in her view no accident that the transition coincides with Christianity's gradual emergence into the role of a state religion (with the great theorist, once again, being Augustine).

All this is ancient history. Yet, even when the fear of hell-fire has faded away, that obviously does not of itself ensure any major re-evaluation of 'the world' and its worldliness. And in fact, despite all the best efforts of the 'political theologians', what that fear originally helped to stop from ever taking root still remains a very tender growth, even today.

In terms of external intellectual stimulus, contemporary 'political theology' has largely been conceived in sympathetic response to the challenge of (dissident forms of) Marxism – but from an Arendtian point of view Marxism represents a classic case of the misguided subordination of worldly politics to a 'social' enterprise. Hence her critique of Christian other-worldliness comes from an altogether different angle: she is concerned, simply, with 'the freedom inherent in action', or with freedom conceived as a space for action, isonomous freedom. The importance of Ancient Athens is just that it is the best example we have of a political culture preserving a high degree of such freedom, over an extended period of time, within the central institutions of the state; even if only for a minority of the male population. She finds something of that same spirit flaring up, in occasional flickering fits and starts, in modern history, above all in the great moments of revolutionary crisis: that is, at those points where the collapse of an old ruling order has issued in a sudden ferment of free-spirited political initiative from below, in the shape of revolutionary councils, clubs, forums, assemblies – as, for instance, in 1989; the first exhilarating moment of liberation, before the descent into violence, the military triumph of reaction, or the lapse of an unprepared people back into materialistic indifference.

Much of her writing, on the other hand, consists of an analysis of 'dark times', when the public space of freedom has been fragmentary or almost non-existent. So, for instance, she adheres to what she calls 'the hidden tradition' within European Jewry, so long kept out on the edge of public life, of those who have positively sought to celebrate the status of 'pariah'. Bernard Lazare, the Dreyfusard lawyer, is one model here – who 'saw that what was necessary was to rouse the Jewish pariah to a fight against the Jewish *parvenu*';[37] for, whereas the *parvenu* has sold out to fashionable society, the 'conscious pariah' – even when emancipation on any terms other than those of fashionable society is impossible – is at any rate helping to enrich the public domain to this extent, that he or she attempts to be a voice for those who otherwise would never be heard; or at least to give some expression to their experience of life. (Besides Lazare, she refers to Heinrich Heine, Franz Kafka, even the non-Jew Charlie Chaplin, as, each in their very various ways, representatives of this 'tradition'.) Or again, she takes Lessing as a model of civilized 'humanity' in dark times: no pariah, but a privileged man of letters, who, however, acutely conscious of the potential for enslavement in any settled social doctrine, effectively devoted his life to the undermining of all such certainties. A man who 'wanted to be the friend of many men, but no man's brother' – always, therefore, preferring humanity to even the truest of 'truths'.[38]

Between freedom at the level of direct participation in the decision-making processes of the state and freedom at the level of solitary witness in dark times, though, there clearly exists another level; less established than the former, but more organized than the latter: the freedom of civil society. By contrast with the other two, this is not in fact a type of freedom which Arendt anywhere systematically considers. The most notable example she does discuss – in her essays 'On Violence' and 'Civil Disobedience' – is the anti-Vietnam War campaign and the student movement of the late 1960s;

and her verdict on this is certainly very positive indeed. She sees it as a remarkable sign of hope:

> A student rebellion almost exclusively inspired by moral considerations certainly belongs among the totally unexpected events of this century. This generation, trained like its predecessors in hardly anything but the various brands of my-share-of-the-pie social and political theories, has taught us a lesson about manipulation, or, rather, its limits, which we would do well not to forget. Men can be 'manipulated' through physical coercion, torture or starvation, and their opinions can be arbitrarily formed by deliberate, organized misinformation, but not through 'hidden persuaders', television, advertising, or any other psychological means in a free society . . .[39]

But, since civil society is also the domain to which most religious life, in so far as it attains a genuinely 'worldly' existence in the Arendtian sense, itself immediately belongs, it is no doubt freedom at this level which has the most direct specifically theological relevance. Thus, by way of an initial response to the element of revelation in the nightmare of totalitarianism, it might well be proposed as at least one fundamental criterion for the spiritual health or sickness of any religious community that one ask: just how creative is it of its own distinctive spaces of isonomous freedom? To what extent, in this way, does that community help to train free-spirited citizens in the art of self-organization?

Auctoritas

Arendt has other, still more fundamental criticisms of Christianity, which however – since they relate directly to Simone Weil's discussion of 'absolute goodness' – I shall leave until I come to that. But, at the same time, there are certain countervailing elements in her thinking that to a significant extent serve to qualify her critique – both of Christianity and of philosophy. Before we turn to the comparison with Weil, we also need to note these.

The first point emerges out of her analysis of the concept of 'authority'. As she recognizes, active participation in public affairs is always likely to remain very much a minority vocation. Important though a popular attachment to, and treasuring of, the possibility of such participation certainly is, therefore, a civilized political culture surely requires something more than that, as well, for its protection. Oakeshott's 'conservative' meditation on the lessons of the totalitarian nightmare may be incomplete, but clearly one of the most basic requirements remains a universal respect for the restraints set by law on the ambitions of those in power. Nothing, after all, is more typical of totalitarianism than its total contempt for the rule of law, as opposed to rule by decree.

But, in order to be fully effective, the rule of law not only needs good policing and an efficient judicial system, which people feel is fair, it also needs an underpinning of moral authority; deriving not only from the intrinsic *gravitas* of legal tradition, but also from the support of other traditions.

This communitarian moment in Arendt's thought is primarily to be found in her essay on authority in *Between Past and Future*. At the heart of her argument here stands her critique of two equally unbalanced analyses of the evil of totalitarianism: the naively 'liberal' analysis and the naively 'conservative'. The liberal interpretation, in its exclusive concern with the 'progress' of negative liberty, tends to see totalitarianism as an essentially reactionary phenomenon: a violent attempt to undo the anti-authoritarian achievements of the Enlightenment. Whereas the conservative view, on the contrary, represents it as a symptom of the collapse of authentic authoritarian tradition, and the consequent opening up of a spiritual void, ready to be filled by all manner of *ersatz* satisfactions. In fact, she thinks, both are right: 'if we look upon the conflicting statements of conservatives and liberals with impartial eyes, we can easily see that the truth is equally distributed between them and that we are in fact confronted with a simultaneous recession of both freedom and authority in the modern world'.[40] But both are also wrong. They are wrong, above all, because of the pervasive failure, in modern culture, to differentiate properly between the type of obedience which is a response to authority and that which is elicited by other means.

The source of the misunderstanding, she argues, is simply that 'authority'– in the strict sense – has to such a large extent 'vanished from the modern world'.[41] For her, this is indeed, alongside the 'social' blurring of the public and the private, another no less essential part of what makes the modern world 'modern'. Of course, we still speak of modern institutions and of individuals within the modern world as having 'authority'; however, the point is that, when applied in this context, the word has changed radically in meaning. The etymological root of 'authority' is Latin, *auctoritas*. But what modern political and social science mostly means by 'authority' is no longer *auctoritas* as the Romans knew it. So she complains of 'the almost universal *functionalization* of all concepts and ideas' in the social sciences.[42] 'Authority' is defined in terms of *what* it does – that is, its function of making people obey – rather than *how* it does so. No political system is more effective in compelling people to obey than totalitarianism; therefore, the liberals conclude, no system is more authoritarian. And yet, she argues, totalitarianism is a type of system entirely devoid of true *auctoritas*. A system grounded in *auctoritas* will naturally tend towards the shape of a pyramid, with authority filtering down, quite openly and visibly, from the top. Whereas, by contrast,

> the proper image of totalitarian rule and organization [is] the structure of the *onion*, in whose centre, in a kind of empty space, the leader is located; whatever he does – whether he integrates the body politic as in an authoritarian hierarchy, or oppresses his subjects like a tyrant – he does it from within, and not from without or above. All the extraordinarily manifold parts of the movement: the front organizations, the various professional societies, the party membership, the party bureaucracy, the elite formations and police groups, are related in such a way that each forms the facade in one direction and the centre in the other, that is, plays the normal outside world for one layer and the role of radical extremism for another.[43]

The true extremism of the leadership is in this way systematically concealed from the outside world, whilst the conviction of the insiders is continually reinforced by their being brought into contact with the external world only in the form of fellow travellers: 'the onion structure makes the system organizationally shock-proof against the factuality of the real world'[44] – in a way which the pyramidical structure of *auctoritas* cannot. *Auctoritas* has nothing to do with such deception.

Neither does it involve violence or any other form of coercion. (And here those she speaks of as 'conservatives' also miss the point.) This is, indeed, surely a crucial distinction: coercion is what has to be employed where *auctoritas* fails, *auctoritas* has no need of it. In fact, true *auctoritas* is, strictly speaking, incompatible with any sort of power backed by coercion. She quotes Cicero: '*Cum potestas in populo auctoritas in senatu sit*, "while power resides in the people, authority rests with the Senate" '.[45] By 'the people' Cicero means the popular assemblies (*comitia*) of the citizens, to which the magistrates were formally answerable. It might be objected that, as a description of actual practice, this formula is somewhat misleading, since for the greater part of the republican period the Senate did in fact exercise a good deal of executive power, albeit informally, and under the emperors, whilst its influence in most respects declined, it took over much of the legislative power that had earlier belonged to the *comitia*. It was only in Cicero's own day – in the last years of the republic – that the practical reality genuinely approximated to his statement of principle. But then, it was just in that period, when it was serving for the most part simply as an advisory body, that the Senate became in the most emphatic and least ambiguous way an embodiment of pure *auctoritas*. Arendt speaks of what she calls 'the Roman Trinity': authority, tradition and religion. The Romans, she remarks, conceived their gods too, in their oracular role, as having *auctoritas* rather than power; inasmuch as these oracles, unlike those of the Greeks, did not claim to reveal the future, but only to express divine approval or disapproval of human decisions. *Auctoritas* rests on a basis of sacred narrative: the Senators were the elders whose responsibility it was to link the present with the past, to make it all one story, way back to the foundation of the city – and beyond, to the earlier, also authoritative history of the Greeks; in every situation recalling relevant precedents, as a guide to the decision-makers. She draws attention to the etymological source of the word *auctoritas* in the verb *augere*, to augment: 'what authority or those in authority constantly augment is the foundation'.[46] Likewise, she points to the link here with '*auctor*', meaning 'author': the *gravitas* of the Roman Senators, she remarks, expressed the weightiness of their role as those who, with regard to their people's history, sought, as it were, to maintain the proper coherence of the plot; preserving the essential character of the tradition, as it had been established from the outset.

The ancient Athenians had no tradition of *auctoritas*, no institutions to embody it. And those modern institutions which have most directly inherited the Roman tradition, namely the Roman Catholic and Eastern Orthodox churches, have always been somewhat deficient with regard to the practice of isonomy. Yet Arendt's tone is by no means entirely hostile when she speaks of the 'miracle' involved in the church's appropriation of 'the Roman spirit'.[47] Of course, the Hebrew tradition also had a potent element of *auctoritas* in it; but the 'miracle' here lies in the transformation of an event, the death and resurrection of Jesus, which had initially been understood in terms of an eschatological judgement on the world, radically undermining all things established, into the opposite: a worldly act of foundation – a positive source of *auctoritas*, just like the foundation of the city of Rome itself, to those charged with commemorating it. And this did at any rate have the merit of presenting the totalitarian regimes of modernity with something not immediately easy to digest. The great problem which appears to present itself is thus: to think through what it might require for traditions to develop – not least, civil religious ones – truly capable of conferring *auctoritas* on the ethos and practices of isonomy.

The Life of the Mind

But even in the darkest of dark times, even when the last spark of public freedom has been extinguished and the laws are openly despised by those in power, people are still not prevented from trying to behave to one another with at least a simple modicum of decency. For the darkness to prevail within a particular individual's soul there remains a further step to be taken, a final moral threshold to be crossed. And, from our present point of view, the third key element in Arendt's analysis – alongside her discussions of freedom and authority – is her account of the crossing of this critical line.

The argument of the book she left unfinished at her death (which is also her one genuinely 'philosophical' work), *The Life of the Mind*, was originally inspired, so she tells us in the Introduction, by what she had observed over a decade earlier, in 1961, at the trial of Adolf Eichmann – the subject of her intensely controversial report at the time, *Eichmann in Jerusalem*. What proved most provocative in the report was her – it has to be conceded – very harsh judgement on the way in which the Jewish leadership had, as she saw it, allowed themselves to be used by the Nazis.[48] Her remarks on that issue, however, are in fact quite incidental to her main argument, which concerns the person of Eichmann himself, and his specific role in the bureaucratic management of the genocide. Again, the basic point is quite straightforward. The prosecution at the trial sought to portray him as a demon, yet what she saw was something quite different:

> The deeds were monstrous, but the doer – at least the very effective one now on trial – was quite ordinary, commonplace, and neither demonic nor monstrous. There was no sign in him of firm ideological convictions or of specific evil motives, and the only notable characteristic one could detect in his past behaviour as well as in his behaviour during the trial and throughout the pre-trial police examination was something entirely negative: it was not stupidity, but *thoughtlessness*.

She even found an element of 'macabre comedy' in his hapless inability to express himself, other than in the most hackneyed 'officialese'. ('Officialese', he at one point admitted, 'is my only language.')

> Clichés, stock phrases, adherence to conventional, standardized codes of expression and conduct have the socially recognised function of protecting us against reality, that is, against the claim on our thinking attention that all events and facts make by virtue of their existence. If

we were responsive to this claim all the time, we would soon be exhausted; Eichmann differed from the rest of us only in that he clearly knew of no such claim at all.[49]

What led Eichmann over the threshold into terrible evil was his sheer, exceptional thoughtlessness, or 'banality'. And hence the famous sub-title of the book: *A Report on the Banality of Evil*.

True, this phrase, 'the banality of evil', can scarcely be taken literally, as a definitive statement concerning the nature of *all* evil, unless the word 'evil' is being used in a peculiar, restricted sense: what she sees in Eichmann is not what one sees in Hitler, nor of course does Arendt pretend otherwise. So she distinguishes between 'evil', which is banal, and 'calculating wickedness'.[50] (Most of the Nazi leadership, on this account, would no doubt have to be said to have shown a mixture of both.) It may indeed be objected to her analysis of Nazism that she tends to minimize the role played by the 'calculating wickedness' of the leadership, to the extent of somewhat distorting the historical picture;[51] thus, one may well question the sharpness of the contrast she draws between totalitarianism and tyranny, and her emphasis on the blind automatism of the totalitarian system; it is debatable to what extent the ideological drive towards destruction really stemmed, as she suggests, from the 'evil' inherent in the mentality of the masses, rather than from the genuine conviction of the ideologues who manipulated them. But her priorities here are surely determined by the fact that she is writing first and foremost as a political moralist, and not simply as a historian. The potential for 'evil' being both far more widespread than the impulse to 'wickedness', and also that which historical reflection may much more readily serve to redeem, for those reasons it is from an ethical point of view the more appropriate focus. In as much as they attempted to demonize Eichmann, the prosecutors at his trial were actually following a universal but very suspect human inclination: the desire that the evil one should always be as easily identifiable, and as reassuringly remote from our own everyday normality, as possible. In *The Origins of Totalitarianism* Arendt herself had written of the holocaust as a manifestation of 'radical evil'; by which she meant an evil that went far beyond any possibility of adequate punishment, an evil that was literally unforgivable, an evil so pointless that it defied all real comprehension.[52] Reflecting on the Eichmann trial, however, she changed her mind: unpunishable and unforgivable though this evil unquestionably was, how does it help to call it incomprehensible? Is this not also a manoeuvre of evasion? And, accordingly, in her public letter to Gershom Scholem, she now wrote:

It is indeed my opinion that evil is never 'radical', that it is only extreme, and that it possesses neither depth nor any demonic dimension. It can overgrow and lay waste the entire world precisely because it spreads like a fungus on the surface. It is 'thought-defying', as I said, because thought tries to reach some depth, to go to the roots, and the moment it concerns itself with evil, it is frustrated because there is nothing. That is its 'banality'. Only the good has depth and can be radical.[53]

Only the creativity of the good truly exceeds the scope of our understanding, to the extent that we ourselves are not good enough to grasp how it is possible. There is plainly nothing incomprehensible in 'calculating wickedness', since one comprehends it in grasping its calculations. But then, neither is there any ultimate mystery in the sort of evil Eichmann represents – it just requires a different sort of explanation.

What, in other words, she sets herself to grasp is the latent evil of banality; evil, the way Augustine described it in his polemic against the Manichees, as in itself a nullity. And this one comprehends when one sees clearly just what it is that is most essentially missing here, the most basic precondition for any form of moral goodness. Banality consists of 'thoughtlessness'. In all his scheming and planning Eichmann never stopped to think what he was doing; that was the problem. And what exactly does it mean to 'think', in this sense? The first volume of *The Life of the Mind* bears the simple title, *Thinking*, and Arendt prefaces it with a quotation from Martin Heidegger:

> Thinking does not bring knowledge as do the sciences.
> Thinking does not produce usable practical wisdom.
> Thinking does not solve the riddles of the universe.
> Thinking does not endow us directly with the power to act.[54]

What was lacking in Eichmann was not any sort of scientific knowledge, practical know-how, metaphysical insight, or even, in the first instance, spontaneity; but what the terrible drama of his criminality helps to highlight above all is the vital necessity of that other activity which gets tangled up with each of these. This other activity cannot, in fact, be reduced to the quest for any particular species of knowledge or truth – not, that is, if one takes 'knowledge' and 'truth' in a positivistic manner, as referring to the irrefutable data of experience and research, such as may come to be incorporated into 'common sense' (whether this be the common sense of the multitude, or of a narrower group of scholarly experts). For what led to Eichmann's moral downfall was not, primarily, his lack of common sense either. But rather,

Arendt argues, what he most spectacularly lacked was any serious concern with what his work meant.

She refers to Kant in this connection:

> Kant's famous distinction between *Vernunft* [reason] and *Verstand* [intellect], between a faculty of speculative thought and the ability to know arising out of sense experience – where 'all thought is but a means to reach intuition' ('In whatever manner and by whatever means a cognition may relate to objects, *intuition* is that through which it is in immediate relation to them, and to which all thought is directed as a means') – has consequences more far-reaching, and even perhaps quite other, than those he himself recognized.[55]

Kant claimed to have denied knowledge in order to make room for faith, but in reality it is not so much faith as 'thinking' which stands in need of decisive liberation from the knowledge of *Verstand* – for it has to be recognised that 'the need of reason is not inspired by the quest for truth but by the quest for meaning. And truth and meaning are not the same'.[56] The difference here lies in the fact that 'the quest for meaning produces no end result that will survive the activity, that will make sense after the activity has come to its end',[57] but consists instead of a pure restlessness, circling its object, never finally satisfied, without any utility recognizable to the thoughtless. Nor is this quest by any means only to be identified with the specialist concerns of those whom Kant ('not without irony') called *Denker von Gewerbe*, professional thinkers. It is a universal vocation. Without it, no form of moral goodness is possible, simply because moral goodness requires choice, and the one who does not think is swept along by life's inertia. Thinking, as such, is just that which interrupts, calls a halt; the most elementary negation of the nullity which is the possibility of 'evil'.

The thinking Arendt means is, thus, where one *stops* and thinks. She refers, for example, to Xenophon's description of Socrates, how on one occasion he stood for some 24 hours stock still in the midst of a military camp wrestling with a problem, as an image of this. Yet she also quotes with approval (both at the end of *The Human Condition* and then, by way of a reprise, at the beginning of *The Life of the Mind*) 'a curious sentence' attributed by Cicero to Cato: 'never is a man more active than when he does nothing, never is he less alone than when he is by himself '.[58] 'Never is a man more active': the thinking ego is what is stirred into action by the admiring wonder at the world of which Socrates speaks in the *Theaetetus*.[59] But by the same token it also pushes towards the infinite scepticism of Cartesian solipsism; and similarly, it was Kant's reflection on the actual experience of thinking which led him to posit his distinction between the phenomenal and the noumenal. Our one direct encounter with a sub- stratum of reality beyond all 'appearance' is in the absolute inwardness of our self-awareness in the process of thought – the thinking ego, she argues, is the primary 'thing in itself'.[60] Indeed, it belongs to the very nature of thinking as opposed to *Verstand* that the world of appearance loses its commonsense reality. In thinking one dies to the world; from the world's point of view this may appear as a somewhat ludicrous absent-mindedness; or, again as in the case of Socrates, it may appear downright dangerous (although this is perhaps rarer than the vanity of philosophers would suggest). And to some extent no doubt rightly so: for that which dissolves common sense *ipso facto* dissolves the common world of ideas which provides the necessary stock in trade for any sort of politics, the best as well as the worst. Nor of course is there anything to prevent one, after thinking about a moral issue, from choosing wrongly, even wickedly. Thinking, after all, is never the only factor involved in ethical choice. Yet herein there nevertheless does lie a remedy, at least against certain ills. 'Never is a man less alone . . . than when he is by himself': in illustration of this she also cites the closing lines of the Platonic dialogue, 'Hippias Major', where, as Socrates bids farewell to Hippias, he jokingly laments his own fate: having to share his home with a most tiresome character, his 'close relative', who is bound to cross-examine him when he gets back, retracing the course of their discussion and taunting him with the inadequacy of the answers he gave (the workaday cousin, one might say, to his *daimon*). How 'blissfully fortunate' the simple-minded Hippias is to be spared such a relationship with himself! Is it not out of just such dialogue that conscience emerges? That is: the sort of conscience which is more than just an internalizing of social norms; which transcends social conditioning; and which can therefore still operate for good even in the most corrupt of social environments – where the norms and the conditioning merely reinforce evil. Such conscientiousness arises out of the habit of internal dialogue, the 'two-in-one' of thinking, itself – to some extent, Arendt intimates, even when the actual subject matter of that dialogue, up to the critical moment, has been unrelated to the choice in question.[61] Thus, it is the sheer process which counts. For

the partner who comes to life when you are alert and alone is the only one from whom you can never get away – except by ceasing to think. It is better to suffer wrong than to do wrong, because you can remain the friend of the sufferer; who would want to be the friend of and have to live together with a murderer? Not even another murderer . . .

When Socrates goes home, he is *by* himself. Clearly, with this fellow who awaits him, Socrates has to come to some kind of agreement, because they live under the same roof. Better to be at odds with the whole world than be at odds with the only one you are forced to live together with when you have left company behind —[62]

when the current of social life is broken.

The Life of the Mind was conceived, in systematic terms, as a three-part work: from 'thinking', Arendt turns in the second volume to 'willing', as the faculty which the apostle Paul 'discovered'; sadly she died just before starting on the third part, concerned with 'judging', in which, it seems, the main focus was to have been on Kant's *Critique of Judgement*. There is an underlying thesis here, a certain hierarchical progression. Just as labour, work and action represent the three basic divisions of the *vita activa*, so thinking, willing and judging represent the three basic divisions of the *vita contemplativa*. (As Agnes Heller remarks, the implication no doubt is that *Verstand*, on the contrary, belongs to the *vita activa*; just as, in the case of both willing and judging, one has to distinguish between two different aspects, their role in the purely interior dialectic of the *vita contemplativa*, and their corporate role, as a collective will or collective judgement.[63]) Thinking entails a pure withdrawal from the world; it is, however, a withdrawal which is necessary, not just for its own sake but, more importantly, also for the world's sake. Where this withdrawal is reinforced by being caught up into a conscious discipline of the will, so much the better. But the act of judging – whilst, as part of the *vita contemplativa*, it remains withdrawn – nevertheless turns back towards the world; and it is, therefore, in the cultivation of this faculty that the *vita contemplativa* comes to its true fulfilment.

Here then, if you like, is the spirituality underlying Arendt's *amor mundi*. It culminates in a gaze directed, not towards the infinite beyond – not, for all her Kantianism, towards 'the starry skies above and the moral law within', not towards the eternal – but, far more, towards history, the domain of potential freedom-in-action, the object of free-spirited judgement. Her wisdom is the wisdom of the always 'innocent' spectator; innocent, yet at the same time profoundly mistrustful of that innocence, inasmuch as innocence alone will never be enough to save us. All her writings, in short, stem from her preoccupation with the flames of the holocaust: how was it possible? The trajectory of her thought is in the direction of an ever-increasing generality of response: from the analysis of the more immediate causes in *The Origins of Totalitarianism* to a more general analysis of the relevant aspects of modernity as a whole, the 'triumph' of the *animal laborans* and the 'vanishing' of *auctoritas*; and from that to the final generality of *The Life of the Mind*. But it is here, in *The Life of the Mind*, that she comes closest to reflecting on her own procedure, throughout her work. For notwithstanding her radical critique of philosophy for its tendency to devalue the *vita activa*, Arendt herself consistently writes very much in a mode of contemplative judgement, largely detached from the turbulent hurly-burly of action.

Her only direct personal participation in any organized form of political campaigning was, for a while in the 1930s and early 1940s, in the context of Zionism; yet she was never in sympathy with the more militantly nationalistic turn which the Zionist movement took under the leadership of Ben-Gurion, following the 1942 Biltmore Conference. And this involvement pre-dated any of her major writings. The ultimate detachment with which she writes about politics is indeed very much of a piece with the way she also writes about religion – as a phenomenological observer rather than as a theologian, with the actual issue of her own faith or lack of it always strictly bracketed. In this regard, perhaps the thinker to whom she is actually most closely akin, of the many she discusses, is that most elusive of controversialists, Lessing. Thus, like Lessing, she too remains publicly uncommitted to anything, in the final analysis – except pluralism.

Simone Weil

Arendt's relative detachment from particular political causes is perhaps a necessary precondition for her radical affirmation of isonomy, as the ideal space for political causes in general. In Simone Weil's thinking, however, the dynamic is just the opposite: thus, whereas Arendt is a contemplative mistrustful of contemplation, Weil is an activist mistrustful of activism.

Unlike Arendt, she is a thinker wrestling with the implications of her commitment to communities which were in direct competition with fascism for people's loyalties: the trade union movement, the church. She was in fact a predecessor of Arendt in adopting the term 'totalitarianism' from fascist theory and reversing its evaluative thrust; although she uses it in a much broader sense than Arendt – applying it not only to the twentieth century but also to earlier phenomena, such as the Roman Empire or Gothic Christendom. But what differentiates Weil's critical approach is that she, as it were, tackles totalitarian ideology on its own ground. Over against the totalitarian movements of the right, with their claim to be the restorers of rootedness to the uprooted, she seeks to rethink the notion of roots at a much deeper level; over against the totalitarian movements of the left, with their claim to represent the true interests of the labouring masses, she attempts an altogether more radical affirmation of the potential dignity of labour. She is combating totalitarianism on its own ground, yet what she mistrusts is the tendency for communities of resistance against barbarism to be dragged down, in the process of such struggle, towards the moral level of what they oppose. Her question is how this can be avoided; and her answer: only by a decisive orientation to the '*absolute* good'. This then results in an increasingly eccentric stance within the labour movement, as an heretical anarcho-syndicalist; and an extremely heterodox form of Christian faith, in which the decision not to be baptized becomes a prophetic act of solidarity with all outsiders.

Déracinement

When, in her last major work, Weil takes up the topic of 'the need for roots' she is grappling with a major theme of Nazi propaganda: the Nazis' inheritance from Romanticism, by way of the *völkisch* ideology arising in reaction to German industrialization; the tradition associated with such diverse names as Wilhelm Heinrich Riehl, Eugen Diederichs, Adolf Stoecker, Julius Langbehn, Paul de Lagarde, Houston Stewart Chamberlain, Heinrich von Treitschke, Moeller van den Bruck. Running through this tradition one finds a polemical lament over the uprootedness of the new urban proletariat, associated with nostalgia for the Middle Ages and an often rather sentimental idealization of traditional village or small-town life; a lament which is, however, further fitted for the 'us'-against-'them' needs of propaganda by being hitched on to the traditional prejudices of anti-Semitism, on the grounds that if uprootedness is an evil, then so much the more reason to struggle against those 'root-less cosmopolitans' the Jews.[64] In France, much the same argument was developed, first by Maurice Barrès, and then by Charles Maurras and his colleagues in the *Action française*. As a matter of fact, there is surely a certain sense in which one of the most remarkable features of the more religious forms of diaspora Judaism has been precisely their extraordinary capacity to put down new roots wherever they have been transplanted; thereby preserving that 'obstinate' separateness of the Jews, against which anti-Semitism is originally a reaction. But, of course, the point is that here that old inherited animosity is neatly transferred elsewhere: to the would-be assimilated Jew.

Weil, an assimilated Jew herself, naturally develops her critique of *déracinement* in a very different way. She is concerned with the nature of totalitarian ideology as a spurious response to a genuine need: totalitarian movements are movements of the uprooted, and their success is for her the prime indication of just how thoroughly uprooted large segments of the population in the affected countries had become. But the cures they propose touch only the symptoms, not the true cause of the sickness; which indeed they only aggravate intensely – reinforcing the problem from which they thrive. The reasons are quite straightforward: the need for roots, as a need common to all cultures, is in the first place a need for peace, whereas totalitarianism issues in war. And then, alongside the violent disruption brought by war, conquest, deportation and the deliberate destruction of traditional culture by government action, the other great positive force working towards the destruction of rooted community is the logic of money, the impulse to economic growth at all costs, to which totalitarian regimes also surrender.[65]

In effect, she tries to refute *völkisch* ideology by turning its own techniques, of argument by caricature and the construction of world-historical stereotypes, against it. Thus, she too associates *déracinement* with the Jews, or rather with the heritage of ancient Israel. And, whilst her critique of that heritage may not exactly be racist in character, it is outrageously one-sided. But then she links it with Rome. She accepts the boast of the Italian Fascists, and of the *Action française*, to represent a renaissance of the true spirit of ancient Rome; and moreover she argues that, notwithstanding the Nazis' hankering after Wagnerian prototypes, this was also true of them. In their lust for world dominion, and in the cynicism of their methods, they were in reality far more Roman than authentically Teutonic.[66] Whereas Arendt, when she thinks of Rome, thinks of civic virtue, the rule of law, and the amazing stability of a system built upon solid foundations of *auctoritas* – all the things that 'Rome' had also meant to the French and American revolutionaries of the eighteenth century – Weil, by contrast, thinks primarily of great massacres committed by Roman armies; which she immediately further associates with all that is most bloodthirsty in the deuteronomic literature of ancient Israel. Rome and Israel, the two powers involved in the crucifixion of Christ, symbolically coalesce for her, as the two classic embodiments of 'idolatry' – a society's worship of the projection of its own corporate identity. With these modes of argument she is clearly playing with fire.

However, she does also have some other more genuinely interesting things to say. In fact, it seems to me that another major problem with her discussion of the need for roots is the way she runs together three quite distinct forms of rootedness: three forms which, again, directly correspond to the basic Arendtian distinction between labour, work and action. One may be rooted in one's experience of labour. One may be rooted in relation to the world of work. One may be rooted in relation to an ethos of action. The first form is to feel oneself at home where one makes one's living; the second is to have a strong sense of belonging, creatively, to a particular cultural tradition; the third means not to feel oneself the victim of political coercion, or continually threatened by it – and therefore not to be subject to aggressive impulses of *ressentiment*. The caricatural element in Weil's argument has to do exclusively with this third level. So, in illustration of the principle that '*qui est déraciné déracine*'[67] she contends that both the Romans and the Israelites were essentially rootless peoples – the former an 'artificial' people from the beginning, the latter a people never fully recovered from the uprooting experience of slavery – who therefore uprooted others (an argument which skips over the centuries with breathtaking abandon). But one certainly could not say that either the Romans or the Israelites were rootless peoples in the sense of lacking a coherent cultural tradition; nor in relation to their land or their cities. And Weil's most interesting insights actually have to do with the modern problematic of rootedness in the experience of labour.

'*Déracinement*' in this sense signifies the experience of alienation in one's job, considered as a *spiritual* problem – and hence in terms of its cultural consequences. Already in *Oppression and Liberty* the connection Weil sees between good employment practice and being well-rooted in a community is clear:

> A team of workers on a production-line under the eye of a foreman is a sorry spectacle, whereas it is a fine sight to see a handful of workmen in the building trade, checked by some difficulty, ponder the problem each for himself, make various suggestions for dealing with it, and then apply unanimously the method conceived by one of them, who may or may not have any official authority over the remainder. At such moments the image of a free community appears almost in its purity.[68]

The workers on the production line have no immediate experience of community in their labour – whereas in an ideal culture 'all human relations, from the most superficial to the very tenderest, would have about them something of that manly and brotherly feeling which forms the bond between workmates', where labour is truly co-operative.[69] (There is obviously also quite a harsh judgement implicit in this particular way of putting the point, on the given social roles of women.[70]) Good working practice both generates rootedness and depends on a context of rootedness; but '*qui est déraciné déracine*'. The key difference between the vicious circle and the virtuous one lies in the quality of the experience of labour involved. In short, whilst Arendt in *The Human Condition* places labour on the lowest level of the *vita activa* and directs her polemic against the corruption of our understanding of that which is the highest, namely, the domain of action to which isonomous politics belongs, by prejudices deriving from the experience of this lower level Weil on the contrary envisages an ideal civilization whose governing principle would be none other than the upholding of the proper dignity of labour. She believes that 'the most fully human civilization would be that which had manual labour as its pivot, that in which manual labour constituted the supreme value'.[71]

But to render manual labour 'the supreme value' in the sense intended here would mean transforming what Arendt fears, the spirit of the *animal laborans*, into quite another spirit. For the *animal laborans* is what one sees (at its most extreme) in Taylorism, the 'scientific management' of time and motion in the factory where the workers are treated as part of the machinery. And Weil's whole concern is with the dehumanizing impact of such attitudes: precisely this being, for her, the basic underlying problem which the success of totalitarianism serves most spectacularly to highlight.[72]

In response, she appeals to a tradition going back, she suggests, to Bacon. 'The idea of labour considered as a human value', she writes,

is doubtless the one and only spiritual conquest achieved by the human mind since the miracle of Greece; this was perhaps the only gap in the ideal of human life elaborated by Greece and left behind by her as an undying heritage.[73]

With regard to Bacon, she admires particularly his saying, 'We cannot command Nature except by obeying her'; of which she remarks,

This simple pronouncement ought to form by itself the Bible of our times. It suffices to define true labour, the kind which forms free men, and that to the very extent to which it is an act of conscious submission to necessity.[74]

The vital word here is 'conscious'. So, she advocates a systematic popularizing of scientific knowledge,

a science whose ultimate aim would be the perfecting of technique not by rendering it more powerful, but simply more conscious and more methodical. . . . Such a science would be, in effect, a method for mastering nature, or a catalogue of concepts indispensable for attaining to such mastery, arranged according to an order that would make them palpably clear to the mind.[75]

It would be a question of demystifying complex technology to those who labour with it, rendering labour as little robot-like as possible – and she thinks that this also corresponds to Descartes's ideal conception of science. In general, she proposes that we judge the moral health of any civilization, first and foremost, by the way labour is organized and valued within it: by asking how far it manages to eliminate soul-destroying drudgery even in the case of the simplest and most monotonous of tasks, so that, whatever anyone is doing, they are enabled truly to attend to it, give their mind to it. It is in this sense that manual labour would constitute 'the supreme value' of an ideal culture. More exactly expressed perhaps, the preservation of labour from drudgery would constitute its supreme priority.

Other literary representatives of the modern tradition which has opened up this ideal include Goethe (notably the conclusion to *Faust*), Rousseau, Shelley, George Sand – 'and, above all, Tolstoy, who developed this theme throughout the whole of his work in matchless accents'.[76] It is of supreme importance, in her view, that what Marx called 'the degrading division of labour into intellectual and manual labour' be overcome;[77] and, at the same time, that the labouring classes themselves should so far as possible take over the organization of their own labour, maybe somewhat along the lines suggested by Proudhon. Weil admires Marx's historical materialism as a methodology, but is profoundly critical of what she terms the 'religious' element in Marxism, the persistent remainder of wish-fulfilling fantasy in the Marxist 'myth of progress'. She is in fact one of the first commentators to emphasize the implicit contradiction between the standpoint of Marx's early writings, with their critical analysis of the alienating quality of modern industrial labour, and that of his later works, dominated by this historicist faith, which tends on the contrary to validate a quite uncritical acceptance of every latest technological development – the sort of attitude which comes out, for instance, in Lenin's enthusiastic advocacy of Taylorism in the 1920s. The one Marxist thinker for whom she – like Arendt – has real admiration is the libertarian, and heretical, Rosa Luxemburg. Against Marx, she sides with Saint-Simon and Proudhon: what counts, as she sees it, is not so much who *owns* the means of production, but far rather the manner in which labour is divided up and *managed*, the relationship of the labourers to the machinery they operate, the potential for oppression inherent in the very rhythm of the production process itself.[78]

What Weil envisages as authentic rootedness is the absolute opposite to *völkisch* rootedness, politically speaking: for, if to be rooted entails any kind of patriotic loyalty, then this in her view can only be to the creative achievements of a cultural tradition. It cannot be to a nation, or to a race; it cannot involve any pride in military conquest, or the status of one's people as a power in the world; it can have nothing to do with the sort of 'heroic glamour' one finds, say, in the dramas of Corneille. But rather, she suggests, in its purest expression it appears as compassion for one's country. It is what we encounter in Jesus, weeping over Jerusalem, foreseeing its destruction:

This poignantly tender feeling for some beautiful, precious, fragile, and perishable object has a warmth about it which the sentiment of national grandeur altogether lacks.[79]

It involves, not least, compassion for those who have been uprooted. Authentic patriotism does not need enemies; Weil, in exile with the Free French forces in London, was actually quite mistrustful of the patriotism inspiring the resistance in France, inasmuch as this was a patriotism essentially defined by its opposition to an enemy; and again she refers back to the New Testament:

There was once a nation which believed itself to be holy, with the direst consequences for its well-being; and . . . it is strange to reflect that the Pharisees were the resisters in this nation, and the publicans the collaborators, and then to remind oneself what were Christ's relations with each of these two national groups.[80]

There need be no clash between national and other loyalties, she argues: one cannot legitimately seek to mobilize patriotism in the cause of political centralization, as a means of melting down regional or ethnic distinctions within a state; nor is it to be confused with the cause of a reactionary nationalism, rejecting moves towards greater international co-operation. Most importantly of all, it has to be kept in strict subordination to the prior demands of faith:

If the word patriotism is used in its strongest sense, its complete sense, a Christian has only one country that can be the object of such patriotism, and that is situated outside this world.[81]

Weil's other-worldliness remains qualified by her concern for real rootedness within the world. She is other-worldly, primarily, in relation to the world of the *Volk*: for her, in total contrast to the conception of *völkisch* ideology, our need for roots is ideally to be satisfied by way of participation in a cosmopolitan community of faith, a truly catholic community. The community must be one which includes both intellectuals and labourers on equal terms, and it has to be one which is as effective as possible in bringing these disparate groups together in a common loyalty – in order that the disastrous gulf between the two spheres of life they represent may eventually be overcome. That is where she moves into territory uncharted by Arendt. But then, at once, she also goes on to raise the basic question: how to attain this goal without taking any type of *völkisch* short-cut?

'The absolute good'

In order to distance her thought, in the most decisive way, not only from *völkisch* ideology but from all forms of corporate egoism, Weil therefore proceeds to distinguish very sharply between the sort of goodness which may indeed come to be bound up with such ideology, and the true Good, which is 'absolute'.

'There are two goods', she writes,

> of the same denomination but radically different from one another: one which is the opposite of evil and one which is the absolute. The absolute has no opposite. The relative is not the opposite of the absolute; it is derived from it through a relationship which is not commutative. That which we want is the absolute good. That which is within our reach is the good which is correlated to evil. We betake ourselves to it by mistake, like the prince who starts to make love to the maid instead of the mistress. The error is due to the clothes.

The absolute good has no opposite in the sense that its demands are infinite: they are not limited by being opposed to any particular evil. And every ideology that falls short of the absolute is in some measure, for her, a species of 'idolatry' – which is, essentially, society's worship of itself. 'It is the social', she goes on,

> which throws the colour of the absolute over the relative. The remedy is in the idea of relationship. Relationship breaks its way out of the social. It is the monopoly of the individual. Society is the cave. The way out is solitude.[82]

Totalitarianism is the most extreme manifestation of idolatry; and the moral of the story of totalitarianism, in her interpretation, is that we need to renounce any supposed good that falls short of the absolute, defined in this manner.

Here again we encounter a radical contradiction between her position and Arendt's. It is not, of course, that Arendt wants to defend corporate egoism as such; and no doubt a good deal of what Weil criticizes as 'the social', in distinction from what pertains to 'relationship', coincides exactly with what Arendt herself criticizes under the same heading – in distinction from what pertains to authentic worldliness. But from the Arendtian point of view Weil's critical strategy is nevertheless, quite simply, far too sweeping. For, in arguing along such lines, Weil does just what Arendt's strict division of the *vita activa* from the *vita contemplativa* is meant to preclude: she takes an evaluative standard deriving from the requirements of the latter and applies it to the former.

This, as we have seen, is Arendt's complaint against the entire Christian-Platonist tradition. Weil, however, represents the agapaic, other-city element of that tradition in its purest and most eloquent form. When she writes, 'society is the cave' – of Plato's *Republic* – her interpretation links the cave directly to that other passage where Socrates compares the species of ethical teaching he rejects to the behaviour of someone confronted with a terrifying 'great beast' which he is anxious to humour, and who therefore resolves to call whatever pleases the beast 'good' and whatever displeases it 'bad'; the great beast being 'society' – which is also the cave. She is, in fact, a quite unequivocal admirer of Plato, whose doctrine she considers a pure anticipation of Christianity.[83] The absolute good is in the first place the Platonic 'idea' of the Good. Yet at the same time her Christianity is profoundly Kantian as well as Platonist; and she reiterates the view formulated in the famous opening sentence of Kant's *Groundwork of the Metaphysics of Morals*, that 'there is nothing in the world which can be termed absolutely and altogether good, other than a good *will* '.[84] Indeed, in Arendtian terms, the innermost core of her metaphysics consists of a meditation on experiences proper to the second level of the *vita contemplativa*, the level of 'willing'; or, rather – it lies in her articulation of the intrinsic conflict between thinking and willing, where thinking is understood as an essentially receptive activity and willing as an essentially self-expressive one (a conflict which, in a non-theistic form, Arendt also finds paradigmatically expressed in the later thought of Martin Heidegger[85]). Weil herself prefers to speak of the appropriation of the absolute Good as a matter of 'attention': thus she says, 'we have to try to cure our faults by attention and not by will'.[86] The absolute good represents the will of God; the relative good is what we may will independently of God – and the path to the absolute is, in that sense, therefore one of willing-not-to-will. She has numerous formulas for this sort of radical 'obedience':

> The extinction of desire (Buddhism) – or detachment – or *amor fati* – or desire for the absolute good – these all amount to the same: to empty desire, finality of all content, to desire in the void, to desire without any wishes.
>
> To detach our desire from all good things and to wait. Experience proves that this waiting is satisfied. It is then we touch the absolute good.[87]

To 'touch the absolute good' in no way implies any lessening of the energy with which life is lived; but, as she puts it, 'we have to go down to the root of our desires in order to tear the energy from its object'. We have to 'desire without an object', that is, without any object deriving from the particular perspective of the self. Neither does this by any means imply an absolute withdrawal from action; but it requires the sort of action which is praised in the *Bhagavad Gita* – a 'non-acting action'; where in place of any self-expressive goal there is simply a 'void'. One comes to the absolute good by way of an attentive 'acceptance of the void'.

She is here, amongst other things, systematically undercutting the spiritual basis for any politics of corporate self-expression, the 'romantic' element, so to speak, flowing into totalitarianism. The way out of the cave is a way of unromantic inner solitude. This contemplative discipline is fulfilled in the test of that most solitary of conditions, the experience of affliction which St John of the Cross called 'the dark night of the soul', where all sense of the presence of God is lost, where there is no longer any desirable 'object' in prayer, no consolation at all – and yet one persists. Weil adds a new metaphysical dimension to the traditional concept of the dark night, and she also takes it out of the cloister and into the work-place. Metaphysically, she presents it as an experience of 'de-creation', the only means by which we may be reunited with the Creator, and indeed 'participate in the creation of the world':

> In a sense God renounces being everything. We should renounce being something. That is our only good.[88]

She views the cross of Christ in this light: 'The crucifixion of God is eternal. "The lamb that was slain before the foundation of the world" . . .'.[89]

Crucifixion becomes for her the definitive symbol of divine creativity, which is itself an act of renunciation rather than of self-expression. And, at the same time, she links the dark night to the experience of degraded manual labour, the experience of the slave, unalleviated by any real reward or compensation. We have here a discipline of the will which is in fact both Christian and Stoic, in more or less equal measure. Weil is Stoic in her radical refusal of wish-fulfilling fantasy, and her love for that beauty which is for her the highest form of beauty, the beauty of the order of the world as a whole, in all its impersonal necessity and even apparent cruelty; the Stoic *amor fati*, or love of reality for reality's sake. Two of the aspects of Christianity which she finds most questionable are the consolatory notion of the afterlife, and the interventionist notion of providence; both of which represent a turning aside from *amor fati*. 'Christianity', she writes,

> will not be incarnated so long as there is not joined to it the Stoics' filial piety for the city of the world, for the country of here below which is the universe. When as a result of some misapprehension, very difficult to understand today, Christianity cut itself off from Stoicism, it condemned itself to an abstract and separate existence.[90]

Yet she is also Christian in her going beyond the prudential Stoic quest for *apatheia*, inner tranquillity; in her orientation towards the infinite demands of *agapé*, the love of one's neighbour understood in a contemplative sense as a form of 'implicit' love for God. Thus, in her thinking Stoic *amor fati* and Christian *agapé* coincide, as a double defence of the integrity of the individual against the (potentially totalitarian) blandishments of the 'social', the Great Beast, with all its illusory hopes and excuses for insensitivity.

And, from the Arendtian point of view, perhaps – so far so good. The problems arise, however, just as soon as Weil seeks to apply these same primarily contemplative principles, without further ado, directly to the public realm, the domain of the *vita activa*. For it is not just the Great Beast which depends upon our attachment to the 'relative' good; the whole *vita activa* depends upon it. Absolute goodness may find expression in 'relationship', but only in private: there can be no *public* agreement to act in concert without clearly definable goals, and hence a clear sense of the particular evils to which one is opposed. The transcendent authority of the absolute good seems radically to dissolve any form of worldly *auctoritas*, and also, at any rate in effect, to devalue the worldly solidarity of isonomous freedom.

1. The denial of auctoritas

The intrinsic tension between Weil's two themes of the need for roots and the absoluteness of the true good emerges with particular sharpness when in the latter context she actually writes, 'It is necessary *to uproot oneself*. To cut down the tree and make of it a cross, and then to carry it every day.'[91] How then, in general, is one to distinguish between the rootedness which is a fundamental need of the human soul, and the rootedness – the real rootedness and not just its ideological glorification – which tends, on the contrary, to enslave us to the Great Beast? Clearly, rootedness as a matter of humane and non-alienating economic practice is an unequivocal good. But what is much more equivocal is rootedness in the sense of a natural predisposition to be loyal to the established authorities; an attitude which – partly depending on the circumstances – may either be judged as legitimately conservative or else as illegitimately reactionary.

Weil is a thinker whose primary political sympathies, to the end of her life, continued to lie with the revolutionary anarcho-syndicalist tradition. Yet she also writes, 'Obedience to a man whose authority is not illuminated by legitimacy – that is a nightmare.' And

> The only thing which is able to turn pure legitimacy – an idea absolutely devoid of force – into something sovereign is the thought: 'Thus it has always been and thus it will always continue to be.'[92]

What this formulation is evidently designed, first and foremost, to exclude is the sort of obedience demanded by totalitarian or other modern political movements, in the name of an ideology of progress. And in much the same spirit – notwithstanding her bitter hostility to what she terms the 'totalitarian' heritage of Gothic Christendom – she also, somewhat curiously, praises the particular form of rootedness represented by the mediaeval feudal system:

> The feudal bond, in making obedience a matter between one man and another, greatly reduces the part played by the Great Beast.
> The law does so better still.
> There should be no obedience except to the law or to a man.[93]

– for the reason, presumably, that in neither of these cases does ideology necessarily obtrude. However, it is not only progressive ideology which is excluded here. There is, equally, no space left for *auctoritas* either. After all, a legitimacy which depends on the thought, 'thus it has been and thus it will always continue to be', is not one which makes much reference to a tradition, or to any historical origins; but, instead, in such circumstances the basis for authority has been completely dehistoricized – the self-reflective-ness of tradition being displaced by unself-reflective custom. (In the passage cited above she goes on to refer to the ethos of Christian monasticism as a model for what she is advocating, and that is admittedly an ethos with a very strong element of *auctoritas* in it. Yet it does not seem to be that aspect of it which she means to praise.)

The only sort of worldly authority, in short, which she will allow is one which does not seek to justify itself in any way, but which is simply there, with the illusory appearance of a fact of nature. Paradoxically, it is just such illusion that she seeks to affirm. Of course, no worldly authority can represent more than a relative good; the absolute is always transcendent of any particular worldly order. But at least – so the implicit logic of her thought appears to run – an authority which does not seek to justify itself, because it does not have to, can never be tempted to press its claims, positively and idolatrously, *against* the absolute.

Weil is radically Christian in her concern with obedience as a discipline of the will. Yet she had also seen how a rhetoric of obedience can degenerate into an apology for collusion with totalitarianism; and this, then, is where she tries to draw the line. The obvious problem, however, is that in modern culture, so saturated with historical consciousness, such a naively ahistorical model of authority scarcely seems to be possible, as a functioning ideal. For, by definition, an ideal of that sort defies conscious appropriation.

2. The effective undermining of isonomy

Nor is Weil's position any less problematic in relation to the Arendtian ideal of isonomy – despite the fact that, in its negative sense of 'no-rule', this is very much something she too would have wished to affirm. Unfortunately though, as Arendt herself argues, the sheer absoluteness of the absolute good effectively seems to undermine any more positive ethos, supportive of such politics.

Thus, absolute moral goodness implies absolute purity of motive. It is good done for the sake of the good itself, and not for any other reward; certainly not, therefore, for the sake of praise or glory; nor even for the sake of feeling good. 'Goodness in an absolute sense, as distinguished from the "good-for" or the "excellent" in Greek or Roman antiquity, became known in our civilization', Arendt remarks, 'only with the rise of Christianity.'[94] It is intimately bound up with the Pauline/Augustinian 'discovery' of the will:

inasmuch as 'will' is precisely a name for desire baptized with the vocation to purity of motive.

It is this which gives rise to the inwardness of the early Christian love ethic – with its attitude 'so admirably summed up in Tertullian's formula: *nec ulla magis res aliena quam publica* ("no matter is more alien to us than what matters publicly")'.[95] If one original source of this was the apostolic church's expectation of the world's imminent end, the other source, she argues, was precisely the unprecedented ethical absolutism inherent in the preaching of Jesus. She refers, for instance, to the Sermon on the Mount, and to the text, 'When you give alms, do not let your left hand know what your right is doing; your good deed must be secret'.[96] What applies to almsgiving presumably applies across the board, to all good deeds: in absolute terms, she remarks, 'goodness can exist only when it is not perceived, not even by its author; whoever sees himself performing a good work is no longer good, but at best a useful member of society or a dutiful member of a church'.[97] Obviously, though, such absolutism is radically depoliticizing in implication. Given the fallen-ness of human nature, anyone who seeks – as Weil does – to maintain the pure claims of the absolute in strict opposition to any compromise with worldly actuality is more or less bound to withdraw from the political domain, as a place of endless temptation, in which one may be rewarded for one's achievements, and can scarcely escape being influenced by the corrupting possibility of such reward. And then one has just abandoned the struggle on which the very possibility of isonomy depends. Nothing indeed could be more alien to the ethos of the *polis* – an ethos essentially constituted by a particular taste for certain forms of public performance. The world of the *polis* had no notion of this sort of goodness, which 'must go into absolute hiding and flee all appearance if it is not to be destroyed';[98] and which is ultimately impossible, inasmuch as absolute concealment is impossible ('Why do you call me good? No one is good except God alone'[99]). Purity of motivation was simply not an issue in that culture; but on the contrary, it was a world which treasured freedom because it valued the display of individual excellence, and so sought to maximize the possibilities for such display, not least in the form of politics. From this point of view, the problem with an unrelieved ethical absolutism is the way in which it tends to confirm people in their inner loneliness.[100] Weil herself never quite withdrew from politics. Nevertheless, her reflections on the claims of the absolute do date from a period when her political engagement was becoming more and more episodic and idiosyncratically individualistic; and in the end the chief value she finds in her experience of politics is the disillusionment it has brought: 'To contemplate the social is as good a way of detachment as to retire from the world. That is why I have not been wrong to rub shoulders with politics for so long.'[101]

There is indeed, in Arendt's view, a curious contradiction in the bonding together of the ideal Christian community – the community that Augustine speaks of as the 'heavenly city' – by love, in the sense of *agapé*. For the authenticity of *agapé* entirely depends on its association with the absolute good, understood in this way: 'love, in distinction from friendship, is killed, or rather extinguished, the moment it is displayed in public'. So that, strictly speaking, 'because of its inherent worldlessness, love can only become false and perverted when it is used for political purposes such as the change or salvation of the world'.[102] The church, of course, as an earthly institution, always retains at least some residual traces of worldliness in practice; but the whole point of the concept of the heavenly city lies in its non-coincidence with the church, its character as an ultimate focus for Christian loyalty transcendent of the church. 'Historically', she remarks,

> we know of only one principle that was ever devised to keep a community of people together who had lost their interest in the common world and felt themselves no longer related and separated by it. To find a bond between people strong enough to replace the world was the main political task of early Christian philosophy, and it was Augustine who proposed to found not only the Christian 'brotherhood' but all human relationships on charity.

She quotes Augustine: 'Even robbers have between them (*inter se*) what they call charity':

> This surprising illustration of the Christian political principle is in fact very well chosen, because the bond of charity between people, while it is incapable of founding a public realm of its own, is quite adequate to the main Christian principle of worldlessness and is admirably fit to carry a group of essentially worldless people through the world, a group of saints or a group of criminals.[103]

All the wordly virtues of free-spirited political action are here discounted as manifestations of sinful pride; hence the high priority given to the twin virtues of obedience and humility in the traditional spirituality of the Christian monastic orders, 'the only communities in which the principle of charity as a political principle was ever tried' as a conscious organizational project.[104] The very fact that the heavenly city is a city, that is, a real community, at least partially embodied within the church, renders it a far more substantial sort of refuge than pagan philosophy had ever envisaged for itself. Consequently, Christianity is able to provide what Platonism could not: a well-established framework to guarantee the option of a spiritual life lived in radical freedom from politics; an option which, to be sure, Arendt also sees as a vital necessity for any truly healthy political culture to preserve.[105] But the trouble is that that option is then extended to a wholesale rejection of worldliness.

Moreover, one might also cite other texts from the Sermon on the Mount to illustrate the conflict between ethical absolutism and the isonomous ideal. Weil defines absolute goodness as the abandonment of one's own particular perspective on life for the perspective of God. And this immediately recalls Jesus's injunction that we should 'love' our enemies. Those, however, who are incapable of holding fast in principled and stubborn opposition to their enemies are also incapable of political loyalty. Perhaps such opposition is not incompatible with 'love'; be that as it may, Weil's view is perfectly explicit: an authentic loyalty to the absolute must in fact tend to relativize and weaken not only patriotic sentiment, as discussed above, but in the same way all other forms of loyalty. Yet, for the 'no-rule' of isonomy to prosper, what could be more necessary than the establishment of strong bonds of mutual loyalty, political friendship, camaraderie – as an alternative foundation for being-together? In Matthew's version of the Sermon on the Mount, the injunction to love one's enemies is set side by side with the injunction not to resist those who wrong you, to turn the other cheek. The context, of course, is the Roman occupation of Palestine: 'If someone in authority presses you into service for one mile', the passage goes on, 'go with him two'[106] – it was the established right of any Roman legionary to conscript a Jewish passer-by to carry his pack. Is the implication therefore that it is illegitimate to be involved in any direct mode of political resistance to oppressive rule? Perhaps not; maybe this teaching is rather to be understood as an early anticipation of the Gandhian politics of *ahimsa*. But, then, consider the saying which Luke juxtaposes to loving one's enemies: 'Do not judge, and you will not be judged.'[107] Compare the role Arendt ascribes to the faculty of judgement, as the meeting point of the *vita contemplativa* and the *vita activa*; is not good judgement of character a basic political virtue? And yet here again, the beauty of the ideal lies in the absoluteness of the prohibition. In the same way: 'Do not be anxious about tomorrow, tomorrow will look after itself.'[108] Such freedom from anxiety may be the necessary precondition for a proper generosity of spirit on the part of an individual, but in political terms it would clearly be absolute irresponsibility. Or what about the prohibition of oaths in Matthew 5: 33–7? An oath does not have to be an outright loyalty oath in order to represent a pledge of political loyalty; any (solemn) oath which invokes what is sacred to one's community has the effect of affirming one's identity as a member of that community. And thus this teaching too may well be taken as yet another symbolic expression of withdrawal from public affairs, in the name of the absolute.

Arendt regards Jesus as the 'discoverer' of one of the most fundamental requirements of the *vita activa*: namely, the practice of forgiveness. No one before Jesus, she argues, had grasped the true 'miracle-working' potential of forgiveness, to make all things new.[109] Over against the ethical absolutism of the Sermon on the Mount, however, she also refers with approval to Machiavelli's notorious contention that, when it comes to politics, one needs sometimes (in the Christian sense) to learn 'how *not* to be good'.[110] This is by no means a sheer denial of morality: Machiavelli, of course, is not suggesting that one should learn how to be evil; but rather that, in the pursuit of political *virtu*, it is necessary, as he expresses it in another place, to 'love one's native city more than one's own soul'.[111] It must at once be said that Arendt is very critical of any attempt, such as Machiavelli makes on this basis, to rehabilitate violence as a legitimate instrument of politics. But – in the most radical contrast to Weil – she too ranks love of the polity decisively above any more introspective concern with individual salvation.

Nevertheless, the sheer moral force of the absolutist vision can scarcely be gainsaid.

A key element in Arendt's analysis of the phenomenon of political revolution is her meditation on the complicity of genuine goodness with impulses towards violence. On the one hand she considers the potential role played by the unreflective goodness of natural innocence, which just because of its inarticulacy lacks any effective alternative to violence in situations of extremity, when it is confronted with open evil. Has there not, after all, always been an element of straightforward innocent outrage behind the more spontaneous violence of revolutionary movements? She illustrates this with reference to Herman Melville's parable of *Billy Budd*[112]: the figure of Billy in this story embodies an almost pure goodness in the Christian sense; only, in the form of natural innocence. In a moment of crisis his 'erring sense of uninstructed honour' (in the strict sense, tragically) betrays him into an act of murder: it is a case of Abel slaying Cain. Arendt interprets this in terms of the need she sees for the emancipation of worldly affairs from any idealizing dream of innocence. Might one not, though, equally take it as pointing in the opposite direction, represented by Weil? That is to say: towards a no longer untutored, but systematically reflective adherence to the absolute good, which therefore recognizes the necessary limitations on its potential for actual political expression, and the measured withdrawal it requires from overt worldly conflict?

On the other hand, another obvious source of revolutionary violence is the generalization of compassion into a kitschy ideology of pity; which then becomes the moral justification for all manner of inhumanity towards those judged to be oppressors (Arendt quotes 'almost at random' from a document of the Parisian Commune in 1870: '*Par pitié, par amour pour l'humanité, soyez inhumains!*'[113]) This is the spirit of Robespierre and Saint-Just, which Marxist ideology later overlaid with its 'scientific' veneer. To pity, Arendt opposes 'solidarity': 'Pity may be the perversion of compassion, but its alternative is solidarity. It is out of pity that men are "attracted toward *les hommes faibles*", but it is out of solidarity that they establish deliberately and, as it were, dispassionately a community of interest with the oppressed and exploited.'[114] Here compassion remains focused on the particular needs of particular individuals; whilst the essential 'dispassionateness' of 'solidarity' at the level of ideological generality leaves it perfectly compatible with isonomy. Indeed, notwithstanding all her admiration for that other aspect of the revolutionary experience, the spontaneous rediscovery of political virtue in the initial moments of each upheaval, nothing could be further removed from the sentimental moral fury of Jacobin or Bolshevik ideology than the Arendtian ethic of solidarity.

But then what happens when such solidarity is divorced *entirely* from any sort of aspiration to 'absolute goodness' – as Arendt would have it? The divorce may help maintain the dignity of the political way of life, the essential moral underpinning of an isonomous culture; and yet does it not do so at the cost of a certain trivialization? In Arendt's portrayal, the public life of the *polis* appears as a sort of beautiful game. And what is there to ensure that the free-spirited solidarity engendered in such a game will be complemented by an equally free-spirited openness to the moral claims of those who remain outside the game; those whom oppression renders politically invisible and inaudible; or foreigners?[115] In fact, such openness to the claims of the outsider surely depends upon a continual alertness to the pre-political requirements of the absolute good; that radical open-mindedness which is enjoined in the Sermon on the Mount. Without at least some sort of ethical sensibility which already, right from the outset, transcends finite loyalties and the dictates of political 'realism', it would be inconceivable – and does this not, therefore, also need cultivating, even to the point of painful conflict with those loyalties? Weil's absolutism represents Christian purity of will pushed to an extreme which excludes even the minimum necessary compromises involved in church membership. But Arendt herself, in *The Life of the Mind*, situates such purity, the purity of pure 'willing', alongside the purity of pure 'thinking', as twin antitheses to 'banality'; implicitly validating it as an aspiration, after all. Thus, in Arendtian terms, what Weil is after may be said to be just the very purest possible antithesis to banality.

Of course, the sheer impossibility of taking the precepts of the Sermon on the Mount literally, as a universal code, has always been apparent. Already in the *Didache*, one of the oldest Christian documents outside the New Testament, we find the beginnings of a double-standard ethic: 'If you can shoulder the Lord's yoke in its entirety, then you will be perfect; but if that is too much for you, do as much as you can.'[116] In subsequent Christian thinking the demands of absolute goodness have often, for example, been understood as applying much more rigorously to the vocation of the monk or the nun than to that of the layperson. Or else, as in Luther's teaching, they are applied to the individual's private life, in strict contradistinction to his or her more public roles. Yet there are two major sorts of objection to such 'solutions'. In the first place, they are undergirded by the traditional reduction, with which Luther concurs, of politics to ruling; understood as the disciplinary remedy for human fallenness. Whereas, to try and relate the Sermon on the Mount to the ethos of isonomy is, by contrast, to pose a much more serious theoretical problem – just because of the far bolder moral claims which that ethos makes for politics, as a vocation within which individuals may find the very highest self-fulfilment. Secondly, any softening of the original absolutes along these lines runs the obvious risk of degenerating, in actual practice, into the merest apologia for banality.[117]

And this then, I think, is what constitutes the basic problematic of an authentic civil theology. Such theology would thus be 'civil' by virtue of its trans-confessional orientation towards isonomy; but would be 'theology' not only because of its concern to confer *auctoritas* on the ethos of isonomy, but also very much by virtue of its counterbalancing orientation towards the absolute.

2 Religion, Civility, Faith

Corresponding to the three modes of 'society' distinguished above, one can also distinguish between three different modes of civil religion (Robert Bellah's usage of the concept, for instance, represents a somewhat uneasy mixture of all three). In the first place, there is civil religion as an expression of the aspirations of 'society *qua* enterprise': the more doctrinaire types of religious socialism would come under this heading, as would all forms of religiously legitimated nationalism attaching to a genuine democracy. Here, the classic example is no doubt the American one: the ideological celebration of the American nation as a chosen people, 'mankind's last best hope', American manifest destiny. (The democracy is necessary, since otherwise – as with the 'faith movement' of the 'German Christians' in the Third Reich – it would no longer be *civil* religion. As remarked above, civil religion has to do with one's identity as a citizen, not one's tribal or religious identity.) Then, secondly, there is the sort of civil religion which belongs to 'society *qua* order': religion, essentially, as an *eirénikon*, a form of social glue. And thirdly, there is that admittedly somewhat frailer growth: civil religion as the spiritual dimension to civil society.

Much of the general criticism of civil religion on the part of Christian theologians (such as Jürgen Moltmann) depends on blurring these distinctions, and focusing exclusively on the first two categories. Civil religion, however, does not have to be tied to an ideology of domination, nor does it have to be conceived as an *eirénikon*. Perhaps it is therefore a misleading term to use. But all theology is, by its very nature, a tussle with a compromised vocabulary. And there is after all, at least to some extent, one important quality which these three phenomena do have in common: they each present us with another basis of loyalty, alongside the theologian's primary loyalty to his or her own faith tradition.

Theology, however, both depends for its creativity upon its loyalties, and is corrupted by them. Every loyalty carries with it the risk that the language it helps to preserve may degenerate into little more, in practice, than a badge of membership, a set of formulas serving merely as a code for for the egoistical self-assertion of the faith community; in which case the very source of critical thinking dries up: the language in which critique would be formulated now means something else. And is there not, therefore, something to be said for cultivating *dual* loyalties? (That is, if they remain truly dual and do not just fuse together into one.) It is, so to speak, a matter of always having an effective basis for self-critique: being able to criticize one's given identity as a citizen on the basis of the ideals embodied in one's faith tradition; yet, equally, being able to criticize one's given identity as an adherent of that tradition, on the basis of one's solidarity with one's fellow citizens – including those of other faiths and of none. That, as I would understand it, is what civil theology is largely about: a ceaseless critical back-and-forth; the practice of that particular type of spiritual agility.

At this point two avenues open up for further reflection. On the one hand, there is clearly a good deal more to be said about the relationship of such theology to the more critical forms of traditional confessionalism. And, on the other, there is the question of seeking out whatever historical precedents there might be for it.

Against Confessional Exclusivism

My argument has been that in relation to all the main religious traditions of Christendom the phenomenon of totalitarianism has a 'revelatory' quality, of a sort that essentially demands a civil theological response. Now, however, I want to turn to consider two fundamental alternative responses to the same experience along strictly Christian-confessional lines. Søren Kierkegaard was perhaps the earliest Christian thinker – and certainly one of the most notable – whose whole theology is decisively shaped by a sense of the unprecedented spiritual crisis inherent in the emergence of modern mass culture. He might very well be regarded as a key prophetic critic of the trends that were eventually to come to such grotesque fulfilment in the regimes of Hitler and Stalin. And Karl Barth's status as the greatest of twentieth-century dogmatic theologians is of course greatly reinforced by his role as a major theological inspiration to the actual resistance of the Confessing Church in the Third Reich. These two represent Christian confessional thinking at its intellectually most authoritative – in the sense of being scrupulously purged of every last trace of self-serving ecclesiastical enterprise-ideology. It would indeed be hard to think of any more formidable representatives of the confessional approach in the present context.

Both are profoundly troubled by what they see as the churches' prevailing sell-out to the false promises of modernity. Kierkegaard, for his part, responds to the 'progressive' meta-narratives of modernity with a wholesale rejection of any form of 'Christian' meta-narrative thinking. Barth by contrast is a meta-narrative thinker, but one for whom the whole point of good theology is always, so far as possible, to revive the original shock-quality of revelation – not least in relation to the new complacencies of modernity. Anything else is what he lambasts as 'natural theology', that is, a mistaken retreat from the grace of revelation to grace-less nature. In this sense, Kierkegaard and Barth represent two opposing poles of confessional thought. And yet at the same time they are also very much at one in the absolutely exclusive nature of their confessionalism, with regard to any civil perspective.

The following critique, it should be noted, is quite limited in its pretensions – at any rate with regard to Barth. In the end I am inclined to think that Kierkegaard's position is incoherent. But Barth's is not. And moreover it is logically quite independent of the particular analysis of modernity with which it is associated. What I would question is merely the supplementary claim that the nightmares of the twentieth century somehow confirm its validity. I also want to show how both thinkers, in the end, close off the path towards civil theology without really considering it as a serious alternative. I propose to take up Dietrich Bonhoeffer's critique of Barth. For in Bonhoeffer's later thought one actually sees a dramatic turning away from exclusive confessionalism. And then I seek, briefly, to re-open the question of the ultimate ecclesiological implications of this sort of turn.

Truth as subjectivity

Like Simone Weil, Kierkegaard too is an absolute devotee of the absoluteness of the Absolute. And what he identifies as the ultimate truth of Christianity is nothing other than the distinctive spiritual dialectic it enshrines, whose origins Hannah Arendt traces back to St Paul, of infinitely escalating inner conflict. This dialectic is grounded in the aspiration to an absolute 'purity of heart', and 'purity of heart is to will one thing'[1] whatever the suffering which such intransigence towards all other desires may entail. Kierkegaard's psychological studies of 'fallenness', in *The Concept of Anxiety*, and of 'despair', in *The Sickness Unto Death*, develop the same theme; as does his discussion of 'Religiousness A' and 'Religiousness B' in the *Concluding Unscientific Postscript*. The further one turns from the ways of sin, he argues, the more acutely aware one becomes of the infinite gravity of the sins that remain. The deeper one's awareness of God, the deeper one's sense of one's own fallenness: that spiritual vertigo; that 'sympathetic antipathy and antipathic sympathy'[2] towards the moral claims of the other, in general, which is the essence of 'anxiety' – the experience of guilt which precedes any actual sin. The experience of fallenness is not only the source of sin, but also the elementary precondition for the possibility of knowing God. By the same token: the more clearly sin appears in its true form, as a conscious movement of despair, that is, as a rebellious turning away from God, the more sinful it is. Yet the closer one approaches to the reality of God, the greater the temptation to conscious despair. And vice versa: the greater the temptation to despair which one has overcome, the closer one comes to God. That, in effect, is what 'God' means.

It is this which then differentiates the Kierkegaardian 'humour' from Romantic, or Socratic 'irony'. Thus, the essential problem with Romanticism, for Kierkegaard, lies in its tendency towards the reduction of spirituality to a matter of 'aesthetics', devoid of any true sense of fallenness. He too is in some ways an inheritor, with the Romantics, of the type of publicly reflective inwardness pioneered by Rousseau – as an expression of the inner withdrawal of 'the individual' from the corruption of society, especially sophisticated modern society. From this point of view he can even speak of the 'romantic character' of Christian faith itself.[3] Over against both the rigid universalism of Kantian moral reason and the communitarian bindingness of Hegelian *Sittlichkeit*, he too – in *Fear and Trembling* – affirms the possibility of 'the exception'. But by no means in the Romantic sense. Abraham, preparing to sacrifice his son Isaac, is the model for this – and it is not the sublimity of his emotional life, nor even the heroic grandeur of his suffering, that serves to exempt Abraham from the moral rules that would otherwise apply. What vindicates his perverse sense of vocation, as for Kierkegaard it may also vindicate all manner of other forms of moral non-conformity, is simply faith – understood as a peculiarly intense consciousness of what it means to sin, and to be responsible.

The truth of Christianity consists, for Kierkegaard, in what he sees as its unique capacity to articulate and so to elicit this sort of sensitivity. To that extent his argument seems to be entirely congruent with Weil's.

Then, however, he makes two further moves – systematically conflated by him, yet logically distinct. In the first place: when it comes to faith, 'truth is subjectivity'. For what is all-important is the subjective appropriation of responsibility. In so far as the gospel is reduced to a merely 'objective' datum, it loses its cutting edge in relation to the new corruption of modernity. All it does is offer to baptize that corruption, as 'Christendom'.

But secondly, a much more dubious move: it is true that a certain minimum of objective revelation is nevertheless needed. This is in order symbolically to represent the absolute objective otherness of God from any subjective – here in the sense of wish-fulfilling – human projection. Yet that is all. There is no further need to look for objective revelation besides this, and therefore no need to identify the saving truth of the gospel, in terms of its objective historical content, with anything more than its most elementary core. Hence, his thinking moves in the exact opposite direction to civil theology. For, whereas the whole gist of civil theology – which is premissed on a much less reductionist understanding of the *need* for revelation – is to expand the range of historical experience which is brought to bear upon our understanding of salvation, Kierkegaard's determination, on the contrary, is to shrink it.

And so it is that he condemns as false 'objectivity' not only the thoughtless folly of the notion that all Danes are 'Christians', on the merely historic basis that all have been baptized as infants, but also any sort of theology, such as Hegelianism, which regards a concrete knowledge of history, in general, as a potentially significant contribution to our knowledge of God. In a sense it is not only the Incarnation, but that there should be *any* 'objective' revelation in history at all is for him an 'absolute paradox' – to be accepted in faith; but the essential, properly historical content of which he nevertheless seeks to reduce to the barest minimum. As his character Johannes Climacus presents the matter in *Philosophical Fragments*, it should be 'more than enough' for the purposes of faith to be confronted with the following minimal '*nota bene* on the page of universal history': 'We have believed that in such and such a year the God appeared among us in the humble figure of a servant, that he lived and taught in our community, and finally died.'[4] Beyond that '*nota bene*' there is indeed very little in his retelling of the gospel story to distinguish it from some quite unhistorical myth or legend – or even one of the little tales he loves to tell in the manner of Hans Christian Andersen. Those historical elements which are inescapable for any version of the story – Jesus's recorded teachings and moral example – he abstracts entirely, or almost entirely, from their historical context. This was the age of the first 'Quest for the Historical Jesus': David Friedrich Strauss's seminal *Life of Jesus* had first appeared in 1835. And yet for Kierkegaard such a quest can have no true theological significance. He rejects it, on the grounds that, for faith, the only relationship with Christ which counts is one of strict 'contemporaneity':

Out with history. In with the situation of contemporaneity. This is the criterion: as I judge anything contemporaneously, so am I. All this subsequent chatter is a delusion.[5]

Kierkegaardian 'subjectivity' is a spiritual inwardness transcending any historical identity, at home only in eternity.

But why should we accept this? Basically, it seems, the only possible theological function Kierkegaard can envisage for historiography in relation to faith is an apologetic one: as an attempt somehow to '*prove*', or at any rate enhance the plausibility of, the claims of the gospel, as something fixed and given.[6] On the one hand, there is the supposed proof of 'the eighteen hundred years': the sheer weight of church history (can so many people over so many years, and some of them such great saints, all have been wrong?). On the other hand, there is the supposed proof by appeal to the testimony of the original witnesses of Christ's life, death and resurrection (they were there, we were not – can we not trust what they tell us?). His rejection of 'history' is essentially a rejection of these two sorts of argument: as entailing a wholesale distortion of the gospel, in that they pander to nothing more than a sinful craving for false security ('making everything easier'); a sheer distraction from theology's proper business of evoking repentance ('making things harder').

That history might be theologically significant in other ways, however – that an educated awareness of the historical background, and the historical distinctiveness, of one's own culture might contribute towards a genuine deepening of an individual's spiritual sensibilities by raising critical questions which would not otherwise arise about that culture and about the way it shapes those who belong to it – and that it might thereby serve not just to reinforce, but also to supplement the moral educativeness of the gospel: this by contrast is a possibility Kierkegaard never considers at all. Hence, for example, his critique of Hegel seems to be grounded in a thoroughly reductive reading of the Hegelian philosophy of history as *nothing but* a rather sophisticated strategy of apologetic proof. Which I think largely misses its true character.

Furthermore, I would contend that in a certain respect the very radicalism of Kierkegaard's repudiation of a constructive engagement with history actually tends to undermine his own position. This emerges most directly in relation to his discussion of the Socratic standpoint.

Thus, the problem with Socratic 'irony' for Kierkegaard is not so much (as with the Romantic version) a mistaken attitude to passion, but rather just that the moral passion involved lacks sufficient intensity. Socrates attributes wrong-doing to a species of ignorance. But this means that 'Socrates does not really come to the category of sin', strictly understood.

> What then is the missing component in Socrates's specification of sin? It is: the will, defiance. Greek intellectuality was too fortunate, too naive, too aesthetic, too ironic, too – too sinful – to be able to get it into its head that someone would knowingly refrain from doing the good, or knowing what is right, knowingly do what is wrong.[7]

The fundamental advantage of (authentic) Christian faith over Socratic wisdom, in his view, is the element of 'offence' in it, the way it polarizes the choice between obedience and defiance, the sheer intensity of the emotional demands it makes upon each individual believer, compelling a more searching honesty.

But the question has to be asked: where then, in actual practice, does this greater intensity *come from*? That is, what makes it possible? What (if anything) makes these demands more than mere empty words?

Kierkegaard gives a very richly substantive analysis of the experience itself, but as regards its manner of rootedness in the proclamation of the gospel, only a quite formal account: the argument he develops in the person of Johannes Climacus, as a 'thought-experiment', in *Philosophical Fragments*. In this work the logical structure of Christian faith is formally contrasted with that of Socratic wisdom, these being considered as two alternative definitions of the highest human vocation. The 'experiment' runs as follows: Socratic wisdom comes from 'recollection', that is, drawing out of oneself what one already unconsciously knows. But just suppose that we have a higher vocation, and that in the light of this higher vocation the phenomenon of human sinfulness begins to appear a much more serious problem. Suppose it means that the truth which counts is *not* already in us, to be drawn out. What then? A completely different form of teaching would be needed. The Socratic teacher of wisdom, as one who encourages the learner to draw from his or her own inner resources, is in Socrates' own phrase a 'midwife', not a spiritual parent: the birth of wisdom does not depend upon such a teacher, the teacher merely assists. But if the truth is to come instead from outside, then it is clear that we would need another sort of teacher, one upon whom on the contrary we would have to depend absolutely. If human sinfulness really were such a major obstacle, in the end no merely human teacher would do; such truth would only be attainable if the teacher were also God; it would require God to take on the role of a teacher – entering into human history for the purpose. Since, however, Christianity as a matter of fact does postulate this, it therefore seems logically to rest on exactly the radical view of human sinfulness that was postulated in the thought-experiment. And this, Kierkegaard concludes, is the basic reason why the absolute paradox of the Incarnation is necessary: its whole point is, in this way, symbolically to refute the sort of wisdom that comes to its highest expression in Socratic philosophy.

But what such a purely abstract argument fails to explain is how – in concrete terms – the absolute paradox might be expected effectively to touch anyone's heart.

There is the promise of an 'eternal happiness' attached to it, true – but why should anyone ever have taken that promise seriously? Where, in other words, does the raw *emotional dynamism* come from, which is now invested in this story? Surely, it derives from just what Kierkegaard scorns: the *auctoritas*, the sheer weight of historical experience stored up in the then 'eighteen hundred years', now approaching two thousand, of Christian tradition: an awe and love for God, mediated through admiration of the finer testimonies to transcendence within the cultural heritage of Christendom, all the beauty it contains, and the memories of suffering. Surely the believer's confession of sin is in practice inextricably bound up with a sense of human loyalty to the tradition which sets the standards in relation to which one has fallen short. Kierkegaard seeks to escape the inevitable ambivalence of such loyalty by theoretically rejecting it, in any form; so he seeks to emancipate faith from the *auctoritas* of the tradition, and ground it instead on some other sort of authority, an authority supposedly found in 'contemporaneity', straight from eternity, quite without any invocation of the historical past beyond the minimal '*nota bene* on the page of universal history'. But even if it were possible – which, in psychological terms, of course it is not – to abstract the central thesis of faith in this way from its *auctoritas*, how would that then, in fact, leave it with any real authority whatever? In the character of Johannes Climacus he ironically presents his thought-experiment as if it were just an idle game with ideas. But why, after all, should it ever amount to anything more than that?

It might be objected that what Kierkegaard is intent on elucidating is that which is unique to Christianity, 'religiousness B' as opposed to 'religiousness A', and that the type of loyalty I am talking about is on the contrary what is common to all religion as such. But he himself acknowledges that the very possibility of 'religiousness B' rests upon the foundations provided by the higher expressions of 'religiousness A'. And what is so questionable is the rigidly individualistic manner in which he presents not only 'religiousness B' but also the truth of 'religiousness A'. What he will not acknowledge, in short, is the way in which his anti-communitarian insights paradoxically depend upon the community-experience he shares with those for whom he is writing. If, as he claims, Christian faith has an advantage over Socratic wisdom for the critique of modernity, then that advantage surely lies in its embodiment within a living tradition of *auctoritas*, which (pure) Socratic wisdom, in any age, lacks. To be sure, by virtue of the intrinsic ambivalence of all religious loyalty, this advantage is at the same time also potentially its very serious disadvantage; and hence there arises the temptation of trying to *relocate* the advantage, as Kierkegaard does. But the problem is that this relocation represents, in the end, quite an arbitrary reduction of the problem. Kierkegaard's thinking both begins from, and ends up by reinforcing, the viewpoint of 'that solitary individual', to whom for instance he dedicates his Edifying Discourse on *Purity of Heart* – which for him appears to mean an individual entirely withdrawn not only from the thoughtless conformity of mass society, but (as with Simone Weil) to all intents and purposes also from any more communitarian loyalty. And yet at the same time he wants to invoke, not just the theoretical or ideal truth of the Christian gospel, but the whole emotional intensity which he finds concretely bound up with that truth. So he invokes that potential intensity as a theoretical datum; even whilst at the same time quite arbitrarily closing off any enquiry into the *practical* conditions of its possibility.

In fact, as Alasdair MacIntyre has argued,[8] the contradiction is already very clearly present well before Kierkegaard enters into his consideration of the 'absolute paradox'. Thus MacIntyre focuses on *Either/Or*, which has to do with the choice between the 'aesthetic' way of life and the 'ethical', as distinct from the specifically 'religious'. The central point of this book lies in its inconclusiveness: the pseudonymous editor, Victor Eremita, remains above the fray. The aesthetic option is to seek, so far as possible, to lose oneself in the beautiful spontaneity of a life lived in the present. The ethical option, by contrast, is the way of responsibility and long-term commitments, such as marriage. Both prescriptions are, on their own premises, equally coherent; both, as they are presented here, are equally honest. No ultimate significance is accorded to prudential egoistic considerations as a means of arbitrating between them, neither is any ultimate significance accorded to communitarian loyalty – not even by Judge William, the spokesman for the ethical way. We must choose. And yet there seems to be no compelling reason to choose either rather than the other; the choice remains open – 'either/or'. But this is the contradiction: the moral commitments of the ethical option are nevertheless supposed to have a stamp of real authority for the one who adopts them. And how can they? For, surely, the authority of any moral precept depends upon the quality of the reasons that can be given for it. What is chosen in the first place out of mere caprice can scarcely then have binding authority over anyone. Authority requires a basis of legitimacy; yet the openness of the choice in *Either/Or* means that no such basis appears.

Indeed, inasmuch as a mass culture is also an atomizing culture, Kierkegaard's thinking, with its principled indifference to the historical, communitarian dimension of the ethical, might well be seen as itself a symptom of the very disease that he is attacking. MacIntyre, in his chronicle of the decline and fall of Western moral philosophy, actually attributes to *Either/Or*, in particular, considerable historical importance: this he suggests is the book, more than any other, in which 'for the first time the distinctively modern standpoint appears in something like fully-fledged form'. It is the most dramatic testimony we have to that pivotal moment of transition in which the initial substitute for classical traditionality, the Enlightenment project for an ethics of pure abstract reason, first began to collapse. *Either/Or*, he remarks, is 'both outcome and epitaph' of the Enlightenment project.

Of course, in Kierkegaard's later writings the priority of the ethical over the aesthetic does come to be guaranteed by the ultimate primacy of the religious. But even then, as we have seen, the same basic contradiction (at its most abstract, the contradiction between his essentially atomistic understanding of authentic existential autonomy and the inescapable nature of both ethics and religion as a submission to the claims of a corporate 'other') still persists. His de-historicizing interpretation of 'the leap of faith' simply transfers it on to another level.

Critical civil theology is about expanding the range of historical experience brought to bear upon the interpretation of religious symbolism, basically as a means of maximizing the critical-communitarian expressiveness of religious liturgy. In this sense it too is an intensification-discipline, like Kierkegaard's thought. Nor does it mean denying the absolute 'paradoxicality' of a faith grounded in the historical; far rather, it simply means re-envisaging the *content* of the paradox. Thus, the paradox lies in the disjunction between form and content, when a finite, objective datum of history is hailed as a definitive manifestation of the infinite. Kierkegaard, for his part, confines the paradox to the gospel story – but does not *all* history, to one extent or another, have the capacity to play this role? For, latent within every historically conditioned communitarian world-view, is there not, always, at least some intimation of the absolute good? Any communitarian perception of the good is, as such, a relativization of the good; a commingling of the demands of the absolute with the demands of community survival. The absolute, on the other hand, is in principle, absolutely other from the relative. And yet – what words, or other forms of expression, can we ever find for it, except those that are drawn from some particular communitarian tradition, informed by some particular history? In this sense, what the uniquely dramatic paradoxicality of the Incarnation represents is a truth which transcends Christianity: the paradox is everywhere.

The irrational element in Kierkegaard's thinking therefore, from a critical civil-theological point of view, is not his insistence on the paradoxical 'absurdity' of the truth of faith. But it is just the way in which – not loyal to church tradition as such, yet still trapped within its mainstream assumptions – he continues to confine the paradox so narrowly: as, before seeking to de-historicize the proper appropriation of biblical salvation history, he first severs it in traditional fashion, completely, from all other history; an initial step which (thanks in particular to his all too reductive dismissal of Hegelianism) he evidently never sees the need even to try and justify.

Faith versus 'religion'

Barth, by contrast, is very much a tradition-builder.

Barth's attack on the 'nineteenth century conquering-hero attitude to religion'[9] is an extension of Kierkegaard's polemic against Hegel. And he too is entirely concerned to make faith not easier but more difficult: therefore, in repudiation of any theology like Schleiermacher's – designed to *justify* 'religion' in general (understood, simply, as a necessary form of human self-fulfilment) to its 'cultured despisers', and Christian faith as the noblest form of religion – his priority on the contrary, like Kierkegaard's, is very much to rescue faith from its un-self-critical adherents.

Unlike Kierkegaard, however, he invokes *auctoritas* against Christendom: a completely un-Kierkegaardian means to achieve the Kierkegaardian goal. And so he writes a meta-narrative *Church Dogmatics*, a systematic interpretation of the church's history and pre-history (understood as *the* history of salvation) to this end.

It is a Calvinist vision – but also an explosive twentieth-century re-enactment of the explosive Lutheran origins of the Reformation. When Barth burst on to the theological scene at the end of the First World War it was as a commentator on that key source-text for the Lutheran dialectic of faith and works, Paul's Epistle to the Romans. In much the same way as the

Reformers had made Paul seem to speak afresh to their day, as a critic of the corrupt 'works-righteousness' ethos of sixteenth-century Catholicism, so Barth made him seem to speak afresh to the twentieth century: as a critic, above all, of liberal neo-Protestantism. No doubt Luther misinterprets Paul, inasmuch as Paul's opposition to subjecting Gentile converts to circumcision was not so much the expression of a general principled opposition to identifying salvation with the doing of 'good works' as such, but simply an objection to identifying the faith with this particular legal code, in this particular way.[10] But the misinterpretation is an inspired one, rendering possible as it does a fundamental recapturing of the sheer eruptiveness of the original eruptive moment of New Testament revelation. And this is Barth's brilliantly accomplished intention, as well. 'Good works', in the abstract, might be defined as the tokens of loyal membership within an empirically definable social group. Faith signifies loyalty to that which constitutes the church as such a group, and conditionally justifies its 'good works'. But only conditionally – as it also perpetually calls into question the church's tendency to relapse towards mere 'works righteousness'; in other words, a form of *self-justificatory* self-assertion. This, in essence, is the underlying critical principle which both Luther and Barth, in such very different circumstances, bring eruptively alive. 'Luther, you do have an enormous responsibility', Kierkegaard complained, 'for when I look more closely I see ever more clearly that you toppled the Pope – and set "the public" on the throne.'[11] Barth, though, applies the same principle which Luther had used against the Pope, this time against the liberal neo-Protestant 'public'.

In the *Church Dogmatics* the role played by Luther's critique of 'works righteousness' is in fact largely taken over by a critique of 'religion'. This is because of the very positive connotations of 'religion' not only in Schleiermacher, but in liberal neo-Protestant thought generally.

Earlier, in the commentary on The Epistle to the Romans, he uses the term in a double sense: corresponding to, and generalizing from, the two main aspects of the Law in Paul's thought. As he puts it there, 'religion' is 'that last and noblest human possibility which encounters us at the threshold and meeting-place of two worlds, but which, nevertheless, remains itself on this side the abyss dividing sinners from those who are under grace'.[12] It is 'the last and noblest human possibility', to the extent that it prepares us for faith by pointing beyond itself. But it is also a phenomenon of human sinfulness – and not of grace. In the first sense, it is what Kierkegaard meant by 'religiousness A': an ever-increasing sense of spiritual need, which the performance of 'good works' does less and less to assuage. Of this possibility Barth writes:

[Authentic] religion is aware that it is in no [ways] the crown and fulfilment of true humanity; it knows itself rather to be a questionable, disturbing, dangerous thing . . . So far from being the place where the healthy harmony of human life is lauded, [it] is instead the place where it appears diseased, discordant, and disrupted. Religion is not the sure ground on which human culture safely rests; it is the place where civilization and its partner, barbarism, are rendered fundamentally questionable . . . Conflict and distress, sin and death, the devil and hell, make up the reality of religion. So far from releasing people from guilt and destiny, it brings people under their sway. Religion possesses no solution of the problem of life; rather it makes of the problem a wholly insoluble enigma. Religion neither discovers the problem nor solves it: what it does is disclose the truth that it cannot be solved. Religion is neither a thing to be enjoyed nor a thing to be celebrated: it must be borne as a yoke which cannot be removed. Religion is not a thing to be desired or extolled: it is a misfortune which takes fatal hold upon some people, and is by them passed on to others.[13]

We attain to the truth of religion, in this sense, when we arrive at 'the very outermost edge of the precipice'. True religion 'is an abyss; it is terror'.[14] Or (this whole commentary is a feast of metaphor) it is a bomb, decked out with flowers.[15] Yet at the same time, in the second sense, 'religion' also remains Barth's term for the muddling of faith and works: so that even in its highest forms it is not only a pointer *towards* faith, but equally what we tend to cling to in our shrinking *away from* faith. 'Religion' in this second sense is essentially defined in the *Church Dogmatics* as: 'the realm of man's attempts to justify and to sanctify himself before a capricious and arbitrary picture of God'.[16] As such, it is 'unbelief'.[17] It is the name for what revelation comes to abolish. Not that the inner struggle of 'true' religion is thereby done away with. On the contrary. But rather the point is that, even at its truest, 'we can speak of "true" religion only in the sense in which we speak of a "justified sinner" '.[18]

For Barth, however, only confessionally Christian 'religion' is redeemable. Civil religion by contrast quite clearly is not. Because the whole point is precisely to have undivided loyalties.

The dividing of loyalties is, after all, the basic heresy against which the Barmen Declaration of 1934 – the foundational document of the Confessing Church – is directed. Its actual wording is largely the work of Barth himself. And it contains, amongst other things, a ringing denunciation of the false doctrine that the Church, as the source of its proclamation, could and should, over and above God's one Word, acknowledge other events, powers, images and truths as divine revelation.[19]

Whilst the primary object of this denunciation was the 'German Christian' movement's attribution of revelatory authority to the ideology of National Socialism, it was certainly intended by Barth to apply much more widely. What he ultimately had in his sights here is *any* sort of 'natural theology' – which in the *Church Dogmatics* covers a very broad range of theological sins indeed.

Thus the basic corruption of confessional 'religion', for Barth, lies in its mixing of loyalty to the original eruptive truth of Christ, as recorded in scripture, with other, more comfortable loyalties, to other principles. Such other principles may also be presented, by 'natural theology', as manifestations of the truth of Christ. But, he argues, it is scripture alone which has to provide the standard: scripture, that is, in its role as the most immediate registering of the actual shock of the revelation which founded the church, the memory of which it is the church's unique vocation to preserve in all its incomparable distinctiveness. This excludes the attribution of any *independent* authority to putative philosophical insight – Platonist, Aristotelian, Kantian or Hegelian. And it also excludes the recruitment of any additional supposedly authoritative narrative resources.

Let us make some distinctions, though. In the first place, 'natural theology' is not yet the full disease. The problem with 'natural theology' is just that, whatever its good intentions, it has the effect of lowering the church's resistance to the disease. This disease may be defined as a succumbing to rival loyalties – but what sort of loyalties, exactly? In the world of Barth's thought there seem to be, roughly speaking, three primary types: the full-blown totalitarian, the bourgeois conservative, and the cosmopolitan socialist.

When the German Christians crassly hailed the Hitler revolution as an act of divine revelation, the evidence they cited was the experience of rapturous enthusiasm it brought with it, the dramatic surge of collective hope, the widespread restoration of public morale in a common enterprise. This surely is in the most direct contradiction to the notion of revelation implicit in the gospel, inasmuch as such euphoria so easily lapses into the very spirit that crucifies.

By the 'bourgeois conservative' view I mean one which tended, or tends, to identify the authority of Christianity, and hence its 'revelatory' character, with its capacity to establish a particular sort of stable community life; with an accent on the *stability* (society *qua* order) – qualifying the particularity. Here again one may very well accept the validity of Barth's argument: that this too, albeit in a less open way, is a distraction from, and so an obscuring of, the authentic critical truth of the gospel. For, to the extent that it thus assimilates the truth of Christianity to the most universal and elementary function of religion in general, such thinking undoubtedly does also very seriously weaken its resistance to ideological exploitation – as it all too easily degenerates into a mere celebration of social stability in *all* its forms, the secular as well. In German theology of the period, the catch-phrase for what was thereby being affirmed was 'the orders of creation'. This theology amounts to a species of Christian thinking which is, in effect, the confessional equivalent to conservative civil theology: the same thing, only with more or less of an overlay of Christian piety, and minus its free-spiritedly civil, or pluralistic, quality.

Barth's own temptation was socialism. He was both a socialist and an internationalist, whose initial disillusionment with liberal theology had been sealed when he saw so many of the liberal theologians of Germany sign up to the academics' declaration of support for the Kaiser at the outbreak of the First World War. And the first edition of his commentary on *The Letter to the Romans* – appearing just after Lenin had come to power in Moscow – was an overtly socialist work, in which he half-identified the eruptive quality of the gospel with the eruptiveness of socialist revolution.[20] The second edition, on the other hand, marks his decisive breakthrough to the anti-ideological radicalism that continues to pervade all his later thought. He does not abandon his Christian socialist commitments here. But the Christian element comes to be seen far less as contributing to the vindication of socialist principle, far more as a countervailing, corrective principle of infinite self-critique.

What I am arguing for, however, does not fall into any of these categories. For all three alike involve compromise with propaganda ideologies. There surely is, I agree, every reason to try and preserve the autonomy of the gospel in relation to ideologies of this kind. I have no doubt that the proclamation of the crucified dissident – if it is to carry conviction – requires a decisive self-distancing from any such will to domination, no matter how noble may be the ideals to which the ideology makes appeal. The particular forms of 'natural theology' Barth evidently has in mind – not only liberal neo-Protestantism but also Catholic neo-Scholasticism – mostly are, I would accept, too soft in their critique here, too easily distracted from the task of critique. Nor do I have any quarrel with the Barthian view of religion, generally, as belonging in the first instance to the order of sin rather than grace, given that it is always so vulnerable to manipulative interests. Indeed, my *only* quarrel is with the narrow confessionalism within which he continues to confine the alternative possibility of redeemed religion.

Faith and religion: these are two different levels. Christian faith clearly requires a singular loyalty to Christ; which, at the level of religion, means a real loyalty to the church as well. But an *exclusive* loyalty to the church? That is quite another matter.

And moreover, whilst the story of the German Church Struggle of the 1930s is in many ways a very vivid illustration of the strengths of Barthian confessional intransigence, it can also be seen in another light, as a no less dramatic illustration of its major weakness. For the question of theological method is, very largely, a question of *with whom* one chooses to be in dialogue, and on what terms. The Barthian approach dictates that the theologian is chiefly in dialogue with his or her fellow church members, and only very secondarily, or incidentally, in dialogue with any part of the outside world. (His polemic against liberal neo–Protestantism was an attack on an approach which set far more store by the theologian's dialogue with his fellow academics, as colleagues.) But this also helps to determine one's sense of political priorities; and, in particular, what one is prepared to take risks for in a situation of crisis. Barthianism naturally tends to accentuate the importance attached, above all, to the church's maintaining its independence and separateness from the secular world. In the Third Reich, however, the group most acutely victimized was not any of the churches. It was the Jews. And next to the Jews, the communists. The persecution of the Jews did also evoke resistance from the churches, but only to any serious degree when the Nazi regime prohibited people of Jewish racial origin from working as Christian clergy; in other words, only when, and to the extent that, it impinged upon the issue of the churches' independence from the state, to order their own affairs. But as Martin Niemöller for instance put it, looking back in 1945 at his own record as one of the most prominent actual organizers of the original resistance:

> If at the beginning of the Jewish persecutions we had seen that it was the Lord Jesus Christ who was being persecuted, struck down and slain in the 'least of these our brethren', if we had been loyal to Him and confessed Him, for all I know God would have stood by us, and then the whole sequence of events would have taken a different course. And if we had been ready to go with Him to death, the number of victims might have been only some ten thousand . . .[21]

Who knows? Barth himself later regretted that he had not attempted to include a strong affirmation of solidarity with the Jews in the Barmen Declaration: 'Of course, in 1934 no text in which I had done that would have been acceptable even to the Confessing Church, given the atmosphere that there was then. But that does not excuse me from not having at least gone through the motions of fighting.'[22] Why, though, was such an act so inconceivable for the church? Partly, no doubt, it was just a matter of natural human frailty, in an extremely frightening situation; a desire not to be over-exposed. Nor is there any reason to suppose that any other church, as churches are, would have done much better. Yet was not that natural reluctance also backed up by a theology based so strictly on confessional difference? One is, after all, far more likely to have some sentiment of solidarity with people with whom one is already actively engaged in dialogue, as fellow-citizens and equals. And still more so, the more open the frame of mind with which one enters into the dialogue. In this particular case the problem was of course further complicated by the large element of anti-Semitism pervading Christian tradition. (The primary Protestant principle itself has ugly anti-Semitic undertones, as it seems to suggest that Catholic 'works righteousness' is corrupt because of its being, somehow, too Jewish in spirit, too much like Torah.) But also, where in the tradition was there any actual analogy that the theologians might have drawn on, for the particular form of solidarity which was surely now called for, in terms of a corporate, self-sacrificial intervention on behalf of the outsider?

At all events, it is interesting to observe how the thinking of one very early and particularly forceful advocate of solidarity with the Jews in the Third Reich was in fact starting to evolve, in response to the unfolding situation: with Bonhoeffer, who begins from a position very close to Barth's, everything changes . . .

It is true that Bonhoeffer does not explicitly link the move he makes, in his posthumously published *Letters and Papers from Prison*, towards a 'religionless Christianity', or a 'non-religious interpretation of Biblical terms in a world come of age', with his perception of the Confessing Church's failure to do enough for the Jews. And yet it seems to me that this is, nevertheless, very much the context in which that move needs to be seen, and assessed. In fact, I think it is one of the main weaknesses in most of the scholarly discussion of the *Letters and Papers*, to date, that the connection is so often overlooked.[23]

One might perhaps summarize Bonhoeffer's critical move beyond Barth – with particular reference to the problematic nature of Christian 'religion' – like this: for Barth the problem lies in the mixing up of biblical faith with other loyalties, but for Bonhoeffer it is the diversion of faith from its proper practical orientation towards the risky business of solidarity with the oppressed, whoever they may be. What Barth is describing is an inevitable and perennial consequence of human fallenness, which 'natural theology' fails to rise above. Bonhoeffer, on the other hand, is describing something which is itself the direct outcome of theological error, and may therefore be superseded. The language in which he expresses this is perhaps somewhat misleading, with its echoes from the rhetoric of the Enlightenment: in particular, the idea of humanity 'coming of age'. This may recall Kant's celebrated definition of enlightenment, that it signifies 'the emergence of man from immaturity that he is himself responsible for', namely, that immaturity which is 'the incapacity to use one's intelligence without the guidance of another person'.[24] No doubt Bonhoeffer does mean that. Yet his is no Enlightenment ideology of the sort that undermines *Sittlichkeit*. It is on the contrary a direct response to the collapse of Enlightenment ideals of rationalized bureaucracy into the hell of totalitarian 'organization'. ('Our immediate environment is not nature, as formerly, but organization. But with this protection from nature's menace there arises a new one – through organization itself'.[25]) And the crucial innovation is, surely, his decisive *methodological* prioritization of the solidarity needed to fight back.

'Religion', in Bonhoeffer's thought, becomes a name for the results of an error in theological method: 'What does it mean', he asks, 'to "interpret in a religious sense"? I think it means to speak on the one hand *metaphysically*, and on the other hand *individualistically*.'[26] This is at first sight a somewhat curious formulation. And Bonhoeffer's death on the gallows at Flossenbürg meant, of course, that he himself was never able to write the book in which he might have clarified at greater length exactly what he intended here. But the one thing these two phenomena, 'metaphysics' and 'individualism', do appear to have in common is that they are both strategies for the privileging of particular religious truth-claims. They are (perhaps) the two main devices available to theologians for exempting the claims they make from the risk of being judged, purely and simply, on the public evidence of their ethical out-working – and so compared on equal terms with the counter-claims of rival belief systems. Metaphysics in this sense would thus be whatever protects theological (or atheistic) truth-claims from the rigours of pragmatic questioning, by means of a systematically rationalized dogmatism; and individualism would be that which does the same by means of an over-hasty appeal to the undebatable data of inner experience, conscientious conviction. If this is right, then what replaces 'religious interpretation' for Bonhoeffer is, essentially, a direct correlation of theological truth with the believing community's *demonstrable* capacity to resist the sort of evil represented by the Third Reich.

Barth's theology, too, represents an emphatic transcendence of metaphysics and individualism. His radical mistrust of the defensive-apologetic motive in theology precludes the former. And we have already observed how he goes beyond Kierkegaard, whose thought is perhaps the most vivid possible illustration of the ultimate limitations of the latter even where defensive apologetics has ceased to be a primary motive. Barth is also a very vigorous champion of political solidarity with the oppressed, as such. Only, he does not make this the *central* thrust of his theology, as Bonhoeffer does. For in his thought such solidarity still continues to be methodologically subordinated to the demands of church loyalty. This, as I understand it, is what Bonhoeffer means when he comes to criticize what he terms Barth's 'revelational positivism'.

Bonhoeffer does not deny his continuing debt to his predecessor: 'Barth', he writes, 'was the first theologian to begin the criticism of religion, and that remains his really great merit.' But the problem with Barth's 'positivist doctrine of revelation' is that it says, in effect, 'Like it or lump it.' Unfortunately – Bonhoeffer writes –

The positivism of revelation makes it too easy for itself, by setting up, as it does in the last analysis, a law of faith, and so mutilates what is – by Christ's incarnation! – a gift for us. In the place of religion there now stands the church – that is in itself biblical – but the world is to some degree made to depend on itself and left to its own devices, and that's the mistake.[27]

There is no retreat being prepared here, back to a liberal apologetics designed to make faith easier. On the contrary! But the point surely is that, in so far as it precludes the appropriate sort of dialogue ('like it or lump it') the Barthian approach can, in general, only hinder the believer's encounter with Christ in the sufferings of the non-Christian world.

In these last letters of his, Bonhoeffer appears to be feeling his way towards a thinking which would bring together the demands of worldly solidarity with those of church loyalty in such a way that neither would be altogether subordinated to the other. This involves a systematic separation between the two tasks of appropriating tradition and communicating with the world: tasks which, in Barth's thought, tend to coalesce, but which Bonhoeffer seeks to hold apart – first, in order to address the world in terms that will be readily intelligible to the widest possible audience, but secondly, also, so as to preserve the tradition from the 'profanation' that must inevitably come from any attempt at its popularization, in traditional form, within a mass culture.

And so it is that, in sharp contrast to Barthian procedure, he aims to protect the integrity of dogmatics proper by setting it somewhat apart from the immediate business of preaching, as what he calls an '*arcane discipline*'.

But what then follows for that other area of theology which remains outside the 'arcane discipline'? It is I think worth noting, in this connection, that *civil* 'religion' – whilst it is clearly an extremely 'religious' form of religion in Barth's sense – would not in fact count as 'religion' at all in Bonhoeffer's. For it does not have anything intrinsically either 'metaphysical' or 'individualistic' about it, in any way.

And what else, after all, would a non-religious yet non-revelational-positivist Christianity actually amount to in practice – if not a faith purged of just those *confessional*-religious attachments that have in the past always tended to enter into conflict with the ethics of civility?

Affinity group/open forum

A dogmatics such as is here conceived by Bonhoeffer draws close to civil theology, in a Christian context, primarily by virtue of sharing the same underlying polemical concern: with the final, and most unambiguous possible, liberation of theology from any trace of corruption into a self-serving ideology of the institutional church. In the former case, the struggle is conducted in the name of 'faith', understood in effect as an uncompromising testimony to the ideal of absolute goodness represented by Christ and embodied in the Sermon on the Mount – the central theme of Bonhoeffer's 1937 treatise on *The Cost of Discipleship*. In the latter case, it is conducted in the name of something else: a deeper spiritual sensibility – or, yes, if one takes the word 'religion' no longer in its extended Bonhoefferian sense, but in its primary meaning of *religio*, bonding-together, one might indeed say a deeper 'religious' sensibility – to the requirements of political freedom, isonomy, as such. Is there not, though, a real possibility of creative *partnership* between these two disciplines? They potentially converge on the practical issue of church reform.

There are, to be sure, a number of levels on which one may develop a confessional critique of over-institutionalized faith. Quite apart from any political considerations, there is in the first place the whole question of spirituality as an open-ended quest, and the proper diversity of spiritual vocations. This seems to be the basic critical concern, for instance, of Schleiermacher, in the fourth of his youthful *Speeches on Religion*. True religion, Schleiermacher there suggests, is a rare gift, inevitably confined to a small elite. The loyalties of this elite should be to their own individual insights and callings, and to each other; therefore, not at all to the great institutions of religion with their mass membership, unified by hierarchical structures, abstract dogma and insistence on conformity in externals.[28] The true church would be a loose-knit federation of communities of the like-minded, or spontaneous affinity-groups; it would be egalitarian in ethos; its preaching would always be an invitation to independent reflection on the part of the individual; it would provide as much scope as possible for the inspired evangelist, of whatever persuasion. 'Instead of the monstrous association whose existence you now bemoan' – he says to his 'cultured' and sceptical post-Enlightenment audience – in an ideal world 'there would have arisen a great number of smaller and less definite societies in which people would, in all sorts of ways and places, have examined themselves regarding religion'. The perennial temptation is for religious enthusiasm to overreach itself. It is when it seeks to convert the whole world that it is itself corrupted. This is especially the case when the cause of religion is taken up by the state, and when the church lets itself be manipulated as an agency of state policy:

> It is certainly an unholy wish, but one I can hardly deny myself. Would that even the most distant inkling of religion had ever remained foreign to all heads of state, all virtuosos and artists of politics! Would that not one had ever been seized by the force of that epidemic enthusiasm, if they did not know how to separate their individuality from their profession and their public character! For that has become for us the source of all corruption.[29]

In order to preserve its quite unsectarian openness and inner pluralism, Schleiermacher's true church will thus, as a matter of deliberate policy, remain as radically set apart from the state as any minority sect has ever been.

As Schleiermacher presents it, on the other hand, this set-apartness also has other more questionable consequences. For, at the same time, such a vision sets distinct limits to the possible *communal* contribution the religious community might make to the state, and to civil society, from a critical point of view. Since it cannot in any way represent, before God, the wider secular society to which it belongs, so neither can it, as a community, really help to articulate that society's corporate conscience. It can only criticize, as it were from the outside. In this respect Schleiermacher's thought remains just as alien to civil theology as Barth's.

Obviously, the affinity group model may also play host to a spirit of prophetic political critique. Schleiermacher's own argument was no doubt largely inspired by his experience among the Moravian Brethren, by whom he had been educated – what he envisages appears to be a somewhat romanticized version of the Moravian Bible Study or prayer group – and Moravian spirituality actually tends not to be all that prophetic, in any worldly sense. But perhaps the best existing example of this model, generalized as the exclusive organizational principle of a whole church, is the Society of Friends (the Quakers); which, from its origins in Cromwell's England onwards, has in fact always been, or at least has aspired to be, an essentially prophetic movement. Quaker worship (in its British form), with its complete lack of clergy or of any set liturgy, and its long silences, functions both as a symbolic letting-be, expressive of the community's respect for the 'that of God' within each of its individual members, and as a waiting, ideally, upon the spirit of prophecy. And – most recently through its participation in the peace movement – the Quaker community has, without any question, made a contribution to the ethical quality of public debate in Britain quite out of proportion to its small size.

Yet the fact remains that, even at its most eloquent, Quaker testimony can never quite recapture the spirit of prophecy one finds in the Bible: for the great Hebrew prophets spoke from out of, and directly back to, the central religious tradition of their people; whereas Quakerism, after all, essentially depends upon its marginality. Had it (as for just one brief moment in the mid-1650s seemed possible) become a mass church, who knows how it would have developed? As things are, though, like the apostolic church the Society of Friends originally took shape as a small, persecuted minority. Having ruled out doctrinal rigidity and hierarchical discipline, the early Quakers maintained the unity-in-distinctiveness necessary for their cultural survival by the alternative means of a rigorous prohibition of intermarriage with outsiders, the adoption of their own peculiar manner of dress (all sober black) and a variety of other 'public testimonies' (always using 'thee' and 'thou', never doffing one's hat, and so forth) as tokens of identity. With the progressive advance of religious toleration in nineteenth-century Britain these more conspicuous distinguishing marks gradually ceased to seem so necessary. But how else can a religious society not held together by clergy or dogma still continue to cohere if not by virtue of some shared, fixed eccentricity of moral vision? The necessary moral otherness, underlying the religious otherness, of twentieth-century Quakerism lies in its continuing attachment to strict pacifism. Indeed, it is hard to see how a pure affinity-group church could exist without at least some such unusual narrowing of the moral options open to its members – as a basis for affinity.[30] And however much one may thank God for the existence of the Society of

Friends, and even though it may indeed be that theirs is a type of contribution which Christendom will always need and never have enough of, it nevertheless by no means necessarily follows that this is therefore the one and only ideal model for *all* churches.

It is a question of the proper representation of the world in liturgy. For if liturgy is to be therapeutic it must, surely, not only mediate a hope for transcendence – from on high – but also do so in such a way as to *draw in* that which is to be transcended, to work on it. Not by coercion, but by being representative, an attractive medium of self-expression. And the world as a whole can only truly be represented in liturgy to the extent that the liturgical community manages to escape its inner set-apartness from its unbelieving or other-believing neighbours; just as much when that set-apartness stems from the evangelic purism of a community like the Society of Friends as when it results from the pursuit of self-aggrandizement by great religious institutions.

A genuinely 'open' church, in this sense, would thus be an *open forum*: reproducing, within itself, the full range of (thoughtful) moral conflict characteristic of the surrounding world; excluding nothing except intolerance; and differing from the world only in the exemplary manner in which it tried to process these conflicts. Like the Society of Friends, in other words, such a church would seek to make an art out of non-coercion; only, so far as possible a more *catholic* art. As a community conferring *auctoritas* on isonomy, its structure would be determined, not at all by the need to suppress conflict or to ensure the clear dominance of some one particular consensus – but solely by the requirements of the very best possible practice of conflict, within an isonomous culture.

That, I think, is what would provide the most naturally hospitable type of confessional environment for the practice of critical civil religion. It no doubt would involve, in the first place, the cultivation – alongside the official structures – of affinity-group 'basic communities', like those associated with the liberation theology of Latin America; or those which developed, for instance, in the very different political circumstances of communist Hungary.[31] Participation in 'broad-based' local inter-faith campaigning organizations would be another ingredient (a British example is to be found in the recently established, and hopefully pioneering, Communities Organized for a Greater Bristol). In general, it would mean a great expansion of the type of grassroots ecumenical co-operation focused on the issues of 'justice, peace and the integrity of creation' which the Germans and the Dutch, especially, know as the 'conciliar process', and which, from the early 1980s, the World Council of Churches has been active in promoting. Indeed, that phrase, 'the conciliar process', exactly captures the need: for an imaginative experimentation with all sorts of new contexts for corporate deliberation.

But what would it require for such developments to become truly central to church life? I very much doubt whether they ever could whilst the prevailing institutional culture of all the mainstream churches remains so very much *a pastoral monoculture.*

In one of his prison letters, Bonhoeffer notoriously proposes that, in order to safeguard its critical freedom, the state-funded German Protestant church should as a matter of principle give away all its property to the needy, and be content henceforth to have its pastors live off the free-will offerings of their congregations, or else earn their keep in secular employment.[32] However, it is highly debatable to what extent this, by itself, would have had the effect he has in mind, of a new opening-up of the church to the world; or to what extent it would merely have resulted in a new, more congregational type of church ideology instead.

For there is surely a powerful impetus towards 'religiousness', in his derogatory sense, inherent in the very role of the pastor as such.

As Michel Foucault once argued, the particular form of power traditionally enjoyed, or claimed, by the Christian clergy (what Foucault calls 'pastoral power') is in fact one of the great practical inventions of Christianity – although in the modern world it has also proliferated, in new configurations, within the agencies of the state.[33] The notion has its origins in the Hebrew scriptures, notably in the Psalter and in the writings of the exilic prophets, where God is represented as the one true shepherd, or pastor, of Israel.[34] The kings and military leaders of the people are also spoken of here as shepherds, although they are invariably ones who have failed and allowed their sheep to scatter – what Israel needs most is better shepherds.[35] The future Messiah, Ezekiel proclaims, will serve as God's co-shepherd.[36] And not surprisingly, therefore, in the New Testament Jesus is 'the good shepherd'[37] But then this same calling is transferred to Peter, to whom at the end of the fourth gospel Jesus says three times, 'Do you love me? . . . Then feed my sheep';[38] and from Peter it is handed down to all his 'fellow-elders' in the church.[39] Thus far, the metaphor is simply a way of underlining the direct accountability of the one set in authority not only for his own behaviour, but also for that of every member of his flock. But in the practice of the early church this then acquires a quite new significance. And, again, I think the reason lies in the formative impact of persecution. For here was an embattled community which, in order to survive, had to be able to inspire in its members a willingness to risk martyrdom, not for the sake of family-related or tribal religious loyalties, but – what was really unprecedented – for a new faith, freely chosen. A major part of the original role of the Christian pastor was, thus, to prepare potential martyrs. Hence the peculiar intrusiveness which distinguishes 'pastoral power': its preoccupation not just with controlling outward action, but rather with the innermost spiritual health of each believer; its association with practices of introspective soul-searching and confession – which were in the first instance a training in the bearing of testimony to a hostile world; its whole character as a radically transformative saving of souls.

But what began in this way then became a fixed feature of Christian priesthood, even when it was no longer strictly necessary. In some religions leadership in worship goes with the role of healer, magician, medium or oracle; in others with that of teacher, or judge; for the most part, however, Christian clergy have always been pastors. Of course. It is taken for granted that that is how it must be.

And yet – what does it do to Christian liturgy? Unfortunately the pastoral approach to sin, and to salvation, still bears the mark of the exclusively confessional and apolitical nature of that formative struggle. So the pastor is expected to be first and foremost a focus for communal unity, and only secondarily, if at all, a stirrer-up of potentially divisive public discussion. In this way a fundamental insensitivity to the phenomenon of *structural* sin appears to be built into the very structure of the church.

In order for religious faith to fulfil that new vocation which it is the essential aim of a critical civil theology to elucidate – its vocation as a medicine against propaganda – a new model is surely required. Or, at any rate, a wider range of models. Outside the academic context, it would need a far greater investment in the work of clergy officially designated as 'community theologians', for instance, whose whole focus would be on issues of public concern relating to a particular locality. So too, there would be a need for many more industrial chaplains, who did not just see their task—the way it has so often been seen in Britain – as an extension of the pastoral work of the parish clergy into a non-parochial context; but who were, also, first and foremost issue-raisers. Certainly, such critique must entail a certain cultivation of spiritual inwardness. Besides new spaces for debate, another thing the faith-community would ideally need to provide, on a much larger scale than at present, would thus be new spaces for contemplative withdrawal from the realm in which propaganda holds sway, with the explicit purpose of prising open the grip propaganda has on our consciousness; so that, at least from time to time, we might stand back from the endless chatter to gaze upon the world again with a purged sensibility. (Although the trouble here is that the contemplative communities within Christendom have, on the whole, also seen their vocation in the most purely pastoral terms.)

There can be no denying the often very considerable educational value of the experience of pastoring for the pastors themselves; in particular, when working among congregations with a very different class or cultural identity from their own (as I can personally testify). The prayer-life of a church in which such work was not done at all would admittedly be impoverished in a great many respects. But it is a question of *balance*. What is at issue is the distribution of limited resources: the balance between what is devoted to the upkeep of the church's pastoral ministry on the one hand, and on the other hand, the resources devoted to developing places of retreat, or to conscious-ness-raising action on problematic issues of public ethics. And one can hardly escape the suspicion that the leaning, within most churches, towards a pastoral *monoculture* may, after all, have something to do with its being found to be the safest option. For even when it is at its least authoritarian, a pastoral monoculture still represents the type of church life in which the possibility of free debate among equals tends to be minimized.

This, in the end, is what seems to me to be really the most fundamental hindrance, at the *practical* level, to the development of a living culture of critical civil theology within Christendom.

Anticipations of Civil Theology in Christendom

But what other traditional resources are there that we might draw on, from the history of Christendom, to help us break free from these constraints? What other, earlier anticipations of the genre? In this category one might perhaps, very broadly, include any approach to questions of religion and politics which has as its starting point, not so much the need to expound and apply a given confessional tradition, but rather an inquiry into the general religious requirements of a healthy political culture.

In the pre-Christian Classical world, in so far as there was such a discipline as theology, it was all of this sort. The actual term, 'civil theology', dates back to the age of Varro (116–27BCE), the great Roman encyclopaedist whose *Antiquitates rerum divinarum* – now, alas, largely lost – provided the most notable actual instance of it.[40] The rise of Christian confessionalism then obliterated the tradition, and in the world of Christendom civil theo-logians, even in this broadest sense, have admittedly been few and far between.

Nevertheless, among those few that can be identified there are some distinguished figures. Consider for instance the progressive series: Machia-velli, Hobbes, Spinoza, Rousseau, Hegel . . .

Niccolò Machiavelli: Discourses on the First Ten Books of Titus Livy *(1531)*

Civil theology certainly can appear in some very dubious forms. And Machiavelli represents it in perhaps the most dubious of all. Thus, as is his usual habit, so too in those passages of his *Discourses* where he discusses religion, he straight away adopts a tone of mischievous worldly wisdom – openly evaluating religion as a potential '*instrument*' of rule.

He praises Numa in particular, the mythical second ruler of Rome, after Romulus, for his use of religion:

> Numa [he writes] finding the people ferocious and desiring to reduce them to civic obedience by means of the arts of peace, turned to religion as the instrument necessary above all others for the maintenance of a civilized state, and so constituted it that there was never for so many centuries so great a fear of God as there was in this republic.[41]

When Numa – in order to reinforce the authority of his laws – 'pretended' to be following the instruction of a Nymph, with whom he consulted, this deception is for Machiavelli an admirable example of his sagacity. Lycurgus and Solon, he presumes, did much the same. They had the advantage of dealing with relatively uncivilized people, among whom the crudest sort of superstition was rife – and

> Doubtless, too, anyone seeking to establish a republic at the present time would find it easier to do so among uncultured men of the mountains than among dwellers in cities where civilization is corrupt; just as a sculptor will more easily carve a beautiful statue from rough marble than from marble already spoiled by a bungling workman.

Yet did not Savonarola, also, contrive to have the sophisticated city folk of Florence follow him, as a holy man inspired by God? Religion will, on the one hand, always remain a useful means of manipulation for the trickster-statesman.

But, on the other hand, there is so far as I can see no reason to doubt Machiavelli's sincerity when he at once goes on to reiterate:

> Those princes and those republics which desire to remain free from corruption, should above all else maintain incorrupt the ceremonies of their religion and should hold them always in veneration; for there can be no surer indication of the decline of a country than to see divine worship neglected.[42]

And his critique of the political role played by the church in his day is certainly quite serious. This critique is two-fold. In the first place, like so many of his contemporaries, he deplores the sheer corruption of the institution, stemming from the bad example set by the Court of Rome. Since this has led to a loss of the moral authority attaching to religious belief throughout Italy, religion has lost much of its power to unify the citizenry. Things were otherwise in Ancient Rome! There, vows made in the presence of the gods had real weight; they provided a genuine basis for mutual trust, and the city flourished as a direct result. Secondly, however – as he makes clear in Book 2 – even when the church is reformed, the other-worldliness to which it then returns remains for him a major stumbling block. Although he also gives advice to princes, Machiavelli's political ideal is the republic of free citizens. But, he observes, if one considers Livy's description of the Italy of the first period of Roman expansion, or if one considers Ancient Greece, there appear to have been many more republics in those days than is now the case in Christian Europe. Why? At this point it is interesting to compare his argument with that of Hannah Arendt (if only to highlight the contrasts). He attributes the greater love of freedom in the early Classical world to the spirit expressed in the striking difference between pagan ritual, and Christian:

> Their ceremonies lacked neither pomp nor magnificence, but, conjoined with this, were sacrificial acts in which there was much shedding of blood and much ferocity; and in them great numbers of animals were killed. Such spectacles, because terrible, caused men to become like them. Besides, the old religion did not beatify men unless they were replete with worldly glory: army commanders, for instance, and rulers of republics. Our religion . . . has assigned as man's highest good humility, abnegation, and contempt for mundane things, whereas the other identified it with magnanimity, bodily strength, and everything else that conduces to make men very bold.

But, without such boldness, freedom is inevitably endangered:

> If our religion demands that in you there be strength, what it asks for is strength to suffer rather than strength to do bold things.
> This pattern of life, therefore, appears to have made the world weak, and to have handed it over as a prey to the wicked.[43]

The republican spirit may have already been extirpated, before the rise of Christianity, by the Roman Empire; but, in his view, it was the triumph of

Christian other-worldliness that represented the main impediment to its resuscitation, following the Empire's collapse. Machiavelli does not deny that the virtues of Christian morality are real virtues – but he leaves us with the resulting paradox unresolved.

Here, then, we have a first, exploratory attempt at a comprehensive rehabilitation of this-worldly religion. It remains a crude one, inasmuch as Machiavelli continues to be trapped within the traditional Christian identification of divine transcendence with other-worldliness; so that, in rejecting the latter, he thinks he has to reject any sense of the former along with it. (For that of course is what his instrumentalizing approach entails.) And, moreover, one also has to question the apparent glibness of this particular blood-and-thunder defence of paganism: for would not the self-same description, after all, apply just as much to the liturgical practice of the early Roman Empire as to that of the Republic? And to the liturgies of all the other great *empires* of antiquity: Egypt, Babylon, Persia and the rest? In the twentieth century the most notable conscious attempts to revive the martial spirit of pagan ceremonial have occurred in the context of Fascism and Nazism. Indeed, that anyone could ever have supposed there to be a natural link between paganism in this sense, and isonomous freedom, can only be regarded now as a somewhat curious quirk of history.

Thomas Hobbes: Leviathan *(1651)*

Whereas Machiavelli is mischievous, it has to be said that Hobbes by contrast writes with grim authority: an authority which derives from the fact that he is responding, in a fresh and cogent way, to the great revelatory trauma of the seventeenth century. Never before had so many Christians been killed by other Christians in wars fought largely over their conflicting interpretations of the faith as in Hobbes's lifetime, and not least in England. Neither had any global resolution of the conflict emerged (as had been the case with the suppression of the Albigensians, say) to remove the risk of further such wars. Never before had Christian intellectuals been presented with such a lesson regarding the potential destructiveness and folly of religious fanaticism.

As Michael Oakeshott remarks,[44] this experience elicited two basic types of critical response: one a turning towards 'natural religion', and the other – which was Hobbes's way – towards civil religion. (Not that Hobbes himself uses the term.) Natural religion is conceived, in the first instance, as the practice of an enlightened peace-making elite, who have withdrawn from any denominational identity and are thereby enabled to mediate with impartiality. Such an elite can have no use for the authority of historical revelation, except in so far as it coincides with what can be independently demonstrated on the basis of natural reason. This is 'natural theology' in the narrow sense (much narrower than Barth's): in England, the way of the Deists. But Hobbes wants to speak to his Christian fellow-citizens as a fellow-Christian – in order to civil-ize Christianity from within. So, in the *Leviathan*, he passes swiftly over 'the kingdom of God by nature';[45] and for the rest of his theological argument – the second and, both in his own view and that of his contemporaries, from a practical point of view much the more immediately important half of the book – he accepts the authority of Scripture as fundamental. Thus he seeks, not to dissolve that authority as the Deists did, but rather, against those who would misuse it in justification for political disruption, to reinterpret it as a vindication of peace. The element of civil theology in Hobbes's thought consists in his closely argued-for definition of the proper political context for dogmatics: namely, the supreme authority of the sovereign to determine the parameters within which public theological debate is to be conducted. And the essence of his dogmatics is then to demonstrate the perfect compatibility of the gospel with that principle; so reconciling the two authorities together.

But this is as far as he allows reason to go, no further. His civil theology, in other words, is a purely *negative* one. It is concerned, exclusively, with the systematic negation of any claims to the Christian believer's loyalty on the part of the institutional church, which might come into conflict with one's loyalty to the sovereign. Hobbes has no more positive view of the potential contribution of religious community to the civil-izing of the state. It was not, after all, an age in which secularization seemed to pose any threat.

Whether Hobbes's profession of faith was sincere, or whether it was just a tactical device, has been much debated. Already in his own day his enemies accused him of being a secret 'atheist'. This was of course the common coinage of ideological abuse in that period. But many of his later admirers, up until recent times, have also been inclined to agree – quite wrongly, I think.[46] True, he was a materialist, which, thanks to the formative influence of Platonism on the mainstream tradition, has often been supposed to be incompatible with Christian orthodoxy. Yet, as he himself argues, there is nothing in Scripture to preclude it; and there is at least the ancient precedent of Tertullian, who was never officially condemned on *that* score.[47] He does go to great pains to establish his theological views. And – rather as in the case of Hegel – the widespread doubt that he can genuinely mean what he says here is perhaps more to be attributed to a drastic impoverishment of the religious imagination in our culture, than to any real ambiguity in the doctrine itself.

At all events, Hobbes does not share Machiavelli's general admiration of paganism. He does, it is true, have a certain admiration for the heroic ethos of Homeric poetry (in his later years he embarked on a project of undertaking his own translation of Homer). But still his brand of Protestantism is one which analyses the fall of the Church of Rome, not so much as a lapse back into the supposed legalism of the Jews, but far more as a matter of accommodation to the pagan superstitions of its Gentile converts.[48] His ideal is a Protestant state. However, it is one in which the clergy have entirely ceased to constitute an independent caste, with its own corporate ambitions; and so he is also an implacable opponent of Presbyterianism, which, as he sees it, still maintains in full force the basic error of Rome: 'that the Church Militant is the Kingdome of God'.[49] For this doctrine is the original source of all church/state conflict; whereas the true kingdom of God – which Christ declared to be 'not of this world' – is strictly the *invisible* fellowship of the Elect.[50] He himself remained an Anglican; yet at the same time enraged the high church party by his denial of the apostolic succession as a source of authority independent of the sovereign's will.[51] And looking across the Channel, from his exile in France, to Cromwell's England of 1651, he expresses cautious approval of the new official latitude in matters of religion. Both the Episcopalians and the Presbyterians had been politically defeated:

> And so we are reduced to the Independency of the Primitive Christians to follow Paul, or Cephas, or Apollos, every man as he liketh best: which, if it be without contention, and without measuring the Doctrine of Christ, by our affection to the Person of his Minister, (the fault which the apostle reprehended in the Corinthians,) is perhaps the best. First, because there ought to be no Power over the Consciences of men, but of the Word it selfe . . . and secondly, because it is unreasonable in them, who teach there is such danger in every little Errour, to require of a man endued with Reason of his own, to follow the Reason of any other man . . .[52]

The great advantage of Independency from the Hobbesian point of view (with the provisos he mentions) is that, by dissolving the political bonds between the clergy, it tends to bring them back to their true role, as instituted by Christ, to be 'our Schoolmasters, and not our Commanders'.[53]

In order that there shall be peace in the world, he argues, the first requirement is that these two roles should be clearly distinguished, and the latter
entrusted solely to the sovereign, in religious matters just as much as in
secular ones.

Hobbes therefore not only approves of the Anglican notion of the sovereign as 'head of the church', but seeks to extend it as far as possible. He
speaks of the Christian sovereign (whether an individual monarch or the
collective person of a sovereign assembly) as 'God's Prophet'[54] and as 'chief
Pastor' in the church.[55] Obviously, the role so often played by the great
Hebrew prophets, as political dissidents, is a potential embarrassment here.
However, he distinguishes between 'Prophets extraordinary', such as these,
and 'Prophets of perpetual Calling', among whom the devout sovereign is
'supreme', and the clergy subordinate. The revelations of the former –
communicated by 'supernatural' means, mostly dreams and visions – possess
immediate authority only if they are both consistent with tradition and
confirmed by miracle; but miracles have now ceased, and so Scripture
has replaced this sort of revelation.[56] Henceforth, therefore, any claim to
the vocation of 'Prophet extraordinary' depends on the validation of the
supreme 'Prophet of perpetual Calling'.[57] And thus the Christian sovereign,
in principle, inherits the role of Abraham, as the sole official 'Judge, and
Interpreter of what God spoke'.[58] In the pastoral domain, too, the Hobbesian view of the rights of the sovereign goes well beyond any established
practice: for not only do these rights include absolute control over the
appointment of clergy, and exclusive jurisdiction with regard to excommunication,

> But if every Christian Sovereign be the Supreme Pastor of his own
> Subjects, it seemeth that he hath also the Authority . . . to Baptize, and
> to Administer the Sacrament of the Lord's Supper; and to consecrate
> both Temples, and Pastors to Gods service.[59]

It may be appropriate that these roles should always be delegated; but his
point is that the clergy should have no source of prestige whatsoever which
is denied to the sovereign, lest they misuse it to justify sedition. Of course,
this can only apply to Christian sovereigns. And yet, for Hobbes, even the
most aggressively *anti*-Christian of sovereigns still has a sacred, God-given *ex
officio* claim to the believer's civil loyalty. If the sovereign requires some
public adherence to an alien faith, there is no necessary merit in refusing a
merely outward conformity; and whereas there may be some who are called
to a more positive public witness – then, well and good, let them accept

martyrdom; but the one thing faith never can justify, in any circumstances, is rebellion.[60]

The vocation of the Hobbesian sovereign entails the very opposite of thought-control:

> A Christian King, as a Pastor, and Teacher of his Subjects, makes not thereby his Doctrines Laws. He cannot oblige men to beleeve . . .

Should he try to do so, the situation is the same as under an anti-Christian sovereign:

> he may . . . oblige men to certain actions, and sometimes to do such as they would not otherwise do, and which he ought not to command; and yet when they are commanded, they are Laws; and the externall actions done in obedience to them, without the inward approbation, are the actions of the Soverign, and not of the Subject, which is in that case but as an instrument, without any motion of his owne at all; because God hath commanded to obey them.[61]

It is only the public expression of thoughts that may have to be controlled – above all, precisely in order to inhibit the rise of parties that would seek, by rebellious violence, to impose their own system of thought-control.

Nothing, on the other hand, could more dramatically illustrate both the underlying continuity, and the sharp discontinuity, between the revelatory trauma of the seventeenth century and that of the twentieth, than the contrast between two of Hobbes's most notable twentieth-century admirers: Michael Oakeshott and Carl Schmitt. For whilst Oakeshott transposed the Hobbesian critique of un-civil religion into a more general critique of un-civil ideology, Schmitt did just the opposite. Schmitt (depite his Catholicism) held fast, instead, to the Hobbesian civil religious celebration of the unitary sovereign state – even where the state itself becomes the prime carrier of a radically un-civil secular ideology. And so it was that Schmitt became one of the leading Christian apologists for Nazism.[62]

It may well be argued that Oakeshott is a good deal truer to the authentic original spirit of Hobbesian doctrine than Schmitt is. And yet – here we have a doctrine which is premised on the unsurpassability of the horror of anarchy, confronted with the actual experience of a form of sovereign rule seemingly more destructive than even the purest anarchy. A twentieth-century civil theology can scarcely *just* be Hobbesian.

Benedict de Spinoza: Theologico-Political Treatise *(1670)*

Spinoza goes beyond Hobbes, in that his thought represents the first major conjunction of civil and natural theology (in the narrower sense). Thus, the nineteenth chapter of his *Theologico-Political Treatise* is, in effect, a summary endorsement of the Hobbesian position on religion and politics. Politically, it is true, he differs from Hobbes in not only vindicating the supreme rights of the sovereign but also specifying how it is wisest for those rights to be exercised: arguing for the desirability of democracy and the value of guaranteeing free speech. But such concerns remain quite external to his civil theology, which is just as negative as Hobbes's. He does not in fact concern himself with the question of whether, or how, religion might positively help promote these values – other than by self-restraint. The one thing he does provide extra is a minimal definition, for political purposes, of natural religion.

This he summarizes in the following seven articles:

1. That God or a Supreme Being exists, sovereignly just and merciful, the Exemplar of the true life . . .
2. That He is One . . . For devotion, admiration, and love spring from the superiority of one over all else.
3. That He is omnipresent, or that all things are open to Him, for [otherwise] we might doubt . . . the equity of His judgment . . .
4. That He has supreme right and dominion over all things . . .
5. That the worship of God consists only in justice and charity, or love towards one's neighbour.
6. That all those, and those only, who obey God by their manner of life are saved; the rest of mankind, who live under the sway of their pleasures, are lost . . .
7. Lastly, that God forgives the sins of those who repent.[63]

Much of the scandal to which the *Treatise* gave rise derives from article 6, with its denial that 'salvation' depends in any way on right belief, as such.[64] But the absence of post-mortem rewards and punishments from the list, in qualification of salvation, is also notable. And, in general, whereas the Deist version of natural religion merely *de-dramatizes* the way God is imagined (God as the celestial clock-maker who does not need to intervene in creation because the mechanism is so perfect), Spinoza both de-dramatizes and de-images. Accordingly, in his *Ethics* he provides us with the means to decode these 'dogmas of universal faith'. That God exists is in fact nothing more than a tautology: 'God', in Spinoza's vocabulary, being simply a name for the totality of all that exists. God is one, inasmuch as there is nothing outside of God; hence, it is only of God that perfect 'freedom' can be predicated, in the sense of being *causa sui*, not subject to external determination. But this is also how he conceives of the human vocation: to attain to the closest possible approximation of freedom; as much self-determined and as little other-determined as can be; not sunk in passive inertia, nor swept along by sudden impulses of passion, but making one's own decisions, and truly *owning* them, through mature, dispassionate reflection. That, then, is what it means to say that God is our 'Exemplar'. For Spinoza, the whole point of philosophical theology lies in getting beyond the level of 'imagination', where stories are told in which God appears as a person; but that God has 'supreme right and dominion', and that God is the omnipresent judge of our lives, are metaphorical ways of expressing the impersonal authority of this vocation. Whilst, as for the affirmations that God is 'just', 'merciful' and 'forgiving', these are projections – on to the impersonality of the divine – of the typical characteristics of the free, rational, happy human individual, in so far as he, or she, is motivated, not by blind passion, but instead by the 'active emotion' of generosity, which article 5 defines as the essence of true 'worship'.

The character of Spinoza's ethics as an enlightened egoism must obviously set strict limits on the inspirational claims of this form of natural religion. Spinoza allows that there is such a thing as authentic 'revelation', and that religious narrative may play a useful role. However, this is only by way of the popularization of moral truth, adapted for the multitude who lack the capacity for philosophy. Just as much as Machiavelli – even if from the standpoint of the philosopher rather than the man of action – he too instrumentalizes faith: 'Philosophy has no end in view save truth', he writes, 'faith . . . looks for nothing but obedience and piety';[65] therefore they do not compete. Herein lies the fundamental argument of the *Treatise*. Revelation does not convey truth, as such; rather, it is an intuitive apprehension, in imaginative form, of what the truth requires in practice. It is, one might say, the historical emergence of natural religion.

But, whatever one may feel about this, from a twentieth-century perspective the fundamental weakness in Spinoza's natural/civil theology surely lies in the sheer narrowness of its critical focus. As a protagonist of seventeenth-century enlightenment, he attacks the 'superstition' of his day. This, though, is superstitious religiosity purely and simply as such, whereas the nightmares of the twentieth century have largely consisted of forms of oppression which – whilst clearly not unrelated, in spirit, to the type of religious tyranny so prevalent in Spinoza's day – have nevertheless been aggressively irreligious. The task for theology today is surely that of tracing the underlying affinities: analysing superstitious religiosity, therefore, as an epiphenomenon of some more general species of corruption which also appears in other forms. There is nothing of this however, as yet, in Spinoza. And so, when it comes to biblical interpretation he has just two primary polemical concerns. In the first place, on the grounds that Reason has no favourites, he challenges the notion of the Jews as a chosen people: writing for a Christian audience, he urges the excision of this Jewish element from Christian tradition, so that the churches will also drop the claims they make, based on their supposed inheritance of that chosenness.[66] Secondly, he challenges the evidence of miracles; thereby seeking to relativize the authority of revealed religion in general. And that is all.

Jean-Jacques Rousseau: The Social Contract *(1762)*

Rousseau, by contrast to Spinoza, then takes off from Hobbes in another way. He praises Hobbes – who, he remarks, is the only Christian writer clearly to have perceived both the full evil of clericalized religion, and that the only way to remove it is by 'reuniting the two heads of the eagle'. Yet he also criticizes him: Hobbes, in his view,

> should have seen that the dominant spirit of Christianity was incompatible with his system, and that the interest of the prince will always be stronger than that of the state. It is not so much the horrible and false parts of Hobbes's system that have made it hated, but the parts which are just and true.[67]

There has to be some system of accountability, he contends, to restrain the potential arbitrariness of the prince: freedom, the highest good for political theory, is (he agrees with Spinoza) far more than just Hobbesian peace and security. And at the same time, still more explicitly than Spinoza, he advocates active state sponsorship of a civic version of natural religion, as a positive counterweight to both the prince and the church. Unlike Spinoza he is a Deist, retaining a conventional doctrine of post mortem rewards and punishments.[68] But his main claim to originality, in this context, consists in his development of a theology, both civil and natural, in which religious superstition is indeed understood as just one symptom amongst others, of the corrupting dynamic of civilization as a whole.

Unfortunately, this analysis is a deeply problematic one. Rousseau's Deism means that God cannot be conceived as an active player, and is left very much in the background of his account; nevertheless, its theological implications are clear enough. Thus, what he is reacting against is the prevailing Enlightenment ideology of progress; and in so doing he also reverses the progressive dynamic of biblical salvation history. 'I concluded', he wrote to the Archbishop of Paris, Christophe de Beaumont, 'that it was not necessary to suppose man to be wicked by nature, when one could trace the origin and progress of his wickedness.'[69] Human fallenness, as he sees it, is not a given, pre-historical state, to be remedied within history, but rather – whilst pre-social human nature is simply unformed, not angelic – the whole of history appears as a process of falling, ever deeper. 'Man was born free, and he is everywhere in chains.' More exactly: man was born perfectible, innately capable of freedom; that is, not needing any divine intervention in the form of special revelation. But the illusion of that need, arising out of the non-fulfilment of freedom, also reinforces the corruption it purports to explain, by mystifying it.

The argument has a compelling underlying simplicity. All corruption originates from the social inflammation of what, in its natural state, is a perfectly healthy phenomenon: *amour propre*, the sense of one's own dignity. It is in so far as people come to affirm that dignity in *competitive* terms that things begin to go wrong. But the more sophisticated a society becomes and the more luxuries it makes available, the more occasions it provides for such competition, in the enjoyment of those luxuries. And hence the illusion tends to grow that it is in one's own best interest to exploit and oppress one's neighbour. So pervasive is the resulting corruption in the modern world that the best hope of salvation, were it possible, would be for a child to be brought up in total isolation from, and total ignorance of, society: the hypothesis explored in *Emile*. The child, Emile, would thereby, in his formative years, be lifted out of history. What we need, not least, is salvation from history, and the competition for historic success. In non-fictional reality, it is the uneducated peasantry, and especially those living in remote mountain districts or in a place like Corsica, whose lives are lived at the furthest remove from history, in the unchanging rhythms of nature. And it is in such places, therefore, in the sort of community displayed in 'rustic feasts', 'village games' and 'joyful harvests', that Rousseau – the wistful intellectual on-looker – considers we come closest to the actual practice of natural religion. Like Simone Weil, he too values community established on the basis of unreflective custom far higher than community founded on conscious tradition; for custom is next to nature. The more sophisticated, and therefore the more corrupt, a society becomes, on the other hand, the more the religious life tends to be reduced to the sublimated competitiveness of fanaticism (with its natural tendency to re-emphasize the myth of humanity's pre-historic fallenness); and the more that then tends, in turn, to elicit the exaggerated reaction of outright atheism – a phenomenon he associates with the final dropping of all moral inhibitions.

In the concluding chapter of *The Social Contract* Rousseau distinguishes between three basic types of religion: 'the religion of the man', 'the religion of the citizen', and 'the religion of the priest'. The first is natural religion, in its absolute universality; which he also identifies with 'the pure and simple religion of the Gospel'; the most complete antithesis to inflamed *amour propre*. The second is civil religion, as it exists without any necessary admixture of the first. The third is what he agrees with Hobbes and Spinoza in totally rejecting. But this is where he also begins to go beyond their essentially negative civil theology: for he is not only concerned with the negation of 'the religion of the priest', his interest is just as much in positively reconciling the other two. (And here we have at least a remote anticipation of the type of problem with which we were concerned above, in the contrast between Arendt and Weil.)

Thus, in Rousseau's view, neither of these two is adequate on their own: 'the religion of the citizen', on its own, is inadequate because it lacks any check to superstition, and because it tends to promote war with other states who worship other gods. But 'the religion of the man' is no less inadequate on its own – and at this point his argument echoes that of Machiavelli:

> It is said that a people of true Christians would form the most perfect society imaginable. I see but one great flaw in this hypothesis, namely that a society of true Christians would not be a society of men . . .
>
> For such a society to be peaceful and for harmony to prevail, every citizen without exception would have to be an equally good Christian. If, unhappily, there should appear one ambitious man, one hypocrite, one Catilina, for example, or one Cromwell among them, that man would readily trample over his pious compatriots . . . Christians would have scruples about expelling the usurper; for that would mean disturbing the public peace, using violence, shedding blood, and all this accords ill with Christian mildness. And after all what does it matter whether one is free or a slave in the vale of tears? . . .
>
> Suppose a foreign war breaks out . . . all will do their duty – but they will do it without passion for victory . . . Set them at war against a generous people whose hearts are devoured by an ardent love of glory

and their country . . . and your pious Christians will be beaten, crushed, destroyed before they have time to collect their wits, or they will owe their salvation only to the contempt which their enemy feels for them.[70]

Rousseau differs from Machiavelli in that he is just as critical of the more war-like pagan 'religion of the citizen'. And his critique of inflamed *amour propre* leads him entirely to reject the sort of agonal politics which Machiavelli celebrates: his ideal of republican liberty may involve the participation of all the citizens in periodic assemblies to renew the social contract between them, but these assemblies would also be characterized by a complete absence of *partisan* conflict. Nevertheless, he agrees that pure Gospel-Christianity is essentially inimical to any sort of republican spirit; its sublime truth lies strictly in its role as 'the religion of the private person'.[71] It has to be supplemented with a civil creed: the formula for a critically transformed 'religion of the citizen'. Among people who might otherwise be seduced away from their duties as citizens by false religious rhetoric, such a civil creed – with the barest minimum of dogmas to quarrel over – needs to be built into the social contract, as a basis for consensus concerning the divine nature of its authority. And herein lies the key difference from Spinoza's 'dogmas of universal faith': that Rousseau in this way makes the connection, which Spinoza does not, with the issue of freedom. Whereas Spinoza's creed is simply supposed to serve the purpose of making peace between sects, so bonding the citizenry together, Rousseau is, at the same time, concerned with religion's potential for positively reinforcing their attachment to what the social contract is meant to guarantee, their freedom from the sort of manipulation by their rulers to which an inflamed *amour propre* would otherwise expose them.

What, however, renders Rousseau's argument so problematic is just the dependence of this freedom on an absolute maximum of social cohesion at the level of the state, coupled as it is in his thinking with a decisive dissolution of civil society. For if the first requirement of freedom is that everything which might ever conceivably give expression to an inflamed *amour propre* should be abolished, then it is hard to see how anything could be left of politically organized civil society – this being so very much a domain of competing groups. And the compensating achievement of social cohesion at the level of the state thereby becomes all the more important.

The great scandal, of course, attaching to Rousseau's civil religion – what has tended to call down so much opprobrium upon it – is that, being written into the social contract itself in order to sanctify this cohesion, in the ideal state its creed must be *binding* on all citizens. (Since one of its dogmas is the 'negative' one that all sectarian religious intolerance is anathema, it follows that the advocates of such intolerance are in principle excluded from citizenship. And so too are those who openly express atheistic opinions, or disbelief in life after death. Both the fanatic and the atheist alike are faced with the stark choice: either exile or death. To be sure, the reason is not the supposed untruth of their beliefs, as theories – Rousseau is not concerned with that; it is just because of what he envisages as the inevitably anti-social consequences of these beliefs, in practice.) It is doubtless a gross exaggeration to charge Rousseau with therefore being a proto-totalitarian: totalitarianism, after all, is also an expression of inflamed *amour propre*, the corporate *amour propre* of a movement, a nation, a race. And, in Oakeshottian terms, Rousseau is very much an advocate of the state as 'civil association', not 'enterprise association'. Yet, even so, his position surely is indefensible. It is not only that twentieth-century experience appears to refute the link he makes between atheism and moral licence. This was a prejudice he shared with some of the most advanced liberals of the age; one finds the same in John Locke's *Letter Concerning Toleration*, for instance, and in Rousseau's case it was exacerbated by his own unhappy personal relationships with the *philosophes*. But a still more fundamental objection is that his sort of civil religion simply does not seem capable of doing the job he has assigned to it.

For how could it come alive? How could it – as it must – really capture the imagination, and speak to whole communities? Its creed is so bland, and the accompanying historiography is so abstract, that the development of a truly compelling spirituality on this basis looks about as unlikely as the writing of great literature in Esperanto. Rousseau rules out 'the religion of the priest' without making any enquiry into the possibility of a purified religiousness at that level, which might mediate between 'the religion of the man' and 'the religion of the citizen', presumably because of the inherent liability of any form of church life to inflamed corporate *amour propre*. He deals with the same problem at the level of civil religion – the risk, in this case, of religious nationalism – in effect, by depriving it of any genuine inspirational force: the sort of force it could only have by virtue of the active participation of religious bodies belonging to civil society. But, when he also wants to deploy this faith in a critical capacity, *against* the inflamed *amour propre* of the private individual, such rigorism is plainly self-defeating.

The Jacobins did their best to institute a civil faith along Rousseauian lines. It is not surprising that they failed, and that their artificial creation seems scarcely to have put down any real roots at all. Or, to put it in other words: 'the religion of the man' – represented in its noblest form by the Savoyard Vicar in *Emile* – is reconciled in this scheme of things with 'the religion of the citizen', only by lifting them both right out of the medium of inherited tradition, within which they might come into conflict. That is: the problem is solved by being suppressed. The Vicar advocates outer conformity to whatever may happen to be the public religion of one's homeland, as an expression of patriotism.[72] Yet his 'profession of faith' belongs in *Emile*, a study of education-through-isolation, because it is essentially a celebration of inner solitude: an assault on the authority of tradition in the name of 'conscience' and 'sincerity'. Emile himself receives no traditional religious instruction. The whole point of the experiment is to ensure that he will learn to think for himself, always directly from his own perceptions and insights, never second-hand from the opinion of others; his tutor, therefore, acts as a gentle guide, never giving arbitrary-seeming commands or imposing any point of view of his own. And so too when it comes to religious faith, the tutor practises the most scrupulous restraint: only when Emile's own spontaneous reflections lead him 'naturally' to the topic – Rousseau imagines, around the age of eighteen – is it time to talk about such matters.[73] But the question then is: has one really learnt to think for oneself when one has nothing to *rebel against*? The basic trouble with Rousseau's Utopian ideal is that it would do away with any possibility of educative rebellion. And so all we are left with are the sentimental effusions of the Savoyard Vicar, with his *faux naïf* refrain: 'I am not a great philosopher . . . It is enough for me to reveal to you what I think in the simplicity of my heart.'[74]

G.W.F. Hegel (1770–1831)

Truly, nothing could be more remote than this from the spirit of Hegel: for not only was Hegel by no means ashamed to be a great philosopher; he was also quite allergic to such appeals to simplicity of heart, in justification of de-historicized theological abstraction!

Yet we know (from the evidence of his contemporary Leutwein[75]) that Rousseau was Hegel's 'hero' during his student days at the Tübingen Stift. And whilst there is no actual discussion of Rousseau in his earliest writings, the central concern of those writings does relate very closely to Rousseau's civil theology.

Indeed one might well see Rousseau's position as the starting point from which Hegel progressively develops away: first dropping the element of coercion in the Rousseauian scheme, and then exploring the contemporary possibilities for a civil religion (in his own terminology, a *Volksreligion*) with just the sort of roots Rousseau fails to envisage. Thus, already in his Tübingen period, we find Hegel setting out the following three basic criteria for a healthy *Volksreligion*:

I.   Its doctrine must be grounded on universal reason.
II. Fancy, heart and sensibility must not thereby go away empty.
III. It must be so constituted that all the needs of life and the public affairs of the state are tied in with it.[76]

It is evident that, in his view, mainstream Christianity fails, above all, with regard to the first and third of these criteria; but where Rousseau's civil religion would fall short is with regard to the second.

Initially, Hegel seems to consider Kant's 'religion within the limits of reason alone' to represent the fullest elaboration of the first criterion; the second and the third, on the other hand, are fulfilled in paradigmatic fashion by the religion of ancient Greece. And it therefore becomes for him a question of reconciling what is exemplified there with Kantian reason. His idealizing enthusiasm for Greek paganism, which he shares with so many of his generation, differs notably, however, from Machiavelli's: it is not the blood-and-thunder aspect which he admires, but simply the vivid way he supposes this religion to have been integrated into the life of the city as such:

> Anyone who did not know the history of the city, the culture, and the laws of Athens could almost have learned them from the festivals if he had lived a year within its gates.

How different from the religion of Christendom! Of course, there can be no absolute division of spiritual from civil history: in Germany the memory of the Reformation, in particular, does provide at least some opportunity of re-uniting the two –

> But apart from the usual annual readings of the Augsburg Confession in some Protestant churches (readings usually wearisome to every hearer) and apart from the dull sermon which follows these, what is the festival which celebrates [that] memory?

And, for the rest,

Christianity has emptied Valhalla, felled the sacred groves, extirpated the national imagery as a shameful superstition, as a devilish poison, and given us instead the imagery of a nation whose climate, laws, culture, and interests are strange to us and whose history has no connection whatever with our own . . . Thus we are without any religious imagery which is homegrown or linked with our history, and we are without any political imagery whatever.[77]

This is the original complaint which gives rise to Hegel's civil theology.

To be sure, there are faintly disturbing undertones here of that all too conventional prejudice against Judaism which in fact rather blights his early thinking as a whole. In his mature thought, however, that prejudice, even if it does not altogether disappear, tends to drop away. For this thinking begins from a general re-evaluation of both Jewish and Christian tradition: issuing from a new sense of the inherent *potential* of Christianity – properly interpreted – to transcend its historic other-worldliness, and actually to fulfil all three of his criteria for a genuine *Volksreligion*. Like Hobbes, therefore, the mature Hegel aspires to be a civil theologian fully within the confines of orthodox Christianity. Yet at the same time he also goes beyond Hobbes in two respects. In the first place, he is much more emphatic than Hobbes in his advocacy of religious toleration. He is very clear that the political coherence of the state ought not to be regarded, in any way, as depending upon institutional religious unity; on the contrary, he even rejoices in the schisms resulting from the Reformation. For

so far from its having been a misfortune for the state that the church is disunited, it is only as a result of that disunion that the state has been able to reach its appointed end as a self-consciously rational and ethical organization. Moreover this disunion is the best piece of good fortune which could have befallen either the church or thought so far as the freedom and rationality of either is concerned.[78]

Ecclesiastical disunity, in other words, has helped to emancipate the modern state from its moral dependence on the church; which in turn has helped to set the church free from its role as an instrument of state power, a role which in his view was always spiritually enslaving. But then secondly, he also goes on to develop a much more positive civil theology than Hobbes: centring on what – in stark contrast to Machiavelli or Rousseau – he now comes to see as the latent symbolic capacities of Christian dogma to represent the requirements of (in effect) isonomous freedom.[79]

Hegel's politics are, on the one hand, strictly anti-Utopian – a reaction to the Utopian horrors of the French Revolution; but on the other hand, within the limits of that anti-Utopianism, they are a celebration of isonomous citizenship (in so far, that is, as the type of political structures conceivable in his day could coherently give space to it).

Isonomy, after all, is a political order designed to maximize the possibilities of each individual's spontaneous participation in public life; its ethos derives from a powerful affirmation of human individuality. In the world of the Greek *polis* this was limited by the divisions between slave and free, citizen and non-citizen. But Christian dogma presents us with an image of God incarnate precisely in the figure of a single human individual; an individual, furthermore, condemned for his challenge to the repressiveness of an extremely anti-isonomous regime; a crucified dissident. The story surely *might* lend itself very easily to interpretation as a symbolic vindication of, in Hegel's own phrase, 'the infinite value of the individual as such'. The fact that the isonomous implications of the gospel have so seldom been realized in practice he attributes to the way in which its essential truth has been obscured by the inevitable ambiguities attendant on the religious medium in which it is cast. The medium particularizes the universal in order to represent it imaginatively – always with the risk that the particularity of the representation will obscure the universality of what is represented. And so too in this case: the universal truth, represented here, about individuality in general is all too easily displaced by an exclusive focus on the particularity of the representative individual, who is the actual subject of the story.

It is perhaps, first and foremost, this perception which leads to Hegel's transition from Rouseauian cultural criticism to (in his own terminology) 'speculative' philosophy. In his critique of the imaginative medium of religious thought as such, he takes up where Spinoza left off. But of course, he goes beyond Spinoza above all in the way he traces the course of revelation through a comprehensive survey of world history – with the Incarnation as its 'speculative mid-point'. Thus, he takes the atonement represented by the Incarnation and places it in the context of an ultimate *need for atonement* conceptualized in terms which entirely transcend the medium of specifically religious language: namely, the need for the at-one-ment of the two halves of 'unhappy consciousness'.[80] 'Unhappy consciousness' is essentially a term for any sort of positive mental servitude. It is the condition, to which all human beings are to one extent or another subject, of being the censor of one's own experience, disallowing the lessons it might teach one, for fear of the consequences. It is a divided consciousness, inasmuch as one is, at once, both the censor and the one whose experience is being censored;

super-ego and ego, unreconciled. Whilst in substantive terms it is an internalizing of the prejudices of a community, Hegel defines it more formally as an internalizing of the 'lord and bondsman' relationship. It is a general name for everything that is *spiritually* opposed to isonomy.

But then the argument progresses more or less as follows. Unhappy consciousness projects its own dividedness on to the cosmos: the censor-self lays claim to lordly, in the sense of unquestionable, authority. Hegel speaks of it as 'the Unchangeable' – what cannot be questioned cannot be changed. However, in order to maintain that authority this self has to understand and present itself as something far more than just the internalized voice of a particular human community. Its impulse is to speak in the name of some transcendent 'Truth', some unchanging cosmological principle of order. And its opposite – the 'bondsman', 'changeable', empirical and censored self – has accordingly, therefore, to be assigned an opposite cosmological status: as belonging to, and representing, an ontologically contrary realm, of disorder and untruth. The resulting dualism here need not be theological or religious. But it is nevertheless only too readily reinforceable by direct identification with the duality of the sacred and the profane, as the cult of a heavenly Lord conceived in the image of the despotic super-ego; and to the extent that that happens, religion is reduced to a system of neurotic compulsions and taboos. The authority of the sacred serves simply to close off unwanted questions as expressions of *hubris*. Teaching becomes fence-maintenance. The questioner comes to be regarded as a trespasser in the Lord's estate.

Admittedly, therefore, no Christian thinker who is indeed a genuine thinker has ever been a positive exponent of the world-view proper to unhappy consciousness. A truly thoughtful affirmative expression of unhappy consciousness is impossible. But what is new with Hegel is just his unprecedented critical focus on the issue, his explicit identification of the inner truth of the gospel with the overcoming of unhappy consciousness.

For unhappy consciousness is sin. But it is not sin as traditionally defined, anywhere, within a tradition largely lacking in the actual experience of isonomy. On the contrary, it is that very dimension of sin which – despite the gospel itself – the tradition fails to recognize, because of its lack of such experience.

It is the most basic outright denial of 'the Absolute'. The Absolute is a landscape without enclosures, no questions barred, no *a priori* specially privileged stories or protected mysteries. And philosophy, defined as the exploration and mapping out of that landscape – the knowing of the Absolute for what it is, or 'absolute knowing' – is at the same time for Hegel the highest form of worship.[81] The more sophisticated a religion becomes, on the other hand, the more the mentality of compulsion and taboo develops into an unhappy discipline of introspection. In his 1827 *Lectures on the Philosophy of Religion* Hegel distinguishes three 'forms' of religious worship, at three different levels of theological sophistication.[82] There is (a) simple 'devotion': the 'becoming vivid' of faith through an 'immersion' in prayer; an affair of sheer 'fire and heat'. There is (b) the more reflective type of thinking concerned with regulating the externals of public worship, shaping and interpreting the symbolism of sacrifice, sacraments, liturgy in general. And then (c) there is the spirituality of 'remorse and repentance'. Here one is not only emotionally stirred in the immediate present; nor is one's spirit of self-sacrifice satisfied with liturgical gestures of renunciation; but what one offers up is nothing less than 'one's heart or inmost self'. These three forms of worship may certainly in his view be paths towards inner liberation. However, they also correspond to the three levels of unhappy consciousness which he distinguishes in *The Phenomenology of Spirit*: first, the mindless religiosity which is 'no more than the chaotic jingling of bells, or a mist of warm incense';[83] second, the formal relationship of humble thanksgiving to a gracious but ultimately despotic Lord God;[84] and third, a move to put down the resistance of the censored self once and for all by way of a spirituality of radical self-loathing.[85] It is above all at this third level, he remarks, that 'the enemy reveals himself in his characteristic shape': that is, in the more extravagant attempts at a penitential mortification of the flesh; or in a view of discipleship as a matter of unconditional obedience to one's superiors in the religious hierarchy, viewed as necessary mediators between one's sinful and unworthy self, on the one hand, and Heaven, on the other; or, perhaps, in an unquestioning devotion to charismatic religious leaders, on the same basis. From the Hegelian point of view these are not more or less flawed practical approximations to gospel truth. They are, precisely, its practical antithesis.

Unhappy consciousness is by no means confined to any one particular faith tradition. Indeed, as I have said, its basic dualism may also, in principle, take on all sorts of other, non-religious forms of expression. Hegel's discussion of it is studded with allusions to Christianity just because he is preoccupied with the intrinsic capacity of Christian dogma to symbolize its overcoming, and with the way in which that symbolic potential is so often obscured. But the historiography which constitutes his philosophy of world history is essentially a civil theology of revelation: presented as the story of the progressive clarification of this issue, in the evolution of human culture as a whole.

Richard Rothe, in his *Theologische Ethik* of 1848, expresses the Hegelian hope for Christianity even more boldly than Hegel himself:

The first necessity for a proper understanding of the stage which Christianity has now reached is to recognize that the church-phase of its development is over, and that the Christian spirit has already entered into its ethical, or political, maturity. . . . The innermost essence of Christianity drives it out beyond the church; it has to seek its embodiment in nothing less than that body which encompasses the entirety of human life, namely the state. What it essentially requires is reconciliation with the world, that is, for it to shed the ecclesiastical form it was obliged to assume at its entry into the world, and to appear instead as the living expression of a universal ethic.[86]

This is not to deny the value of ecclesiastical independence from governmental power within 'the state' (which here means political culture as a whole – implicitly including the politics of 'civil society', in its current, post-Hegelian sense). But what is interesting about the Hegelian argument in this context is the way in which, beginning from a purely civil-theological original problematic, he nevertheless sets out, as it were, to rescue the whole confessional tradition of the church *from* the church, in its traditional in-civility; that is, to civil-ize the tradition – as a vital contribution to the *general* civilizing of politics.

And here I think we do at last begin to draw much closer to what is needed.

3 'The Solidarity of the Shaken': Civil Theology and Historical Consciousness

Civil theology, one might say, is a study of the proper spirit in which the narratives of civil religion are to be handled. Considered as a contribution to the developing self-consciousness of civil society, it could further be defined as the exploration, from a theistic perspective, of the requirements of moral solidarity in the face of oppression in so far as the need is for a spirit of moral solidarity transcending all confessional boundaries – even including those between theist and atheist. So far we have considered such theology as a response to a particular moment of revelation. But now, in these next two chapters, I want to open up the broader methodological question: what, in general, are the most basic preconditions for the sort of transcendence it expresses?

One thing, at least, that it clearly requires in the first place is – against Kierkegaard! – *a maximally heightened sense of history as such*. For the barriers needing to be broken down are always the result of some particular perspective's having been de-historicized, so as to be presented – whether in mythical or in 'metaphysical' terms – as an immutable absolute. Whereas the solidarity in question is essentially a shared pragmatic response to the specificity of a common historical predicament.

The Czech philosopher Jan Patočka actually seems to me to have a particularly apt formula for this when he speaks of what he calls '*the solidarity of the shaken*'. Which for him is also just what it means to overcome nihilism: taking 'nihilism', as he does, to mean the denial of any positive meaningfulness in history, that might serve as an effective basis for solidarity among those 'shaken' by the loss of ahistorical meaning, hitherto inherent in the apparent naturalness of moral and religious custom.

And in this chapter I therefore propose to do two things: first, to take up Patočka's basic suggestion, as an eminently appropriate formula for the proper ideal of civil theology; and then to set it over against the main alternative critical interpretations of 'nihilism', those of Nietzsche and Heidegger. Unlike either Nietzsche or Heidegger, I think Patočka represents a mode of post-'metaphysical' critique which might indeed open out into a genuinely civil theology. Let me try and indicate how.

Jan Patočka's Meta-history of Historical Consciousness

Patočka was one of the original three spokespeople of the Charter 77 movement in Czechoslovakia, alongside Václav Havel and Jiři Háyek (who had been foreign minister in the Dubček government in 1968).[11] He died on 13 March 1977, as a result of an interrogation by the police. His biography mirrors the traumatic history of his country: born in 1907, he had only just qualified as a lecturer when the Nazi invasion led to the closure of the Charles University in Prague. It was a career he was subsequently only able to pursue for two brief periods: just after the war, from 1945 to 1948, and again, following his reinstatement during the Prague Spring, from 1968 to 1972. His first dismissal followed shortly after the communist coup; his second dismissal was part of the so-called 'normalization' process following the Soviet invasion. For most of the communist period he was employed as an archivist and librarian, banned from teaching and of course subject to the most rigorous censorship.

Charter 77 was perhaps a classic example of 'the solidarity of the shaken', in action. The participants in the thriving Chartist counter-culture represented a very diverse group: anti-communists and 'ex-communists' who had been identified with the Prague Spring; intellectuals and 'workers'; Catholics, Protestants, atheists. They were united not by any common political ideology or orientation, but solely by a common concern for the moral quality of political life in their country. In political terms, the Charter was simply an appeal to the Czechoslovak government to observe its own laws, and in particular the guarantees of human rights to which it had committed itself as a party to the Helsinki Final Act. Without such rights, any other sort of political organization was of course impossible. The solidarity of the Chartists was thus not so much political as pre-political: consisting in an effort to reopen the possibility of politics. Hence Patočka's grounding of the movement in a direct appeal to 'the absoluteness of principles that are, in this sense, "holy", principles that are binding on everyone' – transcending, and setting limits to, the instrumental rationality of *any* form of state policy.[2]

He himself was very much an academic philosopher, even if excluded from the academy.[3] His political thinking emerges out of his at first sight quite un-political-seeming attempts to mediate philosophically between Husserl and Heidegger (he was a particularly close friend and associate of Husserl's). In the pre-communist period he published several essays on the philosophical thought of the founder and first President of Czechoslovakia, Tomás Masaryk: critical of Masaryk's over-confident nineteenth-century faith in human progress, but very much affirming the tolerant and open-minded humanism of Masarykian politics. Following the catastrophe of 1968, on the other hand, he turns to reconsider the question of Czech national identity in a series of letters entitled, *What are the Czechs?*. His argument in these letters appears essentially to be a rebuttal of the prevailing mood in the country, of sullen resentment against the all-powerful Soviet invader. Thus, how is a people which has suffered such a soul-destroying reverse to think of its history? The natural temptation is to concentrate chiefly, in a self-pitying way, on earlier experiences of comparable oppression and humilation, so as to construct a chronicle of victimization, culminating in the present. And perhaps all the more so in this case, given the undeniably abundant material which Czech history provides for such a chronicle: not only the more immediate memories of the betrayal at Munich and Heydrich's Nazi Protectorate, but also the 300 years of Austrian rule and in particular the 'dark ages' of the seventeenth and eighteenth centuries, when Czech culture was almost obliterated. But Patočka rejects this way. Instead, he looks further back, to the glory of those periods in the later Middle Ages when Prague was an imperial capital. His argument in fact sounds almost Nietzschean: turning aside from the moral self-righteousness of a slave-people, to the free-spiritedness of a 'lordly people'; and (indirectly) responding to Soviet imperialism therefore, not by denouncing imperialism as such, but rather by reaffirming the intrinsic virtues of political creativity, or 'greatness', even when these take shape in an expansionist imperial context – and (implicitly) criticizing only the way in which this particular imperialism sought to crush them. He protests, not in the name of Czech nationalism, but for the sake of the ideal he calls 'Europe': as an opening towards the fullest possible cosmopolitan interchange of ideas.[4]

In his contemporaneous *Heretical Essays on the Philosophy of History*, he sets out to explore this notion of 'Europe' in a more systematic manner. The *Heretical Essays* are thus, in essence, an attempt to construct a philosophical meta-history of historical consciousness, as this has emerged out of the whole process of European history.[5]

The tale they tell is one of escalating 'shaken-ness': the progressive de-
stabilization of *every* sort of (honestly tenable) comprehensive world-view –
theistic or atheistic, dogmatic or agnostic, religious or irreligious, alike. A
process, the full universality of which Patočka seeks to grasp by placing it
within the conceptual framework of what he calls '*the three basic movements of
human life*', three 'movements' which together serve to determine the pre-
reflective wholeness of 'the natural world'.[6] This tripartite analysis – first
introduced in a short essay written in 1965, entitled 'Comments on the
prehistory of the science of movement: the world, the earth, the sky and the
movement of human life' – is a theme running right through his later
writings;[7] and is perhaps his chief claim to systematic philosophical originality. In the *Heretical Essays* he refers by way of comparison to Arendt's
account of the *vita activa*, in *The Human Condition*. And to some extent, as he
acknowledges, what he is saying actually coincides with her argument there:
historical consciousness, in the full sense he intends, depends upon, and can
indeed only develop in the context of, an ethos focused on the celebration
of action, as opposed, in Arendtian terms, to labour or work.[8] But it does not
only depend on that – and here he goes beyond Arendt. For such consciousness to emerge, what is needed is not just a new attitude to the world as
constituted by the praxis of the *vita activa*. There is also required a no less
fundamental shift in attitude, surely, to the world's initial *given-ness*, prior to
all praxis.

The 'natural world' of prehistory is thus, he argues, an environment
shaped essentially by two 'movements'.[9] Between them, these two movements represent the most elementary necessities of human life, in corporeal
terms. Each embodies a basic prereflective orientation to the constancy of
the earth and the sky, experienced as a theatre for the perennial sameness of
human affairs.

On the one hand, there is the movement of 'acceptance'. Life obviously
cannot well proceed without the will to live. In this sense, it depends first of
all on a simple enjoyment of the given: one has to learn to sense the
possibility of happiness, to love life, to own it – and for that the prime
necessity is to feel that one is 'accepted'. This initial movement is, so to
speak, an experience of being-moved, by love and appreciation, in radical
passivity; primordial rootedness. The need for roots is of course one which
reappears in all sorts of different contexts, at each of the various levels of the
mature individuals's social identity; but it is clearest of all in the case of
the child, the suckling infant. And then it is, primarily, the need of the
persisting child-self within the adult. What Patočka seeks to evoke here is, in
short, the way that this need serves to determine a absolutely primary

orientation to the world, as a benign and welcoming whole, into which – weak and vulnerable – one is received; the experience of belonging; of being situated on earth somewhere within a covered space, as he puts it, full of warmth and light, securely sheltered from the cold, the darkness, the strangeness all around. This is the movement which determines every dream of a golden age; the vague, inarticulate jealousies with which it tends to be accompanied notwithstanding. It is by this means that one first finds oneself, 'becomes a centre'. In the *Heretical Essays*, he further identifies it as the primordial source of the demand for justice.

But then, on the other hand, there is also the movement of 'defence' – which is where his argument rejoins Arendt on labour and work. (Both labour and work together: Patočka does not question the Arendtian distinction, but it is not particularly germane to his concerns.) After the passivity of one's acceptance into the world comes the active struggle to survive within it, and the struggle for biological reproduction, resulting in a quite opposite relationship both to others and to the world. In the *Heretical Essays* he describes it as 'the abdication of self'. Not that there is any sort of altruism involved. It is much more a matter of one's being compelled, by the implacable logic of the life process, to limit or abandon the emotional aspirations inherent in the experience of putting down roots. The subjective 'centre' which the first movement established now becomes, necessarily, at least to some extent an object to be used, in the process of exploiting the fruits of the earth. The loving regard of acceptance is replaced by the cold assessment of one's utility: it being characteristic of this movement that relationships between people are basically cast in terms of what they might have to offer each other as partners, or the threat they might pose to each other as rivals, in purely material terms; giving rise to an ethic focused on the fulfilment of a range of highly differentiated economic roles.

The point Patočka is making, however, is that these two movements, for all the contradictions between them, nevertheless do have at least this much negatively in common: neither of them yet provides any stimulus to historical consciousness – that is, in the proper sense, where history is understood as an ongoing process of human action, a corporate affair of whole communities, in which what is to come in the future may indeed turn out to be significantly different from what has been and is. The first movement, after all, whereby one makes one's entry into a world already prepared is a response to the given, purely and simply as given; it is the affective dynamic by which the underlying, ahistorical continuity of human life is preserved, from generation to generation. And the second movement is a response to the needs of the present only in their most immediate ahistorical urgency; for which the past is of course also present, but only in the tools and physical structures inherited from one's forebears; whilst the future figures solely with reference to one's own, or one's children's, survival and material well-being. The most basic precondition for the emergence of historical consciousness, Patočka argues, is therefore the decisive transcendence of both these mentalities.

Above all, such transcendence must take the form of a fundamental calling into question of the way in which one's culture defines what it takes to be sacred. Patočka is reluctant to apply the term 'religion' to the type of cult which operates within the horizons of prehistory. For him, religion is what develops later, in so far as the experience of the sacred is modified by the new sense of responsibility associated with an entry into history.[10] But in the context of the not-yet-historical natural world the sacred/profane distinction mirrors the interplay of the two movements by which the character of that world is primarily shaped.

Thus, as a pre-religious category, the sacred is that which is encountered most directly in and through the experience of ecstasy. The ecstatic apprehension of the sacred, in the first place, represents a sort of heightened recapturing of the sense of warmth and security which marks the experience of acceptance. And, secondly, as a public phenomenon it is what constitutes a festival – that is, an occasion set over against the everyday, profane world of labour and work, as its antithesis. It is the experience of being lifted out of the self which is burdened with toil, an experience of release. The gods, being immortal, do not need to labour in order to survive; they are what the burdened, toiling self would love to be.[11] In communing with them one enters, at any rate for a while, into a sphere in which the imperatives of work are suspended.

The birth of historical consciousness, he suggests – and, with it, the transformation of ecstatic cult into authentic religion – requires yet a third 'movement', of equal radicality to the first two. And this he calls the movement of 'truth': an impulse towards 'truth' in the sense of a problematically transcendent ideal, to which its devotees can only aspire – as opposed to the apparently unchangeable, and hence unquestionable, dispensations of prehistory. (Compare Hegel on the enslavement to the Unchangeable which constitutes the unhappy consciousness. The difference is that the unhappy consciousness is a self-reflective, spiritual phenomenon; whereas the apparent unchangeableness of the prehistoric natural world derives simply from the *pre*-reflective character of the life it frames.) By contrast to the first movement, this one provides no 'cover', but initiates a process of self-discovery. However necessary, at one level, the shelter and security of the rooted life may continue to be, the whole dynamic of this movement tends towards (an authentic) up-rooting:

> To speak the language of Hegel, everything that was solid and which hitherto served as a support for life has started to totter. The earth itself has been shaken.[12]

By contrast to the second movement, it involves a quite different attitude to death: regarding death not so much as that from which life has to be defended; but, rather, taking the fact of human mortality and finitude as a moral challenge, to make of one's life something of real significance, in its historic context. (Patočka relates this not only to Arendt's critique of the world-views of the *animal laborans* or *homo faber*, but also to Heidegger's analysis, in *Being and Time*, of *Dasein*'s 'fallen-ness', into the deadly, death-forgetting routine of a historic everydayness.[13]) It is the opposite of that. He sees it as an ethical extension of the impulse that inspires 'mountaineers, sea-voyagers, cosmonauts, acrobats': the intensification of life through a deliberate exposure to risk. Beyond the drift to self-forgetfulness which is natural in a life of toil, it is only here that the possibility of an ethic begins to emerge, centred on a radical discipline of self-overcoming, self-giving, self-sacrifice, the 'care of the soul'. In inter-subjective terms, the results are twofold. 'The earthquake which shook the ground beneath our feet has equally destroyed that which separates, that which renders us strangers to one another.'[14] Yet, at the same time, inasmuch as one ceases to relate to others according to any taken-for-granted norms, the self-motivation of this movement is also more or less bound to seem provocative to those who cling to such norms, evoking resistance and conflict.[15] The ensuing struggle is 'the struggle of awakening'. The ever-present danger, on the other hand, is that that awakening may lapse, through bitter disillusionment, into the sheer destructiveness of nihilism. And herein, therefore, lies the moral purpose of Patočka's meta-history: to trace both the growth of this danger – and the evidence of countervailing potential inherent *within* historical consciousness, as such, to contain and overcome it.

Each of the three movements is an essential constituent of human life, in all its forms; but prior to history the third movement remains relatively unexpressed. It is implicit in the mysterious otherness of the gods and other supernatural powers; it is there in sacred art, dance and song, in so far as these represent an anticipation of revelatory experience, an invocation of the hidden.[16] Yet to the ecstatic consciousness the mystery is merely numinous – that is, not yet *thought*-provoking. One can see the dialectic of the movements dramatically encapsulated in the biblical myth of the fall.[17] For this is also a myth about the origin of history. The paradise in which Adam and Eve first find themselves, ignorant alike of death and shame, is an image of the experience of the first movement, just as the curse with which they are driven out of paradise, made aware of their mortality and condemned to labour for their survival, expresses the experience of the second. But the real focus of attention is on the emergence of the third, in the eating of the apple from the tree of the knowledge of good and evil: a symbolic acknowledgement of the properly historic responsibility we all of us – both individually and collectively – share, as the authors of our own destiny.

Clearly, this notion of historical consciousness involves a good deal more than just a preserving of the memory of the past. For Patočka, the chronicles of the early empires of Egypt, the Middle East or China – since they are a recording of events chiefly for the purpose of codifying and celebrating the status quo – still belong to prehistory.[18] But real history, the experience to which the myth of Genesis only gestures, history in all its fulness, begins pre-eminently among the Greeks. Its birth coincides with the birth of politics, as opposed to the exercise of sacred lordship; and with the birth of philosophy, as opposed to myth. These are in essence, he contends, three aspects of a single existential process. There is in his thought none of Arendt's sense of the inherent tension between politics and philosophy, for what concerns him, rather, is their common historic source.[19]

He finds the classic formulation for this original breakthrough in the fragmentarily preserved thought of Heraclitus. So, Heraclitus defines the basis of his thinking as a reliance on 'that which is common to all' (*tó xunó pantón*):

> Those who speak with sense must rely on what is common to all, as a city must rely on its law, and with much greater reliance: for all the laws of men are nourished by one law, the divine law.[20]

Yet this common element (again he uses the word *xunos*) is also defined by Heraclitus as 'war' (*polemos*) or 'strife' (*eris*):

> One must know that war is common and right is strife and that all things are happening by strife and necessity.[21]

The 'divine law', which nourishes the laws of men, as 'war'; 'right' (or 'justice', *dikē*) as 'strife': what sort of experience is it that underlies such paradoxical formulations? It is, Patočka suggests, precisely the history-making experience of everything being called into question, rendered problematic, as affairs of state are by the public clash of free opinions in a *polis*, and as cultic matters are by being opened up to that free conflict of interpretations which is philosophy:

> *Polemos* is thus at the same time both that which engenders the city, and also the original insight which renders possible philosophy.
>
> *Polemos* is not the devastating passion of a savage invader, but that which creates unity. The unity which it founds runs deeper than any ephemeral sympathy or coalition of interests; adversaries encounter one another in the shake-up of all received wisdom, and thereby create a new mode of human existence – perhaps the only one which, in the storm-tossed condition of the world, offers hope: the unity of the shaken, who are nevertheless fearless in the face of danger.[22]

Heraclitean wisdom, as Patočka understands it, is accordingly a matter of the individual rising up above his or her own particular standpoint *within* the force-field of these conflicts, to contemplate, and to affirm, the process as a whole; thereby helping to create a species of solidarity consciously grounded on the principle of 'unity in discord': a culture of mutual respect between those willing, if need be, to take significant risks, each for their personal vision of the truth, as these visions jostle and collide, both with one another and with the more thoughtless prejudices of the world.[23]

During the course of European history, the possibility of such solidarity has appeared in various shapes, the sequence of which Patočka also seeks to trace. In its heyday, that is, whilst it still offered sufficient scope for the active participation of its citizens, the *polis* itself largely met the need. The decline of the *polis*, on the other hand, gave an added impulse to the development of philosophical schools, as an alternative, more restricted type of free-spirited community. Socrates' informal 'gadfly' style of philosophy was perhaps only possible because he still felt spiritually at home in the *polis*, and therefore had no need for anything else, by way of a social context for his thinking. But the rise of formal school metaphysics, whether in the form represented by Plato and Aristotle or in that represented by Democritus, has essentially to be seen as an attempt to re-found solidarity among the shaken – albeit not yet on the basis of shakenness as such, but only as mediated by a particular interpretation.[24] With the absorption of the Platonic notion of the 'care of the soul' into the world of Christian faith, this metaphysical mode of solidarity goes on to acquire cosmopolitan scope, inasmuch as, with its aspirations to a *sacrum imperium*, mediaeval Christendom at the same time spiritualized the inter-culturally unifying ambitions transmitted to it from its Roman inheritance; so that here there began to emerge an ideal of solidarity, at once both spiritual and political, on the scale of the whole *oikoumené*.[25] Meanwhile, though, Christianity also carries forward the process of historicization, in that the grounding of its faith in a still incomplete salvation history further tends to undermine every kind of apparently natural dispensation in the world as it is.[26] And once this has happened there seems to be no way back. Christianity, with its historicism, actually heightens the threat of nihilism against which it defends its adherents; just as do the various secularizing 'scientific'/humanist ideologies of the nineteenth century which are intended to supplant it (Patočka refers in particular to Comte, Durkheim, Feuerbach, Marx).[27]

In 1914, however, there begins the dark night of the European soul, in which we are still plunged. The last of the *Heretical Essays* is entitled 'The wars of the twentieth century and the twentieth century *as* war'. In Patočka's view, we continue to misunderstand the true meaning of the First World War – because we make the mistake of interpreting it in terms of nineteenth-century ideology. That ideology, however, in all its varieties – nationalistic, Marxist, liberal democratic – belongs to the daylight: to an epoch in which peace was the norm and war the exception. Whereas this is the night. For in the twentieth century, he argues, war has acquired a self-perpetuating, technology-driven dynamism of its own, quite apart from any pursuit of goals to be enjoyed in peace; even to the extent that interludes of peace become little more than the continuation of war by other means. The outbreak of war in 1914 followed from the rise, above all in Germany, of a new sort of state: one in which the technological requirements of modern mass-warfare began to be a primary concern; a whole society increasingly structured according to the logic of its role as a back-up system to the war-machine. This distinctive feature of the twentieth-century state is more or less covered up by the day-dreams of official ideology. But in such a world we need to attend especially to the voices of those who have experienced at first had the ultimate consequences, in the raw reality of life at 'the Front'.

It is not merely that we should hear their cries of pain. Patočka refers for example to two writers, one from either side of the 1914–18 conflict: Pierre Teilhard de Chardin and Ernst Jünger. Both men in fact describe their time in the trenches not only as a nightmare – nightmare though it was – but also as an exhilarating taste of life lived to the full, life at its most vivid and intense, a liberating experience, of positively revelatory significance. Teilhard speaks of it as a 'baptism in reality'. His account anticipates his later Christian/evolutionary mysticism:

It seems to me that the Front might be shown to be not only the line of fire, the corrosive interface between the peoples who are attacking each other, but also in some way 'the front of the wave' carrying the human world towards its future destiny . . . one seems to find oneself at that outer limit, where what has already taken shape edges into what is straining to emerge'[28]

Jünger, by contrast, writes as an admirer of Nietzsche. And Patočka cites his image of the two armies, locked in battle, as the two parts of one and the same force, melting together into a single body:

Into a single body – it is a curious comparison. Only he will understand it who affirms both himself and the enemy, who lives both in the whole and in the parts. Such a one may then picture to himself a God allowing these colourful threads to slip through His fingers – with a smile on His face.[29]

But is this not the Heraclitean wisdom again, a direct encounter with *Polemos* as ultimate reality – reappearing here in the most extreme circumstances imaginable? Is it not an expression of the most dizzying possible shakenness?

The examples of Teilhard and Jünger also represent something else for Patočka, though. For he is equally anxious to affirm a straightforward moral reaction of revulsion at the sheer waste of it all; yet that is not a note which either of these writers strikes at all. On the contrary, Teilhard combines conventional French patriotism with a lofty theodicy, whilst Jünger takes flight from his shaken-ness into its apparent opposite, a visceral nationalism. And both sorts of attitude were of course common enough among the survivors, generally. It is as though the horror, as such, was forgotten. How can this be? Patočka asks:

Why has this great experience, the only one which might be capable of drawing humanity out of the state of war and inaugurating true peace, not in fact had any decisive influence over twentieth-century history, even though people have been exposed to it over two four-year stretches, and even though it has done so much to change their lives? Why has its potential for salvation not been developed? [30]

The problem, he concludes, is that the experience to which Teilhard and Jünger give expression remains a strictly individual one: there may be a certain grim camaraderie in the trenches, but the Heraclitean wisdom is in the first instance very much a movement of inner detachment. In order for genuine solidarity to be established at this level, something more is needed – something more by way of a common framework of ethical ideas untainted by, and set over against, the official ideologies by which the enemy's essential otherness is confirmed. Without such solidarity the movement of revulsion is simply futile. And so what, then, might supply this necessary something more – on which it might be built? Patočka, although he himself was not a member of any church, persists in looking above all to the heritage of Christianity for an answer.[31] In the context of his thinking, the gospel story appears as an imaging of the inevitable struggle attendant on the gradual emergence of the third movement, of devotion to truth, out of the other two, and the prehistoric world which they chiefly constitute; he interprets Christ's fate as a definitive symbol of that readiness for radical self-sacrifice which alone confers authentically historic significance on human life.[32] For him, the Christian dialectic of sin and redemption signifies, in principle, both an extension of what Platonism had previously grasped only as the special vocation of the contemplative philosopher ('Platonism for the masses', in Nietzsche's phrase), but also its dramatic deepening.[33] In practice, though, ahistoric habits die hard. Patočka is preoccupied with the problem of nihilism; but nihilism cannot be overcome by wilfully averting one's attention from that which occasions it, or appears most strongly to justify it. There is no salvation from shakenness-without-solidarity in a solidarity-without-shakenness. On the contrary, the possibility of salvation lies only in a complete dropping of one's defences in this regard. And so, like Rudolf Bultmann, he goes on to call for a 'de-mythologized' Christianity.[34] By this however, he means something much more intimately bound up with the actual specifics of twentieth-century history than Bultmann does: namely, a faith entirely rid of that nostalgic lust for certainty which still continues to lure us away from historical consciousness (in this derogatory sense of the word, back to the world of 'myth'); a faith purged, in other words, of every last relic of the ahistorical sacrality of ecstasy; not least, precisely in order that it may come to terms with, and learn the lessons of, 'the experience of the Front' – now extended by modern technology to whole populations – in all its seismically unsettling absurdity.

The History of 'Nihilism'

In taking up the issue of 'nihilism' Patočka places himself in a tradition of debate, whose most notable protagonists are Nietzsche and Heidegger.

However, it is not only in his (detached) philosophical affirmation of Christianity that he differs from those two predecessors. Underlying this, there is already a still more fundamental difference in the very fact that he identifies the overcoming of nihilism with a solidarity of the shaken.

Thus, each of these thinkers uses the term 'nihilism' to cover a wide diversity of phenomena: in general, whatever hinders people from seizing on the unique, new, liberating opportunities of the present, considered as an era of cultural earthquake. But what Nietzsche is interested in is, of course, not solidarity. It is a Dionysian *amor fati*, or exuberant yea-saying to life, of the shaken; envisaged by him as inevitably solitary individuals. And in Heidegger's case one might say that – by virtue of his 'step back' from 'metaphysics' – it is more a principled theological neutrality of the shaken, than their solidarity. (A shakenness decisively expressed in his insistence on the character of truth as *Ereignis*, 'event of appropriation', rather than 'correctness'; a neutrality coupled with fervent belief in the saving power of the poetic imagination – as mediated through the self-consciously salvational poetry of Hölderlin for example. Neutrality, not agnosticism: beyond dogmatic theism, atheism and agnosticism all alike.)

Patočka is in fact highly critical of Nietzsche, rejecting the Nietzschean 'solution' to the problem of nihilism as 'illusory', more a symptom of the sickness, as he sees it, than a cure.[35] He is, it is true, much closer to Heidegger: as a practitioner of Husserlian phenomenology, he comes from the same immediate intellectual background as Heidegger; he also shares Heidegger's methodological critique of Husserl's Cartesianism.[36] His meditation on the 'natural world' is indeed very much a form of post-metaphysical fundamental ontology in the Heideggerian sense. And yet – the meta-history he constructs on this foundation does seem to derive from a quite sharply contrasting sense of politico-philosophical vocation.

Heidegger traces the use of the word 'nihilism' back to F.H. Jacobi, who employed it in his *Sendschreiben* to Fichte, as a polemical synonym for Idealist philosophy.[37] Later one finds it in Jean Paul, as a designation for the content of Romantic poetry. And in his novel *Fathers and Sons* Turgenev has the character Bazarov describe himself as a 'nihilist': in this case referring to a rather crude cult of science, as opposed to both religion and art. But it is of course Nietzsche who – in his posthumously published notes – decisively stamps its current range of meanings on to the term. In Nietzsche's thinking one can distinguish three different levels of 'nihilism'.[38] In the foreground stands what is always the primary sense of the word, for him: 'nihilism' as 'that which stands at the door . . . uncanniest of all guests'.[39] Here his tone is distinctly apocalyptic. 'What I relate', he declares in his Preface to *The Will to Power*, 'is the history of the next two centuries. I describe what is coming, what can no longer come differently: *the advent of nihilism.*' This is the 'nihilism' that ensues from 'the death of God'; not just what Turgenev's Bazarov stands for, but every sort of debris left behind where the old authority of Christendom has collapsed, and nothing else has yet appeared with the capacity to take its place. Such nihilism may be 'active' or 'passive', 'complete' or incomplete – but is, essentially, post-Christian.

Secondly, however, Nietzsche also uses the term in what is at first sight a quite opposite sense: he speaks of Christianity itself as being 'nihilistic'. He compares it in this respect with Buddhism. Buddhism is, to be sure, in his view a far higher religion, inasmuch as it is relatively free from *ressentiment* morality; but both are 'nihilistic religions'.[40] What emerges here is a fundamental ambiguity in his definition of 'nihilism'. Thus: 'What does nihilism mean?' he asks: '*That the highest values devaluate themselves.* The aim is lacking; "why?" finds no answer'.[41]

The highest values may devaluate themselves in two senses. What were hitherto taken to be the highest values may come to be experienced as self-contradictory: then, the devaluation takes the form of a wholesale collapse of traditional authority – as in the death of God. Or else the genuinely highest values may come to be affirmed only in subordination to the authority of other, in actual fact 'lower', values, as is the case with Christianity, Buddhism, 'nihilistic religion' in general. 'Why?' perhaps does in that case find an answer, of sorts; but only an enfeebling and hence, for him, an inauthentic one; no *real* answer, to prompt dynamically free-spirited action. For Nietzsche the death of the Christian God need not issue in nihilism – but the point is, it does so both when it is incomplete, that is, when those who have lost faith still cling unquestioningly to Christian morality; and when (as in the paradigmatic case of the 'European Buddhist', Schopenhauer) it takes the form of what he would see as a debilitating pessimism.

Then, thirdly, there is *der erste Nihilismus* – primary, or original, nihilism:[42] in the first instance, that collapse of authority within paganism which originally opened the way to the rise of Christianity; the problem to which Christian faith, and Christian morality, seemed to provide a solution. This notion remains quite marginal in *The Will to Power*.[43] But it does serve as a direct link between Nietzsche's analysis of nihilism and his earlier work on the genealogy of morals. If it is legitimate to generalize from that particular historical experience, such nihilism might be defined as the despair of those who find themselves the playthings of inexorable socio-economic forces beyond their control; as, if he is right, Christianity was to begin with a response to the nihilistic despair of those who found themselves the victims of sharpening class conflict in the Roman Empire – restoring meaning, albeit still nihilistic meaning, to lives that had, as a result, come to seem altogether meaningless. (Mark Warren has, I think quite justifiably, criticized Nietzsche for his failure to consider the ways in which similar pressures to those he identifies in his prehistory of Christianity are, in fact, still operative today: in the impersonal proceedings of modern bureaucracy, or the erratic movement of market forces.[44] Thus, was it not very much out of a nihilistic reaction, in this 'original' sense, to 'the experience of the Front' that the nihilism of totalitarian politics initially sprang?) The death of God is also a nihilistic phenomenon when its only result is a lapse back into ultimate despair.

For Heidegger though, by contrast, 'nihilism' becomes simply a general name for the void at the heart of traditional philosophy – as metaphysics, onto-theology, forgetfulness of Being; that is, the distraction deriving from attempts, in reaction to shakenness, to invest the metaphors of some particular religious or anti-religious tradition with unshakeable validity. 'Metaphysics as metaphysics is nihilism proper.'[45] Atheism is nihilistic by virtue of what it has in common with theism. The pure thinking of Being is a thinking which supplants the thinking of God, as Creator and Redeemer, not by doubting God or denying God, but rather by simply bracketing the whole problematic of theism, in a stance of perfect neutrality. On the one hand, negatively, the question of Being is what is left behind by that bracketing. Yet on the other hand it is the resulting enrichment of philosophy which he seeks to highlight by borrowing Nietzsche's term and dubbing the mainstream tradition 'nihilistic': in the place where the thinking of Being should be, the tradition has *nothing*. 'The essence of nihilism', Heidegger declares, 'is the history in which there is nothing to Being itself.'[46] It is that which culminates in the onto-theology of modernity: 'the world-historical movement of the peoples of the earth who have been drawn into the power realm of the modern age'[47] – understood (in effect) as the most shaken of ages, the age of 'the death of God'; a movement, however, stretching way back into antiquity, to the first emergence of onto-theology as a strategy of self-defence, on the part of the shaken, against their shakenness.

Nietzsche concurs with the Heideggerian proposition that all 'metaphysics' is intrinsically nihilistic. But he does not make the converse judgment that all nihilism must appear in the shape of 'metaphysics'.[48] For Nietzsche of course also means something different by 'metaphysics': when he uses the word, it is not, as for Heidegger, a term for just any form of onto-theology, as a defence against shakenness; rather, it signifies the identification of wisdom with a particular *form* of onto-theological defence.

Namely, one that carries with it the promise of a *release from suffering*. As he puts it in the following note on 'the psychology of metaphysics':

> This world is apparent: consequently there is a true world; – this world is conditional: consequently there is an unconditioned world; – this world is full of contradiction: consequently there is a world free of contradiction; – this world is a world of becoming: consequently there is a world of being. . . . It is suffering that inspires these conclusions: fundamentally they are *desires* that such a world should exist; in the same way, to imagine another, more valuable world is an expression of hatred for a world that makes one suffer.[49]

The authentic Dionysian wisdom of which Nietzsche himself is the prophet is fundamentally characterized, on the contrary, by the joyful acceptance of whatever amount of suffering may prove to be the price of a life lived to the full. 'Metaphysics', in Nietzsche's terminology, is thus any type of systematically anti-Dionysian thinking: explaining the origins of suffering in terms of error or guilt, so as to prescribe a corresponding remedy, in radical inner detachment from the un-'true' world; thereby slackening life's intensity. It is the attempt to market a morality by promising release, through a transformed perception of reality. Such thinking is therefore a phenomenon of 'decadence'. 'The philosophers', he remarks – meaning the metaphysicians – are 'always decadents, always in the service of the nihilistic religions'.[50] Nevertheless, in Nietzsche's view the abandonment of the consolations of 'metaphysical' philosophy is still only a first step. A Sceptic like 'the nihilist Pyrrho', or Hume, for instance, may not yet be a fully Dionysian spirit. Their Scepticism may be more an expression of weary disillusionment than real *amor fati*, and in the end everything short of that latter ideal remains 'nihilistic'; only, in differing degrees of 'pessimistic' self-awareness.[51] The move beyond 'metaphysics' simply serves to clarify the issue – by leaving us with a final choice between, on the one hand, the Sceptics' *open* nihilism and, on the other, Nietzschean transcendence.

Yet in Heideggerian terms Nietzsche himself remains a 'metaphysician', and hence also a 'nihilist' – because he is not only a methodological, but also (it seems) an ontological atheist. Or perhaps better: for the negative reason that he fails to make the strict Heideggerian distinction between these two possibilities. 'This world', he says of the world his thinking uncovers, 'is will to power – and nothing besides!'[52] That 'nothing besides' immediately excludes any serious notion of God, in such a way as to render his philosophy, for Heidegger, 'a metaphysics of will to power'; or 'a metaphysics of values' – with 'values' ('devaluation of values', 'revaluation of values') being interpreted as expressions, or strategies, of will to power.[53]

There are obvious echoes here of Schopenhauer's doctrine of 'the world as will and idea', even though it is true that by the time Nietzsche came to write this note (1885) he had left Schopenhauer a long way behind. For Schopenhauer, too, is arguing that 'will' is the ultimate reality – as opposed to God. Thus, let us briefly rehearse Schopenhauer's argument. He begins from Kant: the fact that there is apparently providential order in the universe – the appearance of the world as 'idea' – is no evidence that there exists a divine Creator; the order is merely imposed on reality by the rationalizing operations of the human mind; it is not the ultimate reality, but only a secondary reality – decisively shaped, Schopenhauer adds, by the require-ments of the human will to survive. But he also goes beyond Kant. Unlike Kant he argues that we nevertheless do have direct access to ultimate reality (*das Ding an sich*): we may detect it *in ourselves*, precisely in the movement of pure 'will', prior to all rationalization; that is, in the inchoate stirrings of 'blind' impulse. And, in so far as we cannot escape picturing the inner dynamism of the world in anthropomorphic terms, only that experience therefore provides an adequate analogy: despite all wish-fulfilling appearan-ces, in its original and deepest reality this world is just a complex interplay of such blind impulses – and nothing besides. Schopenhauer, however, is of course very much a 'metaphysician', not only in Heidegger's sense but also in Nietzsche's. To perceive the underlying reality of the world as 'will' is, in his view, also necessarily to recognize its ultimate futility, in general; and hence the ultimate futility of one's *own* 'willing', in particular. For if there is no external sanction for one's willing, in the form of a divine Will – then what, in the end, is the good of it all? It leads to at least as much frustration and suffering as satisfaction; and it leads to conflict. But morality consists in the defusing of conflict. And hence it is best that we should focus on the suffering rather than on the satisfactions, and seek release in, so to speak, willing not to will. So he turns to the wisdom of the East, finding confirma-tion for his standpoint in the spirituality of the *Upanishads*, and in the Buddhist notion of *nirvana*; in so far as these (very different) systems coincide in similarly identifying wisdom with the most radical detachment. This is paradoxically a notion of wisdom towards which Heidegger also moves, in his later thought, with his discussion of *Gelassenheit*. Heidegger too – to begin with, in direct reaction against Nietzsche – becomes the advocate of a 'thinking without willing', here; albeit one entirely purged of meta-physics.[54] (He is very scathing about what he considers the 'superficiality' of

Schopenhauer's thought.) For Nietzsche, however, 'willing liberates, for willing is creating'.[55] And whilst at one level he agrees with Epictetus that true wisdom means always willing what *is* – that is, whatever is unavoidably given – he also, of course, positively celebrates conflict.

The metaphysical impulse in Schopenhauer's thought has, Nietzsche moreover insists, completely falsified his whole concept of 'the will'. It leads to a two-fold error:

(a) As a metaphysician, Schopenhauer presents his theory of the will as an explanatory theory: in the sense of bringing peace and tranquillity to the enquiring intellect which grasps it. Yet, in so doing, all he has really done is 'enthrone a primitive mythology'.[56] His doctrine has no more explanatory cogency than the rival theory that all reality derives from the Will of God: both arguments trade on the same illusion, that in introducing the abstract concepts of 'will' and 'causality' one has made a genuinely substantive clarificatory move – as if we *already knew* what 'will' was. Whereas the truth is that 'it is only a word'.[57] 'The will . . . does not explain anything';[58] indeed, considered as a potentially explanatory concept, there is no such thing. It does not exist – just as 'the ego', 'the soul' or 'the subject', likewise, does not exist, as a *given* entity.[59] The only sense in which it does exist is as the substance of a never humanly resolvable *problem*: the problem of what an authentic *amor fati* would entail. So that when Nietzsche himself writes, 'this world is will to power – and nothing besides', what he means is just that this is the absolutely primary problem with which the highest wisdom, that of Zarathustra, will always be turbulently pre-occupied.[60]

(b) In taking the word 'will', for his particular purposes, as a general designation for any sort of pre-rational impulse – 'craving, instinct, desire' – Schopenhauer is, in effect, entirely reversing its traditional meaning; given that, traditionally, it has always meant not so much desire itself, as that which overcomes desire.[61] In this way, though, he is not merely failing to enter into the Nietzschean problematic (the harnessing of desire in *amor fati*); he is positively closing off any entrance into it. Hence, the Schopenhauerian definition is itself, for Nietzsche, 'a great symptom of the *exhaustion* or the *weakness* of the will'.[62]

In this way Schopenhauer's thought becomes the purest expression of metaphysical decadence: an absolutely last-ditch, despairing defence against shakenness.

And yet, even so, Nietzsche still remains very much an admirer of Schopenhauer's particular form of 'unconditional and honest atheism':[63] he admires it, as an atheism which is couched in such a way as also decisively to preclude the sort of humanist substitute-faith advocated by someone like Feuerbach, for instance. He seeks to radicalize Schopenhauer's atheism; and thereby, as Heidegger sees it, comes to represent the final dead-end to the Western metaphysical tradition. So Heidegger portrays Nietzsche as the thinker who 'completes' the turn to 'a metaphysics of subjectivity' inaugurated by Descartes. (Behind the anthropomorphism of both the Schopenhauerian and the Nietzschean description of the world as a force-field of conflicting 'wills' – both animate and inanimate – there lurks in particular the prior anthropomorphism of Leibniz's 'monadology'.[64] Schopenhauer's notion of 'will' is what the 'monad' becomes with Providence removed; Nietzsche's notion of 'will to power' is the same, converted into a problem.) Nietzsche may – by virtue of his overcoming of what he himself calls 'metaphysics' – invert the classical tradition deriving from Plato; yet he still continues to be trapped within its onto-theological frame of reference. The only way out, Heidegger urges, is by way of a philosophical thinking which is neither theist nor atheist – nor yet, as he puts it in his *Letter on Humanism*, 'indifferent' to 'the holy'; but which, on the contrary, seeks to apprehend 'the holy' at a deeper, more 'primordial', level than any onto-theology, in itself, ever can.[65] (Or, as I would put it: not so much theologically as 'hierologically'.)

'Nur noch ein Gott . . .'

In fact, it seems to me that a thinking orientated towards the cultivation – as the true transcendence of nihilism – of a 'solidarity of the shaken' would need to incorporate elements from the thinking of both Heidegger and Nietzsche; whilst at the same time, equally, in other ways moving beyond both.

With regard to Heidegger the point is quite straightforward. For not only is his (de-theologized and de-'subjectivized' Kierkegaardian) notion of *'Angst'* in *Being and Time* very closely akin to Patočka's 'shakenness', but also, since solidarity of the shaken is solidarity simply *on the basis of* shakenness – a phenomenon completely independent of any metaphysical commitment in Heidegger's sense – it is, in pure terms, something which just cannot be conceived, let alone have its implications properly thought through, other than by means of a prior Heideggerian methodological bracketing of the onto-theological. Which (despite his religious sympathies) is indeed very much Patočka's own practice.

And yet onto-theological neutrality is certainly not, by itself alone, any guarantee of shakenness. For after all: consider the Nazis. Their entire ideology expressed the most intense, ecstatic repudiation of shakenness. But, whilst the Nazi 'German Christians' pulled in one direction and the neo-pagans pulled in another, the movement as a whole did actually manage to remain (if only for reasons of tactical shrewdness) just about as onto-theologically neutral as, in the circumstances, it well could.[66] And no doubt this was at least something of a contributory factor – along with his general weakness for *völkisch* rhetoric, and his chimaerical dream of a leading cultural role for his philosophy, as part of the new order – in rendering possible Heidegger's own infamous flirtation with the Party, during the period of revolutionary euphoria just after its initial rise to power.[67]

Clearly, there must be other no less fundamental criteria, as well, which would exclude such an error, right from the outset. But then – how is one to think through those other criteria? How, in other words, is one to think through the critique of propaganda, as such? Is it sufficient that this should be done solely at the level of a 'pure' post-metaphysical philosophy? How can it be? Given that no form of commitment to religious, or anti-religious, tradition is *a priori* excluded here, the issue surely needs to be pursued at both levels: that is, both in pure post-metaphysical terms – and, so far as possible, in the varying terms of each of the traditions themselves. It is a question of, in addition, drawing out whatever capacity the traditions may already have, within themselves, to point *beyond* the particular loyalties they most immediately enshrine, towards solidarity-in-shakenness.

In the interview published in *Der Spiegel*, just after his death in 1976, Heidegger flamboyantly declares that so far as he can see, in humanity's present predicament, 'only a God can save us'.[68] Elsewhere, he speaks of his attack on the God of metaphysics as opening up a path back to what, by contrast, he terms the truly 'divine God'; or the 'last God'.[69] This would be the saviour: the God of pre-metaphysical folk-religiousness at its best, newly rediscovered by a post-metaphysical *poetic* spirituality: a whole new discipline of the religious imagination, purged of any preoccupation with the maintenance of a narrow orthodoxy, and therefore no longer provoking old-fashioned protest-atheism; although also, to be sure, including within its range a good deal more devotional/meditative solemnity than Nietzsche would ever have allowed.

But the problem is that, in stripping away every possibility of ideological distortion in this way, by the same token he also seems to strip away any real capacity for prophetic critique – and, hence, any actual possibility of political effectiveness in modern conditions. There is indeed no longer anything Hebraic about Heidegger's God at all.[70] Instead, he follows Hölderlin: in effect, worshipping a God of world-historical nostalgia, with a bitter-sweet yearning for the beautiful lost world of ancient Greece. Such a God may perhaps inspire a certain quixotic hope – for some restitution, in another form, of what was lost. But not *faith*. For faith, which alone renders possible prophetic critique in the strict sense, requires a living community of adherents to be real. And whereas some sort of faith might after all be supposed to 'save' us, 'salvation' by nostalgia alone – no matter how apocalyptic its context – does seem a rather curious proposition. Surely, something more than that is needed. That is: some altogether bolder process of shuttling back and forth between the pure 'thinking of Being' and whatever is not merely metaphysical in the popular culture associated with actually existing 'Platonism for the masses'; a thinking which *alternates* between the Heideggerian 'step back' and active engagement in onto-theologically framed debate – for critical purposes.[71]

Any such move, however – beyond the standpoint of Heidegger – takes us straight back to Nietzsche again. Not, certainly, to Nietzsche's dogmatic rejection of religious seriousness, as such; but, rather, to his particular critique of 'metaphysics', understood as a flight from suffering. For the reality by which we are 'shaken' is the painfulness of history: the historic collapse of false hopes on which a certain moral culture – whose attractiveness is still felt – had been founded. And such a flight from suffering will always also imply a flight from history – whether it takes the form of a principled *detachment* from worldly hopes, in pursuit of contemplative serenity, or of some dogmatic faith, offering a historical heavenly *consolation*. If there is any truth at all in Nietzsche's (or Hegel's) report of 'the death of God', then the deceased is presumably just the God who helps to shield us from the pain of history. In a culture saturated with historical consciousness, no theology can any longer enjoy full intellectual respectability unless fully exposed to that pain. Three old illusions are hereby ruled out: first, the old God of consolatory myth; secondly, the old God deriving from Plato and Aristotle, elevated above suffering – Himself the model for the contemplative sage, ultimately untouched by things temporal; and, thirdly, the old only-partly-historical God, whose field of action is, in effect, a special, segregated zone of 'salvation history', rather than history as a whole. Hence, the only type of God who might after all have survived the cataclysm would be the God of *a quite radically non-consolatory, this-worldly, world-historical theology*. Such a God, who no longer secures us against shakenness, requires from us only a disciplined, critical openness to the distinctiveness of the historical moment – as a moment of potential revelation, or *kairos*. The true recognition of which, on the other hand, effectively depends – for encouragement's sake – upon a proper solidarity of the shaken.

4 *The Virtues of Discernment*

Solidarity of the shaken, then, is solidarity in maximum exposure to the negativity inherent in any heightening of historical consciousness. However, such exposure is not just what comes to be given in the general atmosphere of a culture. It also implies an answering movement of the will on the part of individuals, not to take flight from the negativity that presents itself. In short, a certain set of virtues is required. Since these are the sorts of virtue which are primarily defined by their contribution to a proper understanding of the signs of the times, let us call them 'the virtues of discernment'. The question I therefore turn to now is: what exactly counts as belonging in this category?

The chief positive obstacle in the way of people's exposure to actual historical reality in the contemporary world is, surely, the all-pervasive influence of propaganda – as a systematically organized interpreting-away of that reality; both reflecting and reinforcing the average thoughtlessness of its target audience. And to this extent one might perhaps also pose the question in terms of an analysis of, so to speak, the ideal psychology of the anti-propagandee. But propaganda appeals to its audience above all by its proffering of some congenially simplified version of reality for mass-consumption. Hence, another possible definition of the virtues of discernment might be: those qualities of character which – over against this – most radically help to open one up to the intrinsic *difficulty* of difficult reality, in general; that is, to aspects of experience from which, on the contrary, the natural propagandee mentality is bound to recoil.

The analysis of such virtue is, surely, *the* basic pre-theological underpinning for any authentically critical civil theology. It is civil theology's – properly quite direct and explicit – groundedness in this prior intellectual discipline which, at the deepest level, secures its methodological independence from confessional theology. In civil-theological terms, the discernment in question becomes a, so to speak, 'civil' discernment of revelation; that is, discernment in identifying the proper content of civil religious narrative. 'Revelation' is what such virtue draws to our attention, or rather compels us to consider, in our capacity as citizens. Unlike confessional theology, with its founding revelation preserved in given texts, civil theology always has to identify its revelation afresh, in this way.

What emerges here, therefore, is a form of what Heidegger calls (and, yes, let us at least provisionally accept the designation) 'the thinking of Being'. The thinking of Being, beyond confessional metaphysics, precisely as difficult reality; a science of the difficulty of difficult reality, at that ultimate level of generality.[1] As such, of course, it is an enquiry into the moral foundations not only of civil theology, but of civil practice in all its modes. With specific reference to theology, however (i.e.'hierologically') this argument sets off from the point where Heidegger coincides with Wittgenstein: it has to highlight the underlying medium-nature of religious discourse, on which all the messages of faith depend; i.e. the nature of sacred belief-systems – not so much as conflicting (pseudo-) scientific hypotheses, but rather as rules of grammar. No doubt, some religious languages are better equipped than others to express certain features of reality. But the rigidification of grammatical rules into the form of hypotheses, which are supposedly 'true' *in themselves*, merely reflects the power-play, down the centuries, of the religious thought-police – with their sundry ideologies of salvation-by-membership. This countervailing pre-theology, or pre-confessional-religious-philosophy, can obviously never replace theology or confessional religious philosophy: there is indeed no aspiration here to a religious Esperanto. But it is simply a question of getting beyond the formal identity of any one particular body of religious narrative and imagery, in its usage by the various members of a community, to focus instead on its always infinite potential polyvalence, as different people may seek to express quite different things by it: an analytical procedure which must indeed also tend decisively to relativize the formal differences between different belief-systems. Or, equally, between belief and unbelief.

Again, in a sense this was just what Kierkegaard meant by the proposition that, in spiritual matters, 'truth is subjectivity'; not just correctness, not just a property of certain statements; but a quality of character.[2] Or it seems to be what Bonhoeffer meant by his critique of religion-as-metaphysics. Except that, of course, in both these cases the insight is then straight away overlaid with a paradoxical strategy of Christian apologetics: the presentation of Christianity as, in principle, that faith which has the greatest power to dramatize this distinction. But let us separate out these two levels of argument. Another, more concrete formulation of the same principle would be that 'truth is the practice of the virtues of discernment'. Let us therefore try to give a systematic account of those virtues, so far as we can, in strictly *pre-*apologetic terms.

We have to describe the ideal psychology of the anti-propagandee – and the issue comes to light most dramatically in circumstances where propaganda is at its most concerted and concentrated, as it is above all under totalitarian regimes. Drawing on the thought of Arendt and Weil, in chapter 1 I considered three, rather awkwardly inter-related, basic types of cultural bulwark against totalitarianism. One was the creation, and continual recreation, of spaces for isonomy; another was the preservation of traditions of *auctoritas*; another, the cultivation of an 'anti-political' ethos of moral absolutism. And in what follows I want to try and trace a correspondingly triangular pattern, to some extent going back over ground already covered, but in another way. Thus there are, it seems to me, three cardinal virtues of discernment, each of which – inasmuch as they constitute the typical modes of inter-subjectivity underlying these cultural formations – refers to a different level of one's relationship to the Other:

1 The first is the virtue of *free-spiritedness*. This takes shape in relation to the Other as 'one of us'; ideally, one's equal as a citizen. It is an opening to those aspects of reality rendered difficult to recognize by their being overlooked by – or, worse, due to their incompatibility with – some prevailing orthodoxy.

2 The second is the virtue of a (critical) *flair for tradition*. It relates to the Other as a participant in, and representative of, experiences often quite remote from one's own; thereby, to the degree that one engages in truly insightful inward struggle with the relationship, giving one imaginative access to perspectives on reality which significantly undermine what would otherwise be one's natural assumptions.

3 The third is the virtue of *generosity*. It is the recognition of the Other as one's 'neighbour', in the sense suggested by the parable of the Good Samaritan: the Other who lies bleeding in the ditch. For – given the unwelcome demands which the suffering of one's neighbour generally implies – this too is a form of difficult reality, from which one is always tempted to turn away.

That each of these is, indeed, a virtue will scarcely be disputed. The art, however, lies simply in finding the very boldest way possible of pressing their claims. It requires a certain disciplined extravagance of thought, to celebrate them just as they would appear in their ideal fulfilment. For what, after all, should moderate any of these virtues – except one another? And the essential point, therefore, of the following (perhaps inevitably somewhat fragmentary) analysis is just to open up the general issue of their interaction.

Free-spiritedness (Heidegger, Hegel, Nietzsche)

This is the virtue to which Heidegger, in *Being and Time*, gives the name *Entschlossenheit*: 'resoluteness' or 'resolve'; his discussion of which constitutes the real moral heart of that book.[3] In his characteristic, painstakingly idiosyncratic manner, he defines *Entschlossenheit* as: 'a way of reticently projecting oneself upon one's ownmost Being-guilty, and exacting anxiety of oneself'.[4]

True, some elements of this definition – the references to 'anxiety' (*Angst*) and 'guilt' – apply not only to free-spiritedness, but to discernment in general. 'Anxiety' is a term for shakenness, as such, at the level of a pre-reflective state of mind. Following Kierkegaard, Heidegger opposes it to fear: fear is a response to some particular danger, but anxiety, in the specific sense he intends, is a response to – nothing, in particular. The threat comes from nowhere in particular, one cannot put one's finger on it. For 'that in the face of which' – and about which – 'one has anxiety is Being-in-the-world as such'.[5] It is the general sense of being displaced, no longer at home in the world, 'uncanny' (*unheimlich*); where 'everyday familiarity collapses'.[6] To 'exact anxiety of oneself' means just the same, in other words, as to stay with one's shakenness.

And that Heidegger then directly associates anxiety with the phenomenon of a 'primordial' guilt is, of course, another echo of Kierkegaard; whose study of *The Concept of Anxiety* is actually subtitled *A Simple Psychologically Orienting Deliberation on the Dogmatic Issue of Hereditary Sin*.[7] What Kierkegaard is aiming to analyse here are the elementary psychological preconditions for an intensified 'subjectivity'. A primordial sense of guilt (or, mythically expressed, of original sin) is the closest related mode of reflective self-understanding to pre-reflective anxiety. As Heidegger himself puts it, this is guilt not at the 'ontic' level, but at the 'ontological': it has to do, not with actual deeds, but with a condition of being, prior to all deeds. *Entschlossenheit*, according to its definition, entails a 'projecting of oneself upon one's

Being-guilty': 'self-projection' (or 'self-sketching') means self-understanding in the sense of a pondering of the various possibilities inherent in one's being; and what he has in mind by 'guilt', at this level, is just the inevitable limitation of those possibilities. Thus, one's primordial guilt lies immediately in one's finitude or, to be more exact, one's 'thrownness' into a particular situation. He reinterprets the negativity of guilt as the experience of 'notness' (*Nichtigkeit*), as one yearns to follow paths that circumstances decree one cannot, or may not take (the repeated 'no' of reality, so to speak).[8] It is not a matter of any actual failure, with regard to some particular, given moral code. But, on the contrary, he wants to speak of a positive '*summons* to Being-guilty' – in the sense of a summons to responsibility, as an owning of one's limitations. (His formula for responsibility, as a mode of Being, is 'Being-a-basis for' – and hence, bizarrely, 'Being-a-basis for a notness'.) Primordial 'guilt' thus becomes the original, pre-moral opening-up of the possibility of authentic (realistic) morality, in any form; as the summons takes the form of an anxious, unsettled '*wanting* to have a conscience'.

So far – to the extent, that is, that *Entschlossenheit* is simply Heidegger's designation for a heightened responsiveness to this universal summons – the argument might, in other words, be said to be a quite basic elaboration of the difference between true moral discernment, in the most general terms, and ordinary, everyday moral myopia. There are, though, two further elements in the definition he gives which also need to be expounded: the adverb, 'reticently', and the adjective, 'own*most* '.

Much of the fascination of Heidegger derives from the conflict, running right through his career in various configurations, between two opposing impulses: on the one hand the *völkisch* Heidegger, the Heidegger who could become a 'resolute' Nazi – and on the other hand, I would argue, precisely the 'reticent' Heidegger, whose radically contemplative thinking may be vulnerable to the general Arendtian critique of philosophy but nevertheless remains the most rigorous post-metaphysical exploration of 'the life of the mind'. So, his argument here might be reconstructed as follows. Primordial guilt implies a corresponding *telos*. To become aware of it is to surrender oneself to an intensified sense of responsibility – for the whole of one's life. It therefore means reviewing one's life from that unique perspective which renders it apparent in its wholeness, namely, in an anticipatory manner, from the perspective of one's death. Death, for Heidegger, is the ultimate difficult reality: Being as time – as the prospect of death. The difficulty lies in a 'Being towards death', as that which jolts one into anxiety; death, as a moment of judgment evoking primordial responsibility. And that such responsibility then immediately becomes 'guilt' is due, essentially, to one's natural repugnance against the reality of death, so encountered. But this is also where *Entschlossenheit* becomes manifest as free-spiritedness. For the one to whom death is a difficult reality is in Heideggerian terminology just that – 'the "one" ': *das Man*. That is, the individual whose life remains unowned, content with the average everyday conformity of doing what 'one' generally does do. (Macquarrie and Robinson's translation of *das Man* as 'the they' seems to me to have faint undertones of paranoia which are not present in the German.) The 'reticence' of authentic *Entschlossenheit* is a reticence in relation to everyday *Gerede*, the 'idle talk' – or more accurately, the 'functional/entertaining talk'[9] – of 'the "one" '; which expresses curiosity about the world, a restless quest for mere novelty and distraction, rather than that authentic 'wonder' (*thaumazein*) which Socrates declared to be the beginning of true philosophy; but equally, also, a quite complacent resting in the suggestive ambiguities of only half-thought-through formulations. The natural habitat in short for any kind of propaganda-ideology – including, not least, the *völkisch*.

The cultivated *Un-entschlossenheit* of 'the "one" ' may well seem highly 'resolute', in the ordinary sense of the word. It has, after all, done away with the inhibitions of anxiety, leaving the way clear for all manner of unquestioned dogma or anti-dogma; the complete codification of conscience in terms of given roles; even the most exhilarating heroic decisiveness. And yet it would all be bravado. Death – as the deadline for this or that particular personal project – is perhaps worried about; but is not allowed to obtrude in any more radical manner, as a prospect calling into question the whole project of one's life. If authentic *Entschlossenheit* is a '*freedom* towards death'[10] this is therefore in the sense of a freedom *from* 'the "one" ': it is the appropriation of one's 'ownmost Being-guilty', by way of a 'Being towards death' in which the reality of one's own death is appropriated as one's 'ownmost possibility'; an appropriation whereby one is 'wrenched away from the "one" '.[11] Such liberation has, of course, nothing to do with how death is metaphysically interpreted: whether as the gateway to extinction, to rebirth, or to eternal life. But it comes as a response to what death is in itself. When 'the "one" ', thinks forwards to death it is always with reference to the relationship between the self dying and the bystanders, or the bereaved ('one' imagines 'oneself', perhaps, as a spectator at 'one's' own funeral). To a properly 'anticipatory' *Entschlossenheit*, by contrast, death appears as a strictly *non-relational* prospect.[12] No matter how many people may be around, one always dies alone. No matter how one dies, death is not to be 'outstripped' as that which sets the final seal on one's otherness from others; that individual distinctiveness, or ownmost vocation, which 'the "one" ' declines to own.

For 'the "one" ', death remains an unsavoury fact of life, a fact like other facts about the world. The full otherness of this certainty from all other certainties, for one's self, is not taken to heart. Nor is the unpredictability of its timing – as a proper source of thought-provoking anxiety, rather than merely calculative fear.

In Heidegger's later writings, these themes of *Being and Time* melt directly into his analysis of pure 'thinking', referred to above.[13] *Unentschlossenheit* – as the absence of 'thinking' in this sense – is surely nothing other than that 'banality', the dreadful potential destructiveness of which Hannah Arendt found so dramatically revealed in the case of Adolf Eichmann. And yes, no doubt a liberating solidarity of the shaken must also be a solidarity well grounded in 'anticipatory *Entschlossenheit*'.

Yet Heidegger's thinking remains clouded by the *völkisch* impulse of his other self. Already evident in the proto-propagandistic discussion of corporate 'destiny' and 'the hero' in *Being and Time*, in his later work this has, for instance, the effect of deflecting his critique away from the culture of propaganda, as such, and on to the much vaguer, Rohrschach-blob target of modern 'technology' instead; the uprooting evil of which so easily, also, becomes a propaganda-theme itself.[14] In general, in order to hold his two selves together he resorts to a brilliantly inventive strategy of blurring abstraction.

For a more concrete – politically sharper – discussion of the ways in which specific patterns of cultural conditioning may actually help either to encourage or to discourage the authentic practice of *Entschlossenheit*, we therefore need to turn back to other thinkers. To Hegel for example, And, again, to Nietzsche. In this respect, it becomes a question of seeking to penetrate through the, in Heideggerian terms, 'metaphysical' overlay of their doctrines, to what lies beneath.

We have already briefly considered Hegel's formulation for this virtue, in *The Phenomenology of Spirit*: the overcoming of 'unhappy consciousness'. 'Unhappy consciousness' is, essentially, a name for the basic spiritual structure of any banality-promoting ideology. And (as I have remarked) the issue of its overcoming is at least arguably the central theme of the Hegelian philosophy of history. So in the Introduction to his *Lectures on the Philosophy of History* Hegel defines his theme as 'the progress of the consciousness of freedom';[15] but this 'consciousness of freedom' is surely identical to that 'freedom of self-consciousness' which in the more abstract – but also more precise – argument of the *Phenomenology* appears, above all, as the transcendence of unhappy consciousness.

Of course, it is true that the resulting meta-history also becomes just the sort of thing that Heidegger, for his part, wants to leave behind: namely, the life story of a single 'metaphysical' subject, *Geist*. But let us distinguish sharply between that metaphysical stratum of Hegel's argument, and its underlying *pre*-metaphysical rationale (a distinction I failed to make in my previous book, on *Hegel's Political Theology*). Hegel's meta-history aims to be a systematic account of the historical preconditions for the possibility of his own basic insight into the nature, and practical implications, of 'freedom of self-consciousness'. These preconditions include, crucially, the civil religious experience of classical antiquity – remembered as a form of public spirituality extraordinarily free, in its naive and relatively un-self-conscious way, from the servitude of unhappy consciousness. And then, opening up the way to a more self-conscious recapture of that freedom, they also include the double inheritance of biblical faith and idealist philosophy: the one for its latent capacity to express the requirements of freedom, directly, in popular religious form; the other, in order to unscramble that potential truth-content of faith from the multitude of ambiguities inevitably inherent in its form. He further sees his own philosophy as intrinsically Protestant and post-Enlightenment: dependent both upon the space the Reformation clears for the radical reassessment of the proper relationship of church to state, and upon the whole new problematicization of political and intellectual freedom in eighteenth-century thought, culminating in the terrible extremity of the French Revolution. For only in such a context could the new intellectual sophistication progressively brought about by the philosophical culture of Christendom finally be deployed, as he deploys it, in the deliberate attempt to recapture something so remote, so alien from everything customary and familiar, as in the modern world the old free-spiritedness of the *polis* had unfortunately become. So the argument, at one level, runs. But, whilst a certain tradition of metaphysics is hereby affirmed, it is affirmed at this level only as background – part of this particular philosopher's essential education. (And in that sense Heidegger himself also affirms metaphysics.) The foreground of the Hegelian system only becomes metaphysical where he moves on from that empirical anaysis of the preconditions for his *own* insight into the truth of freedom, to the assertion that, *equally for anyone else*, such insight depends upon their entering into the selfsame onto-theological tradition.

The difference is encapsulated in the contrast between the following two propositions. On the one hand, Hegel is arguing for the still only hypothetically metaphysical proposition that, if the truth of freedom is to be uncovered within Christian culture, this must above all be by way of his particular rethinking of the significance of the Incarnation: as a direct symbolic refutation of unhappy consciousness.[16] Here, the pre-metaphysical stratum of his thought still shows through. But, on the other hand, he then adds the further proposition that the Incarnation, reinterpreted his way, is the *definitive* symbolic refutation of unhappy consciousness – in the sense that, outside of the Christian (and more especially, the Protestant Christian) tradition, no full experience of liberation is ultimately possible. And hence, for instance, the triumphalist construction of his *Lectures on the Philosophy of Religion*: in which Christianity is systematically presented as 'the consummate religion', towards which all others more or less inadequately point. (An argument obviously marred by the inevitable sketchiness, in that period, of his actual knowledge of other faiths, and his dependence on Christian missionary sources for most of his information about them.) One needs, in short, to discriminate very clearly between Hegel the civil theologian and Hegel the Christian apologist.

In the *Phenomenology* he sets his own interpretation of 'freedom of self-consciousness' over against two other basic modes of interpretation: 'Stoicism' and 'Scepticism'. Viewed in the context not just of that particular passage, but of the Hegelian 'system' as a whole, both of these may be said to fall short in their failure to provide an adequate basis for effective socio-political critique. These are universal phenomena of civilized life, as universal (even if never as common) as the unhappy consciousness to which they are opposed. The names Hegel gives them play the same role as the allusions to Christianity with which he studs his account of unhappy consciousness: thus, the actual philosophical schools of the Stoics and the Sceptics, as these existed in the classical world, are merely particular, exemplary crystallizations of the far more general types of mentality intended here. (Or, as he himself puts it, they are the movements in which those mentalities were first converted into 'universal forms of the *World*-Spirit',[17] and so rendered accessible to a philosophy of world history, as distinct from a phenomenology of Spirit, as such.) This is made clear by the setting of the discussion, in the overall argument of the book. For it is situated, immediately, at that critical turning point where the un-self-conscious pre-formation of the self, through the experience of coming up against one's limits in struggle and toil, first gives way to self-consciousness. In other words, to a conscious sense of the problematicalness of the question, 'Who am I?' – a conscious awareness of one's self as self-shaping. In Hegelian terminology, this is the point where 'conceptual' thinking (*Begriff*) first emerges, as distinct from 'representational' or 'picture'-thinking (*Vorstellung*). It is where the very process of such thinking itself comes to be experienced as the essence of freedom.[18] And 'Stoicism', in this context, refers to any form of wisdom which seeks, purely and simply, to stay with that experience, and to accentuate it.

In fact, were Hegel writing the *Phenomenology* today, it seems to me that he might well refer in this connection not so much to 'Stoicism', but rather, precisely, to Heidegger! (Just as he might also have illustrated 'Scepticism' with Derrida, say, and 'deconstruction'.) Of course, Heidegger is anything but a Stoic: classical Stoicism was metaphysical in every fibre. But, had Hegel read *Being and Time*, his basic complaint would, nevertheless, surely have been the same as his basic complaint about 'Stoicism', at this level. The 'Stoic' notion of freedom, as he analyses it, is essentially a formal one, lacking substantive socio-political 'content': such thinking, he remarks, 'has no content *in its own self* but one that is *given* to it'.[19] It is socio-politically a chameleon-thinking; a state of inward thoughtfulness, equally available 'whether [one is] on the throne or in chains'.[20]

> Stoicism, therefore, was perplexed when it was asked for what was called a 'criterion of truth as such', i.e. strictly speaking, for a *content* of thought itself. To the question, *What* is good and true, it again gave for answer the *contentless* thought: The True and the Good shall consist in reasonableness.[21]

One has only to substitute *Entschlossenheit* here for 'reasonableness'. The 'content'-lessness of this sort of thinking means that it is quite incapable of furnishing any adequate framework for a civil theology of freedom.

'Stoicism' simply does not yet raise the question of what a proper civil religious embodiment of freedom might look like, in any particular cultural environment. Whilst 'Scepticism', being sharper, only makes things worse. For 'Scepticism' goes beyond 'Stoicism' in that it is no longer a chameleon-wisdom, adapting itself to whatever 'content' it is given; but, instead, indiscriminately sweeps all given 'content' aside. It is thought which, revelling in its power to call everything in question, jealously guards its self-possession, in a persistent negativity towards 'desire and work':[22] refusing to submit to any object of desire, or work-project, that would require a restrictive intellectual discipline. It treats everything the same:

> What vanishes is the determinate element, or the moment of difference, which, whatever its mode of being and whatever its source, sets itself up as something fixed and immutable. It contains no permanent element, and must vanish before thought, because the 'different' is just this, not

to be in possession of itself, but to have its essential being only in an other.[23]

That is to say, for 'Scepticism', not only is common sense despised, but also nothing is sacred. Whereas the true at-one-ment of the Absolute, with its recognition of the sacredness of self-conscious freedom itself, relativizes the subordination of spontaneous thought to its 'other' in this sense, 'Scepticism' by contrast crudely abolishes that subordination altogether. And so it leaves no fixed reference points at all for consistency – and ends up 'like the squabbling of self-willed children, one of whom says *A* if the other says *B*, and in turn says *B* if the other says *A*, and who by contradicting *themselves* buy for themselves the pleasure of continuously contradicting *one another*'.[24]

Of course, both 'Stoicism' and 'Scepticism' are also un-Christian. But that is another issue. Hegel, as an inhabitant still of Christendom, is interested only in a specifically Christian civil theology: what he calls *Geist* emerges in the end as the God of a civil-religiously transfigured Lutheranism; and his philosophy of history serves as the systematic excavation of a tradition for that. In a religiously pluralist world, however, the same basic civil theological argument might certainly be presented in a much less narrowly confessional way. And this would require a metaphysical procedure far more transparent to what lies beneath.

What then does Nietzsche's quite un-civil theological thought add to this? Let us set aside for the moment his very different overall assessment of the value of religion as such. At the same time – and in fact quite independently of that – his thinking also represents the advent of a whole new methodology to supplement the Hegelian approach to the phenomenon of unhappy consciousness, and the task of its overcoming.

Nietzsche too defines free-spiritedness as 'happiness': ' "How shall I become happy?". "That I know not. But I say unto you: be happy, and do what you like" '.[25] This Nietzschean reversal of St Augustine's aphorism, 'Love God and do what you like' is no mere advocacy of licence: he is not saying, 'Do what you like, and in that way you will become happy.' And neither, any more than in Hegel's thinking, is it merely another name for adopting an 'optimistic' outlook on life. On the contrary! In *Ecce Homo* Nietzsche describes himself precisely as 'the first *tragic* philosopher'.[26] Yet he at once goes on to add: 'that is, the most extreme opposite and antipode of a pessimistic philosopher'. And a 'tragic philosophy' is also opposed to what, in *Thus Spoke Zarathustra*, he terms 'the spirit of gravity' – a close equivalent to Hegel's 'unhappy consciousness'. Nietzschean wisdom is a mode of 'happiness' in very much the same way that Hegel's is: the happiness of self-acceptance.

Whereas Hegel writes a *Phenomenology of Spirit*, however, Nietzsche writes a *Genealogy of Morals*. What these two projects have in common is that they are both systematic attempts at disturbing our sense of who we are, dissolving the easy self-justifications which constitute the inertia of our identity, and so helping us to change our minds. And both methods therefore display the given 'self' as an epiphenomenon of other forces, endowed with purposes which that self generally fails to recognize: in the one case, *Geist*; in the other, the will to power. *Geist*, though, is a *teleological* principle, the will to power is an *archaeological* one.[27] Hegelian 'phenomenology', in other words, is the study of a series of states of consciousness, unfolding towards an ever more comprehensive rationality. Nietzschean 'genealogy' is far more a study of sub-conscious instinctual motivation, disguised by rationalization. *Geist* is revealed in the end as divine providence, not yet fully comprehended because not yet historically fulfilled. Will to power is an assembly of competing forces, uncomprehended because, as they enter into an individual's thinking, they wilfully disguise themselves, for domination's sake, and distort what they dominate.

So too, what Hegel calls the 'unhappy consciousness' is an internalizing of the 'lord and bondsman', or master – slave, relationship, just as is what Nietzsche calls 'slave morality'. But, in the *Phenomenology*, the precedence of that relationship to its internalizing is strictly a logical one, rather than causal. Nietzsche's speculative account of the pre-history of our common morality, in the experience of servitude, serves by contrast as a metaphor for what he sees as the still persisting sub-conscious basis for its power. Unlike Hegel who is interested in the inheritance of insight, Nietzsche is interested in the inheritance of trauma. His metaphorical narrative, or philosophical myth of origins, actually centres on the primal moment of transition from animal life to human:

I regard the bad conscience as the serious illness that man was bound to contract under the stress of the most fundamental change he ever experienced – that change which occurred when he found himself finally enclosed within the walls of society and peace. The situation that faced sea animals when they were compelled to become land animals or perish was the same as that which faced these semi-animals, well adapted to the wilderness, to war, to prowling, to adventure: suddenly all their instincts were disvalued and 'suspended'. From now on they had to walk on their feet and 'bear themselves' whereas hitherto they had been borne by the water: a dreadful heaviness lay upon them. They felt unable to cope with the simplest undertakings; in this new world they no longer possessed their former guides, their regulating, unconscious and infallible drives: they were reduced to thinking, inferring, reckoning, co-ordinating cause and effect, these unfortunate creatures; they were reduced to their 'consciousness', their weakest and most fallible organ! I believe there has never been such a feeling of misery on earth, such a leaden discomfort – and at the same time the old instincts had not suddenly ceased to make their usual demands! Only it was hardly or rarely possible to humour them: as a rule they had to seek new and, as it were, subterranean gratifications.[28]

This, one might say, is Nietzsche's genealogical portrait of unhappy consciousness. And it leads, in effect, into an elaborate counter-myth to the biblical myth of the fall: an account not of original sin, but of the origins of the *delusion* of sin – where 'sin' is the creation of the censor-self. We have here a mythical representation of the origins of that self; the origins which – if it is to maintain its authority over the censored – it is always obliged to dissemble.

For, in the first place, he suggests, Slave Morality has to be seen as one form in which what has been repressed in the founding of civilization returns. Civilization is, in all its various beginnings, a necessarily violent imposition. It does not originate in anything as already civilized as a 'social contract'. (Hegel agrees.) To discuss it as if it did is immediately to commit oneself to a rationalizing of the event rather than real comprehension. But instead, the state is to be seen as the blood-stained creation of lions: 'some pack of blond beasts of prey, a conqueror and master race which, organized for war and with the ability to organize, unhesitatingly lays its terrible claws upon a populace perhaps tremendously superior in numbers but still formless and nomad'.[29] Out of the mass of those they have subjected to their power these human 'beasts of prey' have worked to shape a docile and manageable human 'herd'. And what Hegel describes somewhat more abstractly, as a fundamental possibility for human self-consciousness in general, Nietzsche describes as something pertaining to the more advanced stages of civilization especially. It is not just that in all self-consciousness there lies the ever-present possibility of an 'unhappy' relationship to self, but with the civilized cultivation of self-consciousness, such unhappiness also tends to escalate. For this is what the advance of civilization is: whereas at first the human beasts of prey have ruled by open violence, with the sanction of savage punishments, later on such violence grows less and less necessary; as the structures of authority become more established, so the threats of punishment can become milder; society can become more liberal, more humane – because the violence is now increasingly internalized, as the guilt of slave morality, promoted by an ascetic priesthood.[30] One obeys no longer out of crude fear, but out of a sense of guilt.

As a return of the repressed however, Nietzsche further argues, slave morality is at the same time also a morality of sublimation. It sublimates the *ressentiment* which it itself, as an imposed unhappiness, causes. And in this as well we have an important development, beyond the Hegelian concept of the unhappy consciousness: if slave morality is a more complex concept than unhappy consciousness, it is indeed, above all, by virtue of the systematic way in which Nietzsche relates the self-hatred of the divided self to this, its natural companion, the hatred of the 'evil' Other.

And yet – even apart from its metaphysical overlay – there is, I think, at least one fundamental flaw in the Nietzschean argument. A flaw which appears most clearly when set against the background of his counterbalancing teleological suggestions, concerning the paradoxical necessity of slave morality as a moment in humanity's ultimate development towards the *übermensch*.

This necessity, as he sees it, may be said to be two-fold. It has to do both with the inadequacies of 'master morality', and with the threat of the mob.

(a) Nietzsche dissolves the question of metaphysical truth, entirely, into a question of honesty. (The basic problem is not *ressentiment* in itself, only its dishonest disguise.) The death of God is, for him, the death of Truth, in any other sense than honesty. Thus, Zarathustra's proclamation of the ideal of the *übermensch* serves essentially to define wisdom as an infinite honesty – a fulness unattainable by humankind. And the doctrine of eternal return defines the courage needed for that: the courage to accept what one is, and to work from there, regardless of how regrettable the various experiences that have shaped one may appear. For, so the underlying logic of the argument runs, only if one can say yes to the hypothetical prospect of living one's life over (and over) again, has one so truly accepted oneself that one no longer needs to pretend, at all, to be anything other than just what one is. Only if one does not actually grieve over one's sufferings, can one truly be free from a distorting rage against those who contribute to them, or from a distorting envy of those who do not share them. Beyond the death of Truth, these doctrines are 'true', for Nietzsche, simply by virtue of what they express – the wisdom of the notion of wisdom they embody, the 'health' of that will to power.

Honesty, however, is also a matter of introspection. And the master morality of the original civilization-shaping 'beasts of prey' is anything but introspective. In this respect, Nietzsche's argument actually has much the same basic meta-historical structure as Hegel's: it has to do with the recovery of a lost original 'happiness' (for Hegel the happiness of the *polis*; for Nietzsche more generally the happiness of master morality). A recovery, however, which – thanks to just those factors which had initially led to the loss of that happiness – is now to take place (beyond the *polis*, beyond master morality) at a far higher level of complexity, and articulacy, than hitherto.

The great merit of master morality, he argues, is its relative tolerance, the amount of space it leaves for the free spirit. The masters may be cruel; but, just because their aggression is vented in that more open way, they do not feel moral hatred for their adversaries. They seek to regulate only what they need to regulate in order to preserve their own privilege, and nothing more; their morality therefore does not seek to impose an inner censor. By contrast, slave morality has to do with the saving of souls – and hence seeks to regulate everything. It institutes the practice of confession; it probes and roots around in the secrets of the heart; it is consumed with a will to inner truth. And yet this will to truth is ambivalent: it is sublimated *ressentiment*, but at the same time also a form of life which systematically lays itself open to critique. It is so important for slave morality that its accompanying doctrines should be true (as weapons of war) that it is continually testing them, weighing them up against counter-arguments, and against the actual evidence of life, to refine them: witness the whole history of Christian theology – its sheer intensity! Until, in the end, it is the Christian will to truth which explodes Christianity itself; even 'Truth' itself . . . [31]

Zarathustra has two animals: an eagle and a serpent. The eagle represents that nobility of spirit which Zarathustra's wisdom has in common with master morality. The serpent represents – what? Is it not that element of introspective penetration which, after all, his wisdom also has in common with the 'ascetic priestly' will to truth?[32] The serpent is an emblem of cunning, a primary characteristic of the priestly spirit in Nietzsche's eyes. It is priestly cunning turned against the priestly spirit: the cunning of the tempter in the garden of Eden, the bringer of 'the knowledge of good and evil'. Zarathustra himself acknowledges his blood-kinship with his enemies, the priests.[33] 'Profoundest gratitude for that which morality has achieved hitherto . . . !', Nietzsche writes in one of his notes. 'Morality itself, in the form of honesty, compels us to deny morality.'[34] But without that prior discipline, Zarathustra's breakthrough would be inconceivable.

(b) Slave morality is, moreover, the sublimation of *ressentiment*. In that sense it is, after all, 'the curative instinct of life' which works through 'the ascetic priest',[35] even though such priests are themselves spiritually 'sick', and their morality is symptomatic of their 'sickness'. For this morality does at least, in so far as it is effective, deflect the underlying *ressentiment* from more overt expression. The ascetic priest or pastor defends his herd, his flock, 'against the healthy . . . and also against envy of the healthy'[36] – in this way inadvertently helping to protect the healthy, too, from the latent violence in that envy.

> He fights with cunning and severity and in secret against anarchy and ever-threatening disintegration within the herd, in which the most dangerous of all explosives, *ressentiment*, is constantly accumulating. So to detonate this explosive so that it does not blow up herd and herdsman is his essential art, as it is his supreme utility; if one wanted to express the value of the priestly existence in the briefest formula it would be: the priest *alters the direction* of *ressentiment*.[37]

For slave morality teaches one to lay the blame for one's suffering not so much on others, as on oneself. It teaches one to see in one's afflictions the wages of sin; turning the discontent back inwards, thereby rendering it relatively harmless.

In Nietzsche's thinking, therefore, just behind the image of the herd there also lurks by implication the menacing shadow of the mob: where on the contrary the destructiveness of *ressentiment* flows unchecked; where the 'orgies' of pious inner feeling, unleashed by the ascetic priest at his most ambitious, give way to orgies of outward-directed sheer mayhem. And it is perhaps for this reason that – paradoxically enough – Nietzsche, the atheist, is so much gloomier than Hegel, the believer, about the prospects for civilization following 'the death of God'. What Hegel sees here is the chance of a resurrected faith, purged of the unhappy consciousness. Nietzsche prophesies 'wars the like of which have never been seen on earth'.[38] It is of course true that mobs can act in the name of God, as well – but the experience of twentieth-century Europe, at any rate, would certainly seem to reinforce this presentiment of his that the loss of religious faith might, in the end, prove yet more dangerous. And that is why free-spiritedness, for Nietzsche, has to be such a radically elitist ideal: not only does he repudiate any compromise whatever with the spirit of the herd, but he is equally anxious not to collude with the God-less mob.

The problem is, however, that this is as far as he goes. The only shortcoming of master morality he allows is its naivety, its lack of self-reflection; and he considers it only as a feature of the distant past. The only two threats to free-spiritedness which he envisages are the herd and the mob.

But what about the persistence of master morality, within the modern world, in the phenomenon of *the gang*? By 'the gang' I mean: the well-organized enterprise-group bonded together not by any supposedly universal morality, but simply by group loyalty. A loyalty, that is, not to one's rivals within the group, but to the group considered as a whole; and therefore to its central leader, or leaders, as the embodiment of its unity. A gang is a group which perceives itself as an elite, into which one is initiated. It is the type of organization ideally designed to maximize the impact of a small group on larger ones. Politically, the gang ethos is that which carves out empires, or establishes patronage systems. Economically, it is what the more buccaneering forms of corporate capitalism have in common with organized crime. Militarily, it is *par excellence* the spirit of the terrorist (although it is hard to imagine any military organization without at least some infusion of it).

The gang is not necessarily 'sick', in Nietzsche's sense. And here we see the basic danger in his materialist predilection for discussing *spiritual* experience in terms of *biological* metaphor. Thus, in opposing what is 'healthy', or life-enhancing, to what is 'sick', or life-inhibiting, he is not – as Hegel is – arguing primarily in terms of the need for an expanded openness to reality. 'Health', in this context, would seem to signify life at its most vital: a purely out-going energy, not turned back on itself, not in any self-consuming conflict with itself – but in conflict primarily with the surrounding world, as the resistant medium for its self-expression; and with itself, solely in the sense of refining its skills in the conduct of the prior struggle. Of course, Nietzsche does want to argue that slave morality, as an expression of the natural *ressentiment* of the 'sick' against the 'healthy', tends to impede people's perception of reality. The trouble is, however, that in his exclusive concern with that problem he does not in fact systematically ask what else might do the same.[39]

The gang may be infected with elements of mob behaviour: when the Mafia is spoken of as 'the mob', for example, the description is perhaps not entirely inappropriate. Gangs may also seek to exploit the herd behaviour of others – political parties are prime mechanisms for this, as are fundamentalist religious movements. But, in itself, the gang mentality may well include quite a positive appreciation of the assertive individual as such. Status within a gang tends to correspond to the individual's proven capacity for aggression, courage, initiative – as channelled by the corporate code of honour (which essentially is that channelling). In sharp distinction to the self-denying uniformity of slave morality, or the chaotic destructiveness of the mob, into which the individual sinks without trace, the gang exists as an ordered hierarchy of self-assertive individuals, bound together by what is seen, by its members, as enlightened self-interest. There are no 'unhealthy' inhibitions here on ruthless action. The gang-member may even be quite honest, in a cynical if not very introspective way. And yet – first because of the purely calculative and non-meditative nature of gang-thinking, and secondly by virtue of its wilful stunting of any sympathy for those who stand outside its confines – it surely does in fact lead to a quite significantly impaired ability to grasp the fullness of reality.

Nietzsche, unfortunately, just ignores this whole phenomenon. At first sight, the 'pack of blond beasts of prey' might appear to be a gang, in the sense I have defined. But later on we find it to be one of the essential characteristics of their master morality that 'the strong are as naturally inclined to *separate* as the weak are to *congregate*'; and that 'the instinct of the born "masters" (that is, the solitary, beast-of-prey species of man) is fundamentally irritated and disquieted by organization'.[40] They form a strange sort of 'pack', then! A gang may be organized on the basis of enlightened self-interest; its whole dynamic, though, is to convert that self-interest into a certain conformity. And, whilst Nietzsche acknowledges that master morality sometimes 'blunders and sins against reality', this is only inasmuch as, out of contempt, it fails to pay sufficient attention to the slave morality which is its opposite, and so fails to comprehend it. Even here the whole thrust of his polemic is to emphasize how infinitely much more distortion there is in the outlook of slave morality.[41]

At the risk of digressing, let us take one particular example to illustrate the point. This is a case of the politics of gang loyalty in its purest and most elegant, because most aristocratic – and therefore, from the Nietzschean point of view, most seductive – shape.

I once worked for a year in a school in Ethiopia: it was during the reign of His Imperial Majesty Haile Selassie I, King of Kings, Conquering Lion of the Tribe of Judah, Elect of God. In Addis Ababa, the fragrant smoke of eucalyptus fires mingled with the stench of the most abject poverty. I am haunted, for instance, by the image of the women who used to go staggering down the road past the school each day, bent over almost on all fours under the weight of the firewood they were carrying down from the steep forests where hyenas howled. At night one heard gunfire. The writing was on the wall: shortly afterwards the regime collapsed.

And in the months immediately following Haile Selassie's overthrow, the Polish journalist Ryszard Kapuscinski sought out and secretly interviewed a number of his ex-courtiers; those few who still remained in Addis Ababa, lying low. The interviews provide a vivid portrait of that curious world in which they had once lived.[42] They describe it with a delicious irony. It may well be that Kapuscinski, in his editing, has embellished the irony for his own purposes. I do not know. But, as a response to affliction, this irony in itself already bespeaks a thoroughly aristocratic culture: in the midst of defeat and despair, these once great gentlemen and court officials decline to indulge in self-pity, or to attempt any sort of self-justification. Instead, they laugh. (These were not philosophers – but compare Nietzsche's remarks on 'the Olympian vice' of laughter: 'I would go so far', he says, 'as to venture an order of rank among philosophers according to the rank of their laughter – rising to those capable of *golden* laughter . . .'[43])

The court politics of imperial Ethiopia was largely the affair of people accustomed from birth to great privilege. There were always exceptions; but those whom the Emperor raised from humble origins immediately became a new nobility, adopting for themselves the habits and thought patterns of the great ones they had joined.[44] The bureaucracy was growing, but it remained strictly subordinated to the palace. It was a Christian culture. But the Ethiopian Church was a peculiar phenomenon: a church of the most purely feudal type; with really very little, besides a respect for literacy, to set over against the traditional warrior ethos of the aristocracy.[45] There was nothing 'levelling' about this form of Christianity; it was more a ritual expression of Amhara tribal pride, an ideological legitimation of their rule over their Moslem or pagan neighbours. And in terms of court life, its chief role seems to have been to help to invest the diminutive figure of the Emperor with a numinous glow – as the venerable descendant of King Solomon.[46] This was, in short, a world which offered virtually no scope at all to the politics either of the herd or of the mob. It is true that, towards the end, there were quite frequently mobs out in the streets of the city, throwing stones; but their disquiet scarcely impinged on palace intrigue. There was no nobleman ready, or able, to speak up for the urban poor.

The irony with which these courtiers describe palace life is in fact a not uncharacteristic feature of Amhara culture generally. The Amhara are tradi-tionally distinguished by their love for the arts of what they call *sam-enná warq*, 'wax and gold': verbal play with every kind of ambiguity and hidden meaning – as the goldsmith builds his mould around a shape of wax, before melting away the wax and pouring in the liquid metal. But the resulting habits of indirectness in communication all too easily translate, as well, into the passion for conspiracy, the profound secretiveness, the radical reluctance to trust one's neighbour which was also so typical of that culture. This is perhaps just the sort of atmosphere in which the gang mentality thrives, as the one and only way to ensure some semblance of social cohesion. Haile Selassie had three separate intelligence networks working in competition with one another. At the beginning of each day he would listen to the informers' reports. He would take a stroll in the palace gardens, with a servant on hand carrying hunks of meat, which he might toss to his lions and leopards. And, one by one, the three rival spy chiefs would sidle up behind him to whisper their news. Always he contrived to remain above the factions, the supreme arbiter – murmuring his instructions, inaudible to anyone else, into the ear of his Minister of the Pen, or his purse bearer. Almost the sole criterion for promotion was loyalty. Everything depended on being favourably noticed by the Emperor. Every decision, every initiative, had to be presented as deriving from him. The whole system was designed to just one end: to maintain the unity of the court as a single, coherent ruling gang.

And the result – was a total isolation from reality! How, after all, could it have been otherwise? When one's whole attention is riveted on court intrigue, and when one knows that ability or achievement counts for nothing, but that the one thing rewarded is loyalty, the more ostentatious the better – what else could be the result? These were moreover very wealthy men, in a near-destitute country; and, as one of Kapuscinski's interviewees remarks, in such a situation

> Money transforms your own country into an exotic land. Everything will start to astonish you – the way people live, the things they worry about, and you will say, 'No, that's impossible.' Because you will already belong to a different civilization. And you must know this law of culture: two civilizations cannot really know and understand each other well. You will start going deaf and blind. You will be content in your civilization surrounded by the hedge, but signals from the other civilization will be as incomprehensible to you as if they had been sent by the inhabitants of Venus.[47]

The gang ethos, as I have said, excludes not only the sort of 'pity' which Nietzsche derides, but *any* form of sympathetic interest in the outsider.

And so the regime went in for great prestige projects: airports rather than roads; the building of one or two fine hospitals for the well-off – such as the magnificent Haile Selassie I Hospital in the centre of Addis Ababa, which for years remained empty because of the lack of trained staff or the money to pay them – whilst the poor went without any health care at all; and so forth. Even right at the very end, with terrible scenes of famine on the television screens of the world, with his coffers empty and his army preparing to abandon him, the old man in the palace was still dreaming up new schemes to ensure his immortality: the construction, this time, of vast dams across the Nile. Ultimately it was just this remoteness from reality which led to the regime's downfall. Reality overtook it, and it fell; to be replaced by another, less aristocratic, more ruthlessly aggressive gang of conspirators, the young officers of the *Dergue* – a new gang better equipped than the old one to exploit the simmering rage of the mob.

How would Nietzsche have evaluated a phenomenon of this sort, for instance? It is clearly a pathological phenomenon. Yet the pathology is quite different from any that he has identified. The ethos here was certainly not slave morality; yet neither was it master morality, quite as he describes it. Does it not, then, very vividly display the inadequacy of a critique which is confined to the terms of that single over-simple contrast?

Deep down, the herd, the mob, the gang can be seen as three different forms of the same. All three, in their various ways, are social constructs which depend on inhibiting their members' sense of reality. All three represent modes of existence for what Oakeshott calls 'the individual *manqué*'; basic elements of society *qua* enterprise. And in the final analysis, it would seem to be the lesson of twentieth-century history that the very greatest horrors depend, precisely, on their all being compounded together.

Thus, take the case of Nazi Germany. First, the 'banal' evil which Hannah Arendt saw symbolized in Adolf Eichmann was the banality of the herd. And, in general, it is clear that the success of the Third Reich depended to a very large extent on the existence of a pliant herd of privately decent, unfanatical, quite ordinary people who, in their herd-like way, were prepared to operate its bureaucracy; more or less typical products of their Christian culture – with a little patriotism, a commitment to diligence and efficiency, and a strong ethic of obedience to their official superiors. Secondly, at the same time, in order to establish its terror, the regime also needed to be able to whip up at will an atmosphere of outright mob hysteria. This was the role of publicists such as Julius Streicher. It was the whole *raison d'être* of the SA, in its glory days prior to the Röhm putsch of 1934; and one can observe the same principle at work, later on, in the *Kristallnacht* programs of 1938. The pathology manifested in such events was, moreover, deeply ingrained in the minds of the Nazi leaders themselves: as appears in their continuing passion for limitless destruction, even at the end of the war when it had become obvious to everyone that defeat was inevitable. But also, thirdly, none of this would have been possible without what Arendt calls the 'calculating wickedness' of a cynical and ruthless gang, to set the herd to work and to control the mob. It still required the *Führerprinzip*: that bond of common loyalty which – despite the bitterness of their endless internecine struggles – welded the leadership into the coherent controlling body it was.

Nor is it difficult to trace the parallels in the case of Stalinism. The only difference is that in Russia, with its more primitive bureaucracy, the element of sheer gangsterism had to be if anything even more widely diffused throughout the system than it was in Germany.

And so too with the political process surrounding the deployment of nuclear 'weapons' today. All three mentalities are involved. Herd-like we feel, 'This is all too big for us, too disturbing, we cannot cope with it, it is a matter for the experts.' We see images of the mushroom cloud, the devastation of Hiroshima and Nagasaki; these images are horrific, but at the same time awe-inspiring, fascinating. There is a dark side of us to which, perhaps, they secretly appeal – the same dark side that comes to the surface in the ecstatic rage of the mob; the pent-up destructive violence of *ressentiment*. At all events, it is evident that many people are rather gratified to belong to a nation which possesses such a terrifying capability; proud to feel that they too have some share in it. Consequently nuclear 'weapons' become symbols of national resolve, of 'great power' status in the world, of strong leadership. But that is not all. For this symbolism is also positively promoted: it gets caught up into the sublimated gang-warfare that constitutes the game of party-political election propaganda – in which the party leadership's ability to project 'strength' is so vital. That, too, is clearly a major factor in the process.

Isonomy would be the absolute opposite.

And surely it is isonomy which is the natural political embodiment for the free spirit: for Nietzschean *fröhliche Wissenschaft* and for Heideggerian *Entschlossenheit* just as much as for Hegelian civil theology. In Nietzsche's case this is obscured by his blindness to the problem of the gang. And the authentic critical implications of Heidegger's thought are also distorted – first by *völkisch* impulse, and then by his retreat into apolitical *Gelassenheit*; or by the apolitical primacy of his emphasis in *Being and Time* on the philosophical study of death, in its 'non-relational' significance. (Hence Arendt's countervailing orientation towards the implications of human 'natality'.) Yet what else, after all, in Heideggerian terms, is isonomy – politics without propaganda – than just this: a political order which systematically maximizes the possibilities for 'resolute' public discourse – transcending the chatter of 'the "one" '? Whatever other factors may have been involved, his lapse in 1933 certainly was a gross inconsistency at that level.

Flair for Tradition (Hegel)

Free-spiritedness, flair for tradition – the contrast between these two is essentially the contrast between two aspects of responsibility: to put it in the terminology of *Being and Time*, responsibility as a response to that which is each one's 'ownmost', versus responsibility as a response to the 'destiny' of one's community as a whole (only purged of any whiff of potential propaganda). And as these are the cardinal virtues corresponding to two quite different political principles, isonomy and *auctoritas*, so too it is inevitable that the relationship between them must tend to reflect the elementary tension between those principles.

'Flair for tradition' is my shorthand for what Alasdair MacIntyre speaks of as 'the virtue of having an adequate sense of the traditions to which one belongs or which confront one'. As MacIntyre goes on to say, 'this virtue is not to be confused with any form of conservative antiquarianism . . . It is rather the case that an adequate sense of tradition manifests itself in a grasp of those future possibilities which the past has made available to the present.'[48] It is the sort of virtue which Hans-Georg Gadamer, for instance, also classically celebrates in *Truth and Method*: a rooted creativity.

It seems to rest on a basic two-fold pre-disposition: to scientific modesty and hermeneutic patience. In the modern world the *auctoritas* of religious or moral tradition clearly does have a major rival in the authority of technical academic expertise. These two conflict in that both serve to legitimate the ideological claims of certain elites: in the first case a, so to speak, informal prophetic elite – the effective spokespeople for a society's corporate conscience; in the second case, a more formal scientific one. But they also do so with this crucial further difference: that only the former at the same time has the capacity to mediate the claims of – to revert to the Kierkegaardian terminology – 'truth as subjectivity'. Herein lies the need for 'scientific modesty'. Theology is itself a science in this sense – but an intrinsically modest one with regard to the moral claims of the scientific elite *as such*; consistently subordinating these to the higher claims of prophecy. This is indeed just what renders theology 'the queen of the sciences'. (And it would certainly be false modesty in her were she not also to criticize the scientific immodesty of other disciplines.)

'Hermeneutic patience', however, is very much what Kierkegaard lacks: a readiness not only to be shaken out of an unquestioned 'progressive' consensus – but also to engage in a replacement project of popular tradition-building; which would patiently aim at the widest possible dissemination of the insights of the shaken, as contributions to authoritative tradition, liturgically embodied. Whereas modernity is characterized by an exponential growth in both academic research into the past and journalistic information about the present, there has by contrast been no equivalent development of new processes for the popular sifting and appropriation of this knowledge, from the point of view of its deeper ethical implications: that is the pressing need here.[49]

Both aspects of this essential predisposition appear, for instance, in a very vivid way in the recent work of John Milbank, *Theology and Social Theory: Beyond Secular Reason*. For what Milbank means by 'secular reason' is, above all, precisely the scientific immodesty of mainstream sociological or Marxist thought, and the hermeneutic impatience of the anti-Christian post-modernists. It is a bold argument, elegantly developed. Sociology, he contends, represents a systematic endorsement of insensitivity to the proper claims of Christian tradition. And this is so of all its forms alike, the Weberian as much as the Durkheimian. In Durkheimian sociology, the critical focus is on religious ideas as pre-scientific, irrational apprehensions of that which sociology scientifically illuminates: the necessary moral primacy of the interests of 'the social whole' over those of the individual. In Weberian sociology, by contrast, the emphasis is on the interplay between religious experience, as that which lies beyond sociological explanation, and religious organization, which alone falls within its scope; the distinction between the arbitrariness of 'the charismatic' and the instrumental rationality of its 'routinization'. But what both approaches have in common (and hence all the various other cross-bred strains of sociology too) is their methodical adoption of a 'secular' viewpoint on religious traditions, and their claim that this offers some sort of privileged insight into the intrinsically irrational domain of the religious. That is the specific 'sociological' extra to the anthropological or historiographical analyses they develop; the only real difference which their spurious invocation of 'society' in the abstract makes, as a principle of explanation. Sociology as such, Milbank argues, is essentially an ideological promotion of the secular (that is, the repudiation of *auctoritas*) dressed up as science – a 'policing of the sublime'. By way of 'genealogical' analysis he resituates this supposedly 'scientific' discipline within theology: tracing back the sources of Durkheim's thought, through Comte, to the reactionary Catholic 'social theology' of the Restoration period (de Bonald and de Maistre) which

Comte had secularized; and highlighting the Kantian element which also enters into Durkheim's thinking, but still more into Weber's. What we have to deal with here, he concludes, is really itself a form of 'faith'; or, rather, an irredeemable heresy.

By contrast, there are aspects both of Marxism and of post-modernism that he affirms. Marx gains credit at any rate for his refusal to concede the economic sphere to the technicians of liberal capitalism. But the Marxist critique of religion is premissed on just as arbitrary a commitment to 'scientific' secularity as the sociological one; and Milbank is also highly critical of 'liberation theology', in particular, for what he sees as its excessive concessions to the 'scientific' pretensions of Marxism. The 'secular', or 'Nietzschean', post-modernists (including Heidegger, along with such as Derrida, Lyotard, Foucault and Deleuze) have the great merit of totally rejecting the technocratic ideology of 'social science', in both its bourgeois and its Marxist forms. They therefore do not pretend that their repudiation of Christianity, as the chief actual repository of popular ethical tradition in Western culture, is ultimately anything more than a matter of taste. However, their impatience with it, and lack of interest in any other popular alternatives, is also compounded by a 'nihilistic' prejudice (this is how Milbank uses the term 'nihilism'): their belief in 'original violence'.[50] Traditions originating in acts of violence, and nothing more, cannot found *auctoritas*. Notwithstanding their scientific modesty, in other words, these believers in original violence have *still* – quite arbitrarily – ruled out, right from the outset, the very possibility of valid *auctoritas* attaching to a popular tradition. And they have therefore (he suggests) effectively sold the pass to fascism – the all-too-natural form of popular politics in a world which has lost its faith in the myths of Enlightenment, yet remains secular.

What Milbank celebrates, however, is authoritative traditionality only in its very purest confessional form. And so his argument is framed as a polemical defence of confessional theology – against any kind of moral philosophy not explicitly subordinated to it.

Indeed, he criticizes MacIntyre for the essential generality of *his* promotion of the principle of authoritative moral tradition.[51] Unlike MacIntyre, Milbank does not first argue for authoritative traditionality in general and then for Christian tradition in particular. Such detachment is itself, in his view, already too much of a concession to secular modernity. Far rather, he writes as a straightforward Christian apologist. 'Once', he declares,

there was no 'secular'. And the secular was not latent, waiting to fill more space with the steam of the 'purely human', when the pressure of the sacred was relaxed. Instead there was the single community of Christendom . . .[52]

Whilst he is not here simply advocating an impossible return to the past, he is nevertheless seeking to imagine how things might have developed otherwise, and how the broken project of Christendom might once again be taken up, and purified, in future.

This is a position not altogether unlike Barth's. Milbank does not discuss Barth. His theology is not Reformed, but (Anglo-)Catholic; nor is it a dogmatics, directly built upon biblical exegesis, as Barth's is. But it is, nevertheless, a type of apologetics that might very well serve as a propaedeutic to Barthian dogmatics. And from a civil-theological perspective the fundamental problem is much the same as with Barth. The solidarity that such thinking points to as its ideal is not the solidarity of the shaken – but a solidarity among *saints*. Saints, to be sure, are *also* shaken. They are shaken out of the easy ways of what St Augustine calls 'the earthly city': its banality and vainglory, its complacent reliance on coercive violence to maintain order. And yet this shakenness remains limited by their inhibiting loyalty to a church-ideal entirely dedicated to the preservation of confessional, *as opposed to* civil, tradition.

Augustine is Milbank's key authority.[53] That is to say: he returns precisely to that great decisive moment of missed opportunity in Christian history, when the no longer persecuted, no longer even remotely endangered church could after all have afforded to drop its defences against 'the world', and so relax its militant drive to institutionalized uniformity, but by virtue of natural inertia (the inertia of human fallenness, I would suggest) did not. And he takes as his prime reference-point the very theologian who did most to sanction the conversion of that drive into a fully comprehensive scheme of cultural hegemony.

'The revolutionary aspect' of Augustine's social thought, Milbank argues, rests on his ontology. His genius 'was to deny any ontological purchase to *dominium*, or power for its own sake: absolute *imperium*, absolute property rights, market exchange purely for profit, are all seen by him as sinful and violent, which means as privations of Being'.[54] So Augustine turns the Christian notion of a creation *ex nihilo* into a principle of social critique. The sheer plenitude of divine power establishes the real possibility of 'the other city', set over against the conflictual city of this-worldly power: the city of God, in which all relationships of domination are supposed, at last, to be set aside.

The difference between Augustine's two cities certainly is a very different difference from that between the religious and the secular in the thinking of modern social science; Augustine's whole argument being orientated towards the supersession of the earthly city by the heavenly. And yet this ideal nevertheless still remains very questionable. For the 'peace' of the heavenly city is a peace which excludes not only the violence of imperial rule but at the same time, equally, the agonistic politics of isonomy; the ethos of Athens just as much as that of Rome. Augustine – in the circumstances not surprisingly, but most regrettably – does not discriminate between these two at all. It is a peace of (to use Milbank's phrase) ideally 'absolute consensus'.[55] Milbank takes Augustine's collapsing of 'the antique antinomy of *polis* and *oikos*' (city and household), in the ideal of a church-community that would be both at once, essentially as a critical affirmation of the dignity of women and slaves – excluded from citizenship in the earthly city yet equal members of the heavenly one alongside their husbands and masters.[56] Might it not, though, merely mean that the supposed single-mindedness of the patriarchal household is being transferred here, as an ideal, to the public domain? And when it happens also to be in the perceived interests of the rulers of the earthly city that a heresy such as Donatism should be suppressed with violence, is it not then quite consistent for the Catholic church to rejoice, that in this way a malignly disturbing, anti-consensual influence is done away with, for it? Is that not a real, albeit indirect, contribution to the up-building of the harmony of the heavenly city, towards which the harmony of the earthly church is to point? Milbank deplores the fact that Augustine reasoned along such lines. He sees it as a lapse.[57] He wants, so to speak, all the sweetness of Augustine's rhetoric without any of the accompanying bitterness. But – no matter how excellent one's intentions – is it ever possible, in fact, fully to safeguard this sort of Utopian dream against its always potential corruption into a mere ideological disguise for a programme of priestly, as opposed to military or plutocratic, domination? Is it not, in the end, just a bit too good to be true?

At all events – compare the very different *Hegelian* vision for the church. The comparison is clearly not inapposite, since Hegel is of course a notable predecessor of the 'communitarian' strain in contemporary philosophy, to which both MacIntyre and Milbank belong. One can see this already in his critique of 'Stoicism' and 'Scepticism'. So too he deplores not only the de-traditionalizing irreligion of the militant Enlightenment, but equally the sort of privatizing view of religious truth which one finds in the popular Romanticism of Schleiermacher's *Speeches*, on the grounds that the 'pervasive atomism' of such an ideal precludes any adequate appropriation of the proper traditionality of a 'universal church'.[58] He celebrates the civil religion of ancient Athens for the sheer coherence of the *Sittlichkeit*, or 'ethics of belonging', that he supposes it embodied. And his whole philosophy may be seen as being orientated towards a maximal restoration of the same, in a world to which (because of its greater complexity) such coherence no longer comes so naturally; a restoration therefore in another form – in effect, by means of of a systematic invocation of *auctoritas*. Thus he invokes, for this purpose, nothing less than the accumulated *auctoritas* of all the traditions within history, in so far as their claims are not in direct competition with those of Reason, or claiming to pre-empt it, but are simply intended as an opening towards Reason: prior to any actual arguments, each in their own way authoritatively compelling attention to the open question of Reason's requirements. This is, indeed, a major part of what is meant by that basic presupposition of the Hegelian system, that

> What is rational is actual;

and

> What is actual is rational.[59]

It is not just any 'fortuitous' phenomenon which counts as 'actual' here. But whatever perdures in the form of an open, and therefore evolving, tradition certainly does; for Hegel defines 'actuality' as 'the unity, become immediate, of essence with existence, or of inward with outward'[60] – and what else is such a tradition if not the progressive outer, existential manifestation, through time, of the inner, essential principle on which it is founded? If one wants to understand the nature of Reason in relation to human life, he is saying, it is not enough to proceed in the Cartesian manner, as if the best way to begin were by wiping the slate clean. The very opposite is the case: one has to immerse oneself in the study of evolving traditions, on the simple presumption that the more respect one is in the first instance prepared to accord them, the more one will be rewarded. Which is precisely his own practice.

Yet the Hegelian ideal of restored coherence entails, crucially, the 'reconciliation' of the *Sittlichkeit* of the church with that of the rationally reordered wider world. And this implies quite another notion of 'the city of God' from Augustine's. The Hegelian city of God is not a half-concealed remnant of the righteous, as the Augustinian one is. Instead, it is the whole community of the earthly city – only provided with better institutions. Revelatory history is not just the history behind the church. It is the history of 'the state': as already noted, not the state as opposed to civil society – either in the current sense of that term or in his much narrower sense; but the state, simply, as the largest existing unit of coherent political culture (also inclusive of civil society in both senses). The vision is a circumspect one since Hegel is, as a matter of principle, so mistrustful of Utopianism. The argument of *The Philosophy of Right* is thus primarily a defensive one: conceived (as the Preface spells out) in sharp opposition to the species of gang/herd/mob enterprise-politics then sheltering under nationalistic rhetoric glorifying '*das Volk*', or Jacobin rhetoric glorifying '*le peuple*'. It is a celebration of 'the state' as the defender of a pluralistic public life. But the point is that this defence of plurality is at the same time also the prime guarantee of the possibility of rational, uncoerced, non-coercive traditionality. And is not that, in itself, the prime precondition for divine revelation? So Hegel affirms the Lutheran Reformation for its (partial) dissolution of clericalism, and its consequent opening towards a much more positive assessment of the civil order as such. He seeks only, as we have seen, to get beyond that narrowly ecclesiocentric outlook on history and revelation which traditional Lutheranism still has in common with what it rejects.[61] He is a prophetic religious reformer, in that sense.

Milbank is not unsympathetic to Hegel. But he develops two basic criticisms of Hegelianism. First, he attacks what he calls the Hegelian 'myth of negation':[62] that is, the 'myth' that, without any prior *positive* methodological commitment to a particular tradition, it is possible to construct a universally valid ideal framework for *sittlich* consensus simply by way of a process of dialectical negativity. In actual fact, Milbank argues, all that this really does is to hand a methodological victory to that very 'Cartesianism' the de-traditionalizing impact of which Hegel is otherwise so anxious to overcome. Indeed, he suggests it represents something of a regression from the earlier, more radical critique of modernity in the thinking of Hamann and Herder; who by contrast entirely reject the typical Enlightenment ambition to think transculturally, in any sense whatever.[63] Secondly, he also argues against Hegel's anti-Utopianism: that in his concern to counter the 'bad infinite' of the endless Kantian 'ought' (or, from a more immediately practical point of view, the limitlessness of the romantic nationalist or Jacobin striving after an impossibly perfect consensus) Hegel ends up over-compensating; with the result that he excludes not only what he is attacking in the first instance, but the true radicality of Christian hope, as well.[64] Hence, so the argument runs, he is all too submissive to the brute givenness of capitalist property relations, or the disciplinary regimes of (liberal) modern states. He fails to grasp the full extent of the critical otherness of the gospel from any actual aspect of the status quo within Christendom.

And yes, no doubt there is a distinct element of truth in both of these criticisms; one which even non-Augustinians may very well recognize. With regard to the first point: it is certainly true that Hegel is far from being a perfect model of scientific modesty. In terms of the contrast developed above, be it noted, the Hegelian 'science of wisdom' is 'science' with a major admixture of prophecy. It is as much an art as a would-be science: an art of moral and religious tradition-building. And its immodesty is therefore quite different from, and far less damaging than, that of the sociologists or the Marxists. Yet let us immediately concede that the 'myth of negation' does indeed become a myth, in so far as it gets caught up into what is supposed to be a finally definitive metaphysics.

As I have already remarked, though, the metaphysical pretensions of Hegel's thought are very much bound up with his own distinctive strategy of confessional apologetics. And this needs to be clearly differentiated from his prophetically civil-theological critique of the church of his day.[65] Nor does there appear to be any great practical danger, nowadays, of any *excessive* enthusiasm either for Hegel's metaphysics or for his particular form of political caution. Anti-Utopianism may remain widespread, but not on the whole due to any special authority of Hegel's. Nor do many people feel nostalgic for the political realism of the 1820s. If there is a danger, it seems to me, it is only that these excesses will unfortunately obstruct people's appreciation of the more abiding elements of insight which he nevertheless still continues to represent – as *the* great pioneering reconciler, among modern thinkers, of free-spiritedness with traditionality, in a civil (as distinct from a 'secular') context.

Is such a reconciliation truly possible, though, without betraying the free spirit? If we now turn back to Nietzsche, his answer by contrast would certainly appear to be 'no'.[66]

The thinker who, from the Nietzschean side, has most emphatically confronted Hegel is Gilles Deleuze. Deleuze's study, *Nietzsche and Philosophy*, is a classic attempt at a twentieth-century vindication of Nietzsche; but it is also notable for the radical stress he places on the opposition between Nietzsche and Hegel. For Deleuze, 'There is no possible compromise between Hegel and Nietzsche.'[67] In fact, 'Anti-Hegelianism runs through Nietzsche's work as its cutting edge.'[68] On the face of it this is a curious suggestion: Nietzsche nowhere discusses Hegel in any detail, nor does he ever deal with particular texts of Hegel's; and much of what he does say about Hegel appears quite favourable. Nevertheless, Deleuze is undeterred:

The philosophical learning of an author is not assessed by numbers of quotations, nor by the always fanciful and conjectural check lists of libraries, but by the apologetic or polemical directions of his work itself. We will misunderstand the whole of Nietzsche's work if we do not see 'against whom' its principle concepts are directed. Hegelian themes are present in this work as the enemy against which it fights.'[69]

At all events, Hegel is the enemy Deleuze himself wants to fight on Nietzsche's behalf. And one can well see why. It is not only that the intellectual world which forms the background to Deleuze's book, the Paris of the early 1960s, was one in which (largely thanks it should be said to the somewhat imaginatively reconstructive Marxist reading of the *Phenomenology* by Alexandre Kojève[70]) the influence of Hegel bulked far larger than it did in Nietzsche's own day. But, still more importantly, in Hegel we have perhaps the prime witness for the defence, against Nietzsche's caricatural indictment of Christianity; inasmuch as what Hegel purports to find right at the very heart of the gospel itself, heavily overlaid yet none the less recuperable, is precisely a vindication of the free spirit – in a sense that (as I have argued above) does seem to be quite close to Nietzsche's own. So that, if one is intent on saving the Nietzschean attack on Christianity, there is indeed every reason to try as Deleuze does, so far as possible, to dispel that initial impression of affinity.

Deleuze's strategy for this is to focus on Nietzsche's distinction between 'active' and 'reactive' forces, and to take that as the fundamental schema for his whole interpretation. He then goes on to argue that just as slave morality is a 'reactive' phenomenon (morality founded not in the active quest for beauty, but in reaction against privilege), so too dialectics, and especially Hegelian dialectics, is an essentially 'reactive' type of methodology; and therefore sick.

How plausible or helpful, though, is this basic elision? To be sure, it is certainly not just Deleuze's personal invention. One finds it in Nietzsche's own writing – most strikingly in his critique of Socrates. Thus Nietzsche writes:

> With Socrates Greek taste undergoes a change in favour of dialectics: what is really happening when that happens? It is above all the defeat of a *nobler* taste; with dialectics the rabble gets on top. Before Socrates, the dialectical manner was repudiated in good society: it was regarded as a form of bad manners, one was compromised by it. Young people were warned against it. And all such presentation of one's reasons were regarded with mistrust. Honest things, like honest men, do not carry their reasons exposed in this fashion. It is indecent to display all one's

goods. What has first to have itself proved is of little value. Wherever authority is still part of accepted usage and one does not 'give reasons' but commands, the dialectician is a kind of buffoon: he is laughed at, he is not taken seriously.[71]

By 'authority' here Nietzsche of course does not mean *auctoritas*; he simply means masterfulness. Masters do not need to persuade. If they think, it is only in order to explore the possibilities of their own self-expression. And hence they can also afford to be blithely indifferent to the errors of others – except in so far as those errors trigger some insight of their own. They do not react against them. For the masterful spirit, the only serious objection to any train of thought is just that it is boring. Which is presumably therefore the bottom line of Deleuze's polemic here, too.[72]

Hegel, it is true, is by no means just concerned with fending off boredom. And his preoccupation with the problem of establishing an adequate foundation, in tradition, for isonomy does indeed lead him to a notion of intellectual 'good manners' quite different from either the Nietzschean or in fact the Socratic. Unlike the thinking 'master', he is very anxious to persuade, and so his method is grounded in a radical respect for the Other. He is a dialectical thinker, like Socrates, by virtue of his aspiration always, so far as he can, to criticize the Other only on the Other's own terms, by the highlighting of unthought-through implications and self-contradictions. But this sort of dialogue is at the same time also the process of *Geist*: which means that in all the various forms of error discussed Hegel wants to emphasize the countervailing latency of a deeper truth, as well – basically because his aim is always the establishment of the widest possible basis for rational solidarity, in defence of a civilization rendered dangerously fragile by 'the death of God'.

Whilst dialectics is a problem in general, on the other hand, Deleuze actually concentrates his fire above all on Hegel's dialectical discussion of the (external) master–slave relationship in the *Phenomenology*[73] – the passage which, above all others, had so fascinated Kojève. In fact, if one transfers this passage into the (non-Hegelian) context of herd, mob and gang, it effectively amounts to a simple definition of what all three have in common, as corrupt modes of intersubjectivity. Thus, if the process of *Geist* is one of progressive self-opening to reality, then the question Hegel is raising here is: what do we need, at the most elementary level, from our relationship with others, in order to grow in self-knowledge – that is, in critical awareness of the real potential of our own selves? We need a certain balance between self-assertion and self-abnegation; a certain mutuality of 'recognition' between the persons involved. That, one might say, is what herd, mob and gang fail to provide – because they fail to mediate adequately between the dominant and the dominated. In so far as such mediation is lacking, the dominant one in the first instance wants his claims recognized without in any way having reciprocally to recognize the claims of the Other, whom he treats as a mere 'object'. But no *learning*, of any critical value, is possible from another who is so despised; one just can not hear them. The more one extorts recognition from another, the less spiritually satisfying that recognition therefore becomes – this is the self-contradiction of the master (as a spiritual being). And neither can one, if one is in the submissive role, learn anything much about one's own possibilities from a relationship with a master whose whole way of life must always remain so utterly alien to one. The herd recognizes only in this servile mode; the mob escapes only by recognizing no one; gang members recognize only each other. As the initial problem lies in the one-sidedness by which the claims of the dominant alone are recognized, it is clear that the solution must lie in those who remain unrecognized pressing their claim for recognition as well. It is a matter of the dominated overcoming their fear of the dominant, for the spiritual benefit of both. The fear of the Other is perhaps the beginning of wisdom, as one is thereby compelled at least to pay serious heed to the relationship; but the fulfilment of wisdom must lie in the development of a countervailing culture of 'recognition', grounded not in any capacity for violent coercion or resistance, but solely in the intrinsic worth of the work each one does. That is the really quite straightforward gist of Hegel's argument.

Yet Deleuze replies: from the perspective of the *Übermensch*, the desire for recognition is itself a morally slavish phenomenon.[74] In his quest for recognition, the master whom Hegel portrays is nothing more than a 'successful slave', a natural herd-animal. True freedom does not lie in a maximum of mutual recognition – for on what basis does one achieve such recognition? Always, it is on the basis of some already established value-system. Whereas true freedom is to be the creator of one's own value-system.

Perhaps. And indeed in a sense this is also the Hegelian view. Unfortunately, Deleuze completely ignores the way in which Hegel's conclusions in this passage are later – at least by implication – modified in the 'unhappy consciousness' passage, where the (implicitly slavish) 'master'-self, who upholds established values against critical questioning, is dethroned. For after all, in so far as one is inwardly reconciled and at peace with oneself, one no longer needs to be propped up by one's neighbour's approval. And to that extent one has already transcended the terms of the earlier argument.

But the real problem seems to be that Nietzsche – and Deleuze – systematically equate isonomy with democracy; interpreted as herd politics. They

completely miss the potential isonomy-building rationale of dialectical philosophy, as a contribution to dialogue internal to popular traditions. Instead,
dialectics is damned on the basis of the sweeping assertion that wherever it
prevails 'the rabble gets on top'. In its ignoring of the claims of isonomy
Nietzschean wisdom becomes a cult of free-spiritedness arbitrarily cut off
from its natural political expression; a free-spiritedness in splendid isolation,
quite indiscriminately devaluing *all* forms of politics open to popular participation, across the board – completely blind to the necessity of such politics,
not least as a defence against gang-rule, which always seeks to atomize its
victims.

The contrast between the general Hegelian and Nietzschean evaluations of
ancient Athens further illustrates this point. Thus, Hegel in this regard
belongs to the same tradition as Arendt: for him, the beauty of ancient Greek
art is essentially an advertisement for isonomy. The civil religion of that
world marks a key transition from 'nature religion' to a 'religion of humanity', which is also a 'religion of art'.[75] Many of the Greek gods still retain
an intimate connection with the forces of nature (Zeus with the sky and the
weather, Phoebus Apollo with the sun, Poseidon with earthquakes and the
sea, Dionysus with the crops, fruit and wine, Demeter with the harvest,
Hephaestus with fire); yet in artistic representation they are human, as no
other gods before them. Hegel interprets Hesiod's story of the war between
the gods and the titans as a metaphor for the conflict between these two
different ways of understanding and representing the divine; with the anthropomorphic approach eventually victorious.[76] And this victory, he suggests,
springs from a worship directly celebratory of the worshippers' own potential
freedom and creativity as spiritual beings: here, 'humans honour the divine
in and for itself, but at the same time as their deed, their production, their
phenomenal existence; thus the divine receives its honour through the
respect paid to the human, and the human in virtue of the honour paid to
the divine'.[77] In nature religion what is celebrated are the special powers of
particular individuals, with a special relationship to the forces of nature;
shamans, sorcerers, lamas, holy men of all sorts, priests, sacred emperors.[78] A
'religion of humanity', however, finds the divine much more directly in
whatever expresses the isonomous, the *Sittlichkeit* of the worshipping community. 'At the festival of Pallas', for example, 'there was a great procession.
Pallas is the people or nation itself; but the nation is the god imbued with
life, it is this Athena who delights in herself.'[79] At least to some extent, it was
the same with all the festivals. They celebrated the beauty of isonomous
citizenship – that activity through which the human, as a political animal,
becomes fully human.

For Nietzsche, on the other hand, this same legacy appears in quite another light. It is, essentially, an advertisement for master morality. So, in his early essay, 'The Greek State',[80] he provocatively argues in defence of just those aspects of Greek antiquity which appear the least attractive to a 'progressive' modern sensibility: its economic dependence on the institution of slavery, and its continual wars. For an artistic culture to flourish, he suggests, it has to be needed. The only people who can come to feel such a need at all intensely are the leisured classes, that is, those who are set free from the other more fundamental needs of life by the labour of others. 'Accordingly', he concludes, 'we must accept this cruel sounding truth, that *slavery is of the essence of culture*'.[81] The highest purpose of the State is to serve the cause of culture, not least by safeguarding the socio-economic preconditions for its flourishing, along these lines. To this end, however, it also has to win the loyalty of the enslaved, and uphold the clear conscience of their overlords. But no means of doing so is more effective than that of waging war: the labouring masses uniting with their leisured rulers in a common purpose, against a common enemy. It is in that sense that Nietzsche decries what he sees as the 'dangerous atrophies of the political sphere' in his own day.[82] As he goes on to make clear, the 'danger' he envisages here is the prospective rise of a new international order, from which war would be excluded – in the interests of protecting the markets for capitalist enterprise. In his mind this is further coupled with the rise of socialist egalitarianism; as an unprecedented new threat to the very existence of the leisured classes. What he fears is that, as a culture, 'we shall perish through the lack of slavery'.[83]

Of course, Nietzsche does also have other original insights into the achievements of ancient Greece. And, in the end, his general rejection of authoritative traditionality includes the traditions of master morality too. Unfortunately, though, the essential *inverted sentimentality* of this essay – an early work which however he never rejects – continues to close down the space, in his philhellenic thought, where a proper appreciation of the potential role of isonomous art and religion, as a traditionalizing of the free spirit, might most naturally be expected to appear. And so he is also blind to the true purpose of (at any rate) Hegelian dialectic – as an uncovering of that potential.

'That the History of the World, with all the changing scenes which its annals present, is . . . the realization of Spirit – this is the true *Theodicaea*, the justification of God in History': so Hegel declares at the conclusion of his *Lectures on the Philosophy of World History*.[84] It is perhaps an incautious formulation. And the one place where Nietzsche himself develops any direct polemic against Hegel by name is in his early essay of 1874 'On the Use and Disadvantage of History for Life', where he attacks this doctrine in particular, criticizing it as an 'idolatry of the factual'.[85]

Here Nietzsche embarks on a critique of the whole 'historical culture' of his age: the nineteenth century, he suggests, is an age suffering from a 'malignant historical fever'.[86] An excess of historical consciousness of a certain sort becomes a spiritual burden, inducing a certain weariness, an exaggerated self-consciousness which tends to inhibit creative action. This is the case when one feels bound to the past by nostalgic reverence; but it is also, and still more dangerously, the case when one views the whole of world history in the first instance as a story of progress. He identifies Hegelianism as the prime philosophical embodiment of progressivist ideology. 'In learning to duck and scrape before the power of History' – as the Hegelians do, he argues – 'one finishes up like a Chinese doll, nodding "yes" to every sort of power – the power of governments, of public opinion, of the numerical majority; jumping at the tug of a string.'[87] Even though this attitude is not itself a direct expression of *ressentiment*, it does imply a quite excessive tolerance for that which does express *ressentiment*. It is the same spirit as is represented in *Thus Spoke Zarathustra* by the figure of the ass – which brays 'ye-a' (I-A, *ja*) to everything.[88] The last great obstacle which holds back the 'higher men' from the vision of the *Übermensch* is their idolatry of the ass. The 'ugliest man', the free-thinker who has 'murdered' God, sings a litany of praise to the ass on their behalf, with echoes from Christian liturgy; and Deleuze is no doubt justified in supposing that, here too, Nietzsche probably has Hegelianism in mind.[89]

It has to be said, though, that this is really a very crude caricature indeed. At the time of writing 'On the Use and Disadvantage of History for Life' Nietzsche was still perhaps under the influence of Schopenhauer's almost fanatical anti-Hegelianism; he is not so much attacking Hegel in person as the whole 'Hegelian' school; he makes no reference to any specific texts; and he simply overlooks Hegel's own very sharp critique of the prevailing incivility of the age, the 'discordant note' which is to be heard not only at the conclusion of his 1821 *Lectures on the Philosophy of Religion*, but more or less throughout his work. And, besides, Nietzsche wants to affirm *amor fati* too. True, the Hegelian philosophy of history does remain quite alien to him in its deliberate cultivation of traditionality. Yet what is the real point of the statement about history as theodicy which I have quoted? Is it not, in fact, very largely a rejection of any other, more *consolatory* theodicy, invoking other-worldly promise; the setting out of an alternative, entirely this-worldly mode of hope? Of course, Hegel nowhere goes anything like as far in his repudiation of consolatory myth as Nietzsche. He does not presume to produce an anti-consolatory counter-myth, he has no doctrine of eternal return. That is not his style. But is this not, essentially, at least a gesture in that same direction? (In one of his later notes Nietzsche actually seems to acknowledge that it is: he implicitly retracts his earlier attack, praising Hegel for the 'almost joyous and trusting fatalism' he shares with Goethe.[90] Which, in view of Nietzsche's general reverence for Goethe, is in fact for him almost the highest possible accolade.)

Among the other objections to Hegelian 'theodicy', it is sometimes argued that the only sort of history which could fulfil this role is that one-sided tale of 'progress' which is told by the victors in its various struggles. To take just one example here – this criticism is developed in an especially striking way by Mircea Eliade: 'It would certainly be interesting to know', Eliade remarks, 'if the theory according to which everything that happens is "good", simply *because* it happened, would have been accepted without qualms by the thinkers of the Baltic countries, of the Balkans, or of colonial territories . . .'[91]

Eliade belongs to that whole tide of thought which is anti-'historicist' first and foremost because reacting against the horrors perpetrated in the name of History, by the governments of the Soviet Union and its satellites.[92] (His political inclinations were in fact extremely right wing.) What is distinctive about this particular version of that critique, however, is the way it is grounded in his work as an historian of religions: so he sees historicism, essentially, as a spurious means of filling the void left by the decay of authentic religious sensibility in the modern world, and invites us to think our way back into a world-view for which the meaning of events derives, not from their place in history, but instead from the way they relate to a structure of mythic archetypal symbolism. 'Whatever be the truth in respect to the freedom and the creative virtualities of historical man', he argues, 'it is certain that none of the historicist philosophies is able to defend him from the terror of history'[93] when he is not on the winning side. By contrast, he contends, the archaic ontology of primitive societies both can and does 'defend' its adherents from that 'terror' far more effectively. For where no meaning is supposed to attach to historical events as such in the first place, they have in consequence that much the less power to hurt one when in actual fact they appear cruel and meaningless. Here again, therefore, we find historically conscious tradition being unfavourably compared to a historic custom. (We have already seen a similar attitudes in Simone Weil and in Rousseau.) With regard to Christianity in particular, Eliade distinguishes sharply between its urbanized and its rural expressions: thus, writing of the folk-Christianity of the peasantry in the less-developed areas of rural Europe, he comments, 'we must recognize that their religion is not confined to the historical forms of Christianity, that it still retains a cosmic structure that has been almost entirely lost in the experience of urban Christians'.[94] The dominant urban tradition of Christendom is for him very much more a religion of 'fallen' humanity – fallen, that is, from the original harmony of the primitive.[95] Primarily, he sees it as a defensive response to the 'fall'; with the Christian doctrine of divine providence as a way of preserving at any rate some tenuous orientation to the eternal, even in the midst of an encroaching historical consciousness, so to speak, as a last line of defence against it. In that sense, like Kierkegaard he suggests that 'Christianity entered into history in order to abolish it'.[96] Oriental religion, on the other hand, even in its more urban forms, remains far more akin to the 'primordial, ahistorical Christianity' of the European peasantry. Sadly, he thinks it probable that for Europeans 'the discovery of India will not be accomplished until the day the creative forces of the West shall have run irremediably dry'.[97] But his polemic against historicism is an attempt to break open at least a chink in the wall that in the meantime conceals from us the immemorial, yet ever new, wisdom of the East.

Or then there is also the – thoroughly 'Western' – sort of objection to Hegel represented by someone like Richard Rorty, say. This is a critique which embraces both Hegel and Nietzsche together, from a 'liberal' point of view – 'liberalism' being defined by Rorty, in the broadest of terms, as the creed of those 'who think that cruelty is the worst thing we do'.[98]

Unlike Eliade, Rorty does not oppose Hegelian history in the name of the contemplative's eternity, but in the name of a basic irreverence, which is both liberal and post-modern, for all forms of grand 'theory' alike. He admires the method of the *Phenomenology of Spirit*:

> Instead of keeping the old platitudes and making distinctions to help them cohere, Hegel constantly changed the vocabulary in which the old platitudes had been stated; instead of constructing philosophical theories and arguing for them, he avoided argument by constantly shifting vocabularies, thereby changing the subject. In practice, though not in theory, he dropped the idea of getting at the truth in favor of the idea of making things new.[99]

At the level of practice Hegel is therefore a classic '*ironist*' – for this is the essence of irony. And irony is for Rorty the great 'private' virtue of the free-thinker, needing to be reconciled with the 'public' virtues of liberalism; to which, however, it bears no necessary relationship. Irony is what dissolves 'the idea of getting at the truth', or 'metaphysics': in a relatively narrow sense here, which excludes Hegel. Metaphysics, in this sense, may offend against the dogmatic thoughtlessness of militant 'common sense' (or the unhappy consciousness) – but it never offends enough, because it still offers the intellectual fixity and security of a definitively established set of answers. Over against this, the dialectics of the *Phenomenology* immediately dissolve every would-be fixed position as soon as it appears; in contrast to Nietzsche, an ironist of another type, Rorty therefore has no quarrel with the practice of Hegelian dialectics. But his quarrel is just with the way this practice is then built in by Hegel to a 'theory' – about the nature of 'Absolute Truth', about God and the workings of divine revelation. 'For is that not intrinsically illiberal?', he asks. Rorty has basically the same objection to the Nietzschean doctrine of the *Übermensch* and to the Heideggerian doctrine of Being: in all three instances, he suggests, things have gone wrong because 'the ironist theoriest . . . still wants the kind of power which comes from a close relation with somebody very large'; for Nietzsche the *Übermensch*, for Heidegger Being, for Hegel the World-Spirit, Or Christ.[100] And this unbridled will to power, he argues, then has the effect of desensitizing them to the spectacle of cruelty.

So how much weight do such criticisms have? To begin with, let us note the clear polemical distortions in the accounts both Eliade and Rorty give of the Hegelian project. It is obviously true that, as Eliade says, the perspective of oppressed peoples on world history will always be quite different from that of non-oppressed peoples; and also that the world-historical status, in the Hegelian sense, of the particular art forms, religious beliefs and philosophical ideas he considers most significant does rather tend to be associated with the military and political success of their host-cultures. But that does not mean that Hegel is celebrating success for its own sake. What he is celebrating is only the use that has, in certain cases, been made of the ensuing freedom – the opportunities for sophisticated, free-spirited cultural experimentation, of which the oppressed are unfortunately deprived.

And as for Rorty's insinuation that Hegelian 'theory' is ultimately just a covert justification for coercion, the fact is that this flies in the face of all the actual evidence. Nietzsche's illiberalism is quite overt. Heidegger is more ambivalent. Yet Hegelian theory is surely not so much a bid for 'the kind of power which comes from a close relation with somebody very large', but far rather an invocation of the kind of wisdom which comes from a close attention to the widest possible range of traditions. Nor is it at all obvious why his religious faith should be regarded as 'illiberal' in the particular sense Rorty defines; however much it may offend against 'liberal' prejudices in a narrower sense, the prejudices of mainstream modern liberal democracy. On the contrary: if the liberal is one who 'thinks that cruelty is the worst thing we do', then a true liberal state is presumably one which consistently minimizes the scope for cruelty. But the state which Hegel describes in the *Philosophy of Right* – envisaged by him as the best imaginable as a practical possibility in contemporary circumstances – arguably does just that. What he seeks to celebrate as the movement of the World–Spirit through history is indeed nothing other than a progressive reinforcement of the human dignity against which cruelty blasphemes. Precisely that is what is sacred to him, underneath all irony.

From the Hegelian point of view, moreover, the basic question that has to be put back to the critics is of course whether, in downgrading as they do any appeal to the *auctoritas* embedded in given historical tradition, they can offer any adequate alternative, as an effective basis for moral community, or *Sittlichkeit*, in the contemporary urban world? Eliade offers only a religious nostalgia for pre-urban unshakenness. Rorty, on the other hand, proposes a solidarity in liberal sentiment, tinged with a 'light-minded aestheticism'; a solidarity of the sort which is cultivated by the reading of fine novels, and the like – as a means of entering imaginatively into the problems of other people, in other social *milieux*, seeing the world through other eyes; for novels help extend our understanding, without imposing any dogma on us. And that, for him, is enough.

But how *can* it be? What binds the consumers of literature and other sorts of art-product together is after all only their experience as consumers; no matter how well they may be sensitized, they are still not yet necessarily a moral community, capable of an effectively organized corporate response to moral issues. A coherent process of alliance-building surely does require more than just raw sympathy alone. Authentic solidarity of the shaken signifies more than just a highbrow consumer-fashion. By definition it must relativize the claims of more coherent modes of *Sittlichkeit* – but that does not have to mean abandoning them altogether. I would certainly accept that the actual Hegelian meta-narrative belongs to a species which is decisively outmoded; representing, as it does, the self-assertion of the modern state over against the dominant older ecclesiocentric meta-narrative of Christendom. Hegel had no concept of what is now meant by 'civil society'. But why should the collapse of that particular species of meta-narrative necessarily entail the wholesale abandonment of macro-solidarity-reinforcing 'theory'? Is not civil society also in need of such theory? As a theory proper to civil society rather than the state (a possibility Rorty simply does not envisage), there is no reason to suppose that it has to be in any way repressively dogmatic.

Hegelian theory affirms the traditionality of religious tradition, in the name of pure Reason. So he develops an approach in direct opposition to that of the militant Enlightenment, from Deism to Logical Positivism; the approach so perfectly summed up in Kant's formula, that the goal should be to establish a 'religion *within the limits* of reason alone'. For Hegel, one might say, the point is thus not so much to define the 'limits' which corrupt religion is supposed to have transgressed – but far rather the false limits which it has itself imposed: the disastrous blockage it represents to the infinite restlessness of freely questioning thought. This is a strategy of immanent critique – which may indeed lead to loss of faith, but need not; a process of reinterpretation, systematically probing the expressive capacities of the religious medium. It is not so much a matter of building walls, but rather a spiritual pathway: to adopt an old phrase, one might call it the *Via Negativa*, a pathway of determinate negation.

To express it in Hegelian terminology, what the *Via Negativa* negates is, first, any system of '*Vorstellung*' – imaginative 'representation' or 'picture-thinking' – which would lay claim to perfect self-sufficiency, or which would stigmatize critical questioning as a form of sin. For here the various symbolic images and stories of the tradition, having degenerated into mere emblems of communal identity, turn opaque. And, second, any sort of self-sufficient '*Verstand*', that is to say, any attempt to fix the truth into some rigidly abstract conceptual framework – to the exclusion of that free play of ever-shifting meanings and associations by which a tradition properly unfolds. From this point of view, the problem with the theological minimalism of the Enlightenment is that it too (along with so much of the dogmatic theology it attacks) remains confined within the limits of *Verstand*.

Over against the perfectly legitimate Enlightenment mistrust of *auctoritas* as a potential defence against shakeness, Hegel therefore in effect identifies true *auctoritas* with *the very history of shakenness itself*. More particularly, one may see his thinking as a systematic attempt to draw together two opposing aspects of the spiritual heritage of ancient Greece, in a modern context: the element of shakeness in the civil religion of the *polis* is here conjoined with the quite un–civil element of shakeness in Neo–Platonist philosophy. Thus, it is a question of bringing together two basic interpretations of the sacred, understood as a transformative irruption into the lives of the shaken: on the one hand, the civil theological interpretation, which identifies the sacred with whatever contributes to an excellence of political creativity; and, on the other, the purely philosophical interpretation, which identifies it with whatever contributes to an excellence of contemplative negativity. Neo-Platonism in effect lifts the Platonic celebration of philosophic shakenness out of its original context in Plato's own radically anti-isonomous civil theology. And Hegel then reinstates that celebration into a civil theology which is, on the contrary, genuinely open to isonomy.

The Hegelian philosophy of history is essentially the assembling of a would-be sacred tradition to embody this projected reconciliation of the *vita activa* with the *vita contemplativa*. In order to clarify the point, let us just briefly recapitulate its un-civil Neo-Platonist pre-history.

Classical Neo-Platonism

Plato defines that which is truly sacred as 'the Idea of the Good'. An idea. Nothing less. In the first place this means: not something or someone materially present; nor yet something or someone either imagined or intuitively felt to be present; but, precisely, the goal of the most rigorous thoughtfulness, envisaged as the original source of all goodness. At the same time though – as Heidegger complains – in this notion there nevertheless also lies the original source of all metaphysics. For an idea is, first, a perception. Not only are the words *idea* and *eidos* etymologically linked to *idein*, 'to see' or 'to look'; but in his parable of the cave Plato specifically describes the highest truth as being sun-like, luminous; hence that which pre-eminently renders things visible. This is what the cave-dwellers are deprived of, having to make do instead with a paltry fire, and seeing only the shadows which that fire casts. The problem, as Heidegger identifies it, is that such an interpretation of 'truth' tends to imply a decisive narrowing in the word's meaning, and its actual power to evoke thought: a loss of the original breadth still preserved in the etymological connotations of the Greek *alétheia*, 'unconcealment'. 'Thus springs from the primacy of *idea* and *idein* over *a-létheia* a transformation of the essence of truth. Truth becomes *orthotés*, correctness of perception and expression.'[101] Nothing more. The Platonic *idea* is a prototype, a standard of measurement; metaphysics, in general, envisages truth as a quality of theoretical description – rather than of life itself. Truth as a way of being – being 'un-concealed' – shrinks here into truth as a way of perceiving, only. (Here too, in its very different, trans-'subjective' mode, the Heideggerian critique of Plato, and his associated turn back to the Pre-Socratics, indirectly echoes Kierkegaard's 'Socratic' critique of Hegelian 'objectivity').

In *Neo*-Platonism, however (a tradition which Heidegger generally ignores), things are somewhat different. For here one finds the first of these two aspects of Plato's argument, his identification of the sacred with the experience of thinking, at least partly emancipated from his metaphysical commitments.

This is particularly the case with Plotinus: Plotinus is a much less purely theoretical thinker than Plato – for all his loyalty to Plato, going beyond him in two key respects: (i) in Plotinus' thinking the emphasis is not so much on truth in the form of correct perception; far more on truth as an infinite movement of self-transcendence, the various stages of which he seeks to trace; a movement towards an ever-deeper participative in-dwelling of the divine; and (ii) he picks up Plato's enigmatic description of 'the Idea of the Good' as an ideal that lies 'beyond Being',[102] and – shockingly – goes on to speak of a good that lies not only 'beyond Being' (in the Platonist as opposed to the Heideggerian sense); but – beyond any 'idea'! This is 'the One', the highest truth, the ultimate overflowing fulness of truth. If the Good is only an idea, then, Plotinus affirms, the One lies even beyond the Good.[103] It is the source of all form, measurement and limit, but itself formless, unmeasurable, infinite; the source and lure of all thought, but itself beyond thought – and hence entirely immune to being metaphysically pinned down. Indeed, in this later respect Plotinus' philosophy is not only less metaphysical than Plato's; it also remains much less metaphysical than Hegel's.

Yet at the same time the Hegelian notion of *Geist* is in a significant way prefigured by the Plotinian doctrines of *psukhé* ('soul', 'life-principle') and *nous* ('intellect', 'intelligence', 'intellectual principle'), inasmuch as these are two levels of perceptive insight, but also equally two modes of the human thinker's self-identification with the divine, in its activity of self-giving, vivifying, ordering and purifying the outer world.

The first of these 'hypostases', *psukhé*, refers to rational thought in its more elementary aspect: analytically, as the interpretation of particular phenomena of temporal experience; morally, as a rising above brute carnal instinct. My 'soul', for Plotinus, is myself always at risk from the temptations of the flesh and yet able to subdue them; but in so far as I succeed in this I am already participating in God – here conceived as 'the Soul of the All'. The Soul of the All is partly, therefore, the community of all rational souls.[104] From another point of view it is a term for divine immanence within the material world, in general; as the rationality of all rational souls mirrors and shares in the rationality of divine Reason, untainted by the corruption of that to which it gives birth. By contrast the second 'hypostasis', *nous*, refers to rational thought at a more sophisticated level of reflection: this is rationality as a rising above what is particular or contingent – my own personal experience, my own personal concerns – towards a perception of what is universally and necessarily true. It is the thinking of the unchanging forms or ideas underlying all experience of being; an intuitive apprehension of the timeless wholeness of all reality. At this level, then, the basic moral triumph of the rational soul develops into a profoundly contemplative wisdom. It is, so to speak (like the subject matter of Hegel's *Logic*) the wisdom of God 'before' the creation of the world; into which I may nevertheless also begin to enter, in so far as I can think my way free from the limitations of my own particular worldly perspective on things. *Psukhé* and *nous* are both more or less distorted expressions of the One, equally in human thought and in the shaping of the world. For both are characterized by a basic unity-in-multiplicity: in the case of *psukhé* the multiplicity of the many rational souls unified by the in-dwelling of *nous*; in the case of *nous* the multiplicity of the many ideas unified by the ultimate immanence of the One.

In Plotinus' thinking, in short, the sacred is that which unifies, breaking down the barriers of dogma. Yet he also precludes any short-cut: the soul's path back to the One lies through the most rigorous participation in the disciplined life of *nous*. 'The One', he declares,

> is in truth beyond all statement: any affirmation is of a thing; but 'all-transcending, resting above even the most august divine Mind [*nous*] – this is the only true description, since it does not make it a thing among things, nor name it where no name could identify it: we can but try to indicate, in our own feeble way, something concerning it.[105]

It is the homeland from which we are exiled; the Truth we long for, but will never in this life have attained.[106] It may be directly attained only in a mystical experience of union, beyond thought. But nevertheless, far from absolving us from thinking, this insight essentially serves to *liberate* thinking from the fixity of any supposedly given certainties. As two levels of restless thought, *psukhé* and *nous* still continue to be sacred.

The assimilation of other-worldly Platonism into Christianity

With the Christianization of classical culture, the Neo-Platonist *Via Negativa* is then transposed into the context of a 'positive' religion premised on monotheism and historical revelation. And this poses new problems. Polytheism, on the whole, sits much more comfortably with philosophy than monotheism does; as one can also observe in the case of Hindu culture for

instance. (The martyrdom of Socrates is very much an exceptional phenomenon in this respect.) There is not the same element of competition: the
guardians of the popular cult of particular local deities can afford without any
difficulty to surrender the domain of the Absolute to the philosophers, since
their authority does not depend, as the authority of the clergy of a mono-
theistic religion depends, on their own privileged access to that domain.
Their claims are a good deal more modest. But how is one to reconcile the
one God of the Christian Bible – 'the God of Abraham, of Isaac and of Jacob'
– with 'the God of the philosophers'? In both instances we are confronted
with a claim to knowledge of the Absolute, yet the two approaches could
scarcely be more different. On the one hand, we have a specific set of
particular stories and images which are pronounced to be the definitive
revelation of God: a God who chooses, in inscrutable freedom, to create the
world, and who continues to intervene in it here and there with equally
inscrutable freedom. Whereas on the other hand we have a tradition which,
as a celebration of *nous*, seeks to grasp the unchanging universality of the
Good, beyond any particular or contingent manifestation; which consistently
therefore undercuts the authority of stories and images, of any sort; and
which is always acutely aware of the metaphorical nature of whatever
imagery it may allow itself to use. The Socrates of Plato's dialogues may use
myths as a medium of philosophical instruction, but this is a very self-conscious sort of pedagogic device; and whilst there are various different types
of story in the Bible, none of them is like that. The problem of reconciling
their religious beliefs with the philosophical education they had, in some
degree, all received was indeed a central preoccupation for the Christian
theologians of the Patristic period.[107] It was against this background that the
orthodox doctrine of the Trinity actually first began to emerge.

In theory at any rate, for Patristic theology the authority of scripture always
takes precedence over that of philosophy; however, scripture is read as a set
of allegories for a deeper truth which is largely philosophical in character.
That is already the case, for example, in the pre-Christian Jewish Platonism
of Philo of Alexandria (*c.*20BCE–50CE), for example, who in turn borrows his
allegorizing methods from the Stoic tradition, in its reading of Homer. As a
Platonist and at the same time a believing Jew, Philo distinguishes two
different levels of reality in God. Ultimately God is *apoios*, qualityless: this is
his particular formula for the higher truth of philosophical negativity. But
then, at another level, there is also the 'Logos', the Word of God: God made
manifest in the world, as Goodness or 'Creative Power', and as Sovereignty
or 'Regent Power'. It is the Logos which is revealed in history and scripture,

which appeared to Moses in the burning bush and on Mount Sinai, which spoke through the prophets; a secondary level of divine reality, indivisible from and yet subordinate to the God who is *apoios*. It is debatable how much direct influence Philo exercised on his Christian successors; the Logos theology of the prologue to the fourth gospel probably derives from other sources.[108] However, the way thinkers such as Justin Martyr and, above all, Origen go on to develop the idea is clearly determined by the same basic pressure that we see at work in Philo. Their theology has become trinitarian rather than binary, but it is equally subordinationist, and for the same reason.

That subordinationism was of course subsequently condemned – perhaps, in the final analysis, at least partly in reaction against the clear potential for intellectual elitism inherent in a theology like Origen's: in so far as the Logos comes to be regarded as God for the less sophisticated. This had the unfortunate result that the authentically critical element in the Origenist doctrine was lost as well. Nevertheless, it still allowed the *Via Negativa* to reappear in other forms: namely, in the mystical tradition of the church – which has consistently been the most shaken area of Christian theology.

It reappears for instance in Meister Eckhart's distinction between God and 'God'; or between the Godhead and God. All three persons of the Trinity are here, it would seem, regarded as divine agencies at the lower level of 'God' as distinct from God; or of God as distinct from the Godhead.[109] For the dogma of the Trinity, notwithstanding all its unquestionable authority in Eckhart's view, is still a structure of *bilde*, or mental imagery; and, so he teaches, true knowledge of God can only come by way of a radical 'detachment' (*abegescheidenheit*) from all *bilde*. Thus, in Eckhart we have a theologian whose whole thought is centred on the inevitable ambivalence – because of its potential corruption into a form of dogmatism – of even the truest dogma; one who carries the *Via Negativa* right to the very heart of Christian faith, without reserve. 'Where the creature stops', he says in one of his sermons,

> there God begins to be. Now God wants no more from you than that you should in creaturely fashion [i.e., as or to the extent that you are a creature] go out of yourself, and let God be God in you. The smallest creaturely image (*bilde*) that ever forms in you is as great as God is great. Why? Because it comes between you and the whole of God. As soon as the image comes in, God and all his divinity have to give way. But as the image goes out, God goes in. God wants you to go out of yourself in creaturely fashion as much as if all his blessedness consisted in it.[110]

When Eckhart speaks of *bilde* he is not referring to false images; he means good and valid ones. But they are human productions, they are our property and to that extent their truth can never be complete. What is required, he urges, is that we abandon all such property: 'I pray God that he may rid me of "God". '[111]

Like Plotinus but in another way, Eckhart too wrestles with language in order to grasp the all-pervasive immanence of God. God is not one truth among others, not one reality among others, not one being or level of being among others; but is either, as the Platonist tradition would have it, 'beyond' Being; or else – Eckhart actually puts it both ways[112] – the only true Being that there is, so that 'all creatures [in so far as they are other from God] are a pure nothing'. All creatures without exception, that is the point: the *Via Negativa* negates any attempt to confine God within one particular, privileged area of creaturely experience:

> For whoever thinks to get more of God in internal piety or devotion, in sweet consolation and in unusual happenings than in kitchen work or in the barn, then you are acting as though you were to take God, wrap his head up in a cloak, and throw him under a bench. For whoever seeks God in a specific way takes the way and leaves God behind.[113]

'The way', in this positive sense, becomes the property of the ego, like the *bilde* that go with it.

In Eckhart's preaching the *Via Negativa* is not something set over above the Christian gospel. But, rather, the gospel now *is* the *Via Negativa* – nothing more and nothing less. 'Why did God become man? That I be born God the same.'[114] This theme, of salvation as 'deification', is widespread among the theologians of Eastern Orthodoxy, much less so in the West.[115] But Eckhart takes it up and develops it with an unprecedented boldness. The irreducible otherness of the God of authoritarian religion is understood here as an illusion produced by *bilde*. Hence it is that Plato's 'sun' becomes here a 'spark' within the soul, 'such that, if it were totally thus, the soul would be uncreated'.[116] As a discipline of the intellect our transcending of *bilde* – the fanning of this spark into life – is a direct participation in the divine Intellect: 'The same knowledge in which God knows himself is the knowledge of every detached spirit. There is no difference.'[117] As a discipline of the will, it is a direct participation in God as Justice.[118] It is the birth of the Son of God in the soul. (Again, there are Patristic precedents for this way of speaking, but in Eckhart's thinking it attains a quite new emphasis.[119]) The gospel story is no longer a tale of God's arbitrary intervention in the world, once upon a time. Not at all: but

The Father gives birth to his Son in eternity, equal to himself. 'The Word was with God, and God was the Word' (John 1:1); it was the same in the same nature. Yet I say more: He has given birth to him in my soul. Not only is the soul with him, and he equal with it, but he is in it, and the Father gives his Son birth in the soul in the same way as he gives him birth in eternity, and not otherwise. He must do it whether he likes it or not. The Father gives birth to his Son without ceasing, and I say more: He gives birth not only to me, his Son, but he gives birth to me as himself and himself as me and to me as his being and nature. In the innermost source, there I spring out in the Holy Spirit, where there is one life and one being and one work.[120]

The traditional *bilde* representing the interactive life of the Trinity are grasped here, in the boldest possible way, as *bilde* for the process of doing away with *bilde*. This is confessional theology pushing urgently up against its limits, in direct celebration of shakenness. The tendency of *bilde* is to fix the identity of God, in relation to the individual, in quite static terms. We try to fix God into a given identity in order to help shore up our own unregenerate, self-centred or 'creaturely' identity. As Eckhart presents them, therefore, the *bilde* of God-in-Trinity are precisely *bilde* for the energy that breaks through in so far as we abandon our defences.

The God of dogmatic set-apartness is left no hiding place in Eckhart's thinking. The detached spirit is born as 'God's only-begotten Son'.[121] But at the same time: 'What good does it do me that the Father gives birth to his Son if I do not give birth to him also?'[122] The soul is also to be united with the Father. And, in the same way, with the Holy Spirit too: 'the Father's essence is that he give birth to the Son, and the Son's essence is that I be born in him and like him; the Holy Spirit's essence is that I be consumed in him and be completely fused in him and become love completely'.[123] All that is required for this is that we abandon the *bilde* we cling to, the illusion we have of already knowing what 'God' means; we simply have to 'let God be God'. Eckhart's genius lies in the unique poetic skill with which he seeks, as it were, to harness the particular resources available in Christian dogma to express that fundamental necessity.

Hegel's reconciliation of Christian Neo-Platonism with civility

Hegel's thought is a meeting place for numerous traditions. But this is surely the particular one to which, in religious terms, it most profoundly belongs.

It is not that either Plotinus or Eckhart appear to have been significant *influences* on Hegel. He cites Eckhart once, approvingly, in his *Lectures on the Philosophy of Religion*; and Franz von Baader records a conversation he once had with Hegel, in which Hegel expressed the deepest admiration for Eckhart.[124] He discusses classical neo-Platonism generally, and Plotinus's philosophy in particular, in his *Lectures on the History of Philosophy*, where again – although he is critical of its unsystematic nature, and of Plotinus's tendency to argue in images rather than the strict logic of conceptual thinking – it occupies an honoured place.[125] In so far as his own thought may be counted as an extension of the same tradition, however, this seems to be essentially by virtue of his having made his own independent way there.

Nevertheless, he too makes the basic Neo-Platonist move: directly identifying the truly sacred with *Geist* – that is, *psukhé* and *nous* combined – interpreted as an infinite process of self-negating thought, or the self-unfolding of the absolute 'Idea'; which he, like Eckhart, further baptizes in the form of a renewed trinitarianism. And, moreover he not only shares the essential neo-Platonist ambition, to supply the philosophers' celebration of the life of the mind with the most powerful possible *religious* idiom; he also builds that ambition, for the first time, into a systematic history of philosophy, as a tradition with its very own *auctoritas*.

Meanwhile, as I have said, he seeks to incorporate his Neo-Platonism into a proper civil theology. This entails, in the first place, his developing a comprehensive critique of the other, non-Platonist approaches to civil theology current in his world: notably, the approach of Rousseau and Kant on the one hand, and that of Spinoza on the other. For both of these, in their repudiation or devaluation of revelation, stand condemned in his eyes as imposing arbitrary restraints on the philosophical appropriation of religious tradition. But then, secondly, he also has to reject the quite other-worldly ideal of wisdom as *apatheia*, a serenity of radical detachment, which remains presupposed in all previous forms of Neo-Platonism. The dialectic of *Geist* is a dialectic of passion as well as of thought – in its relentless negativity it is even a pan-historical 'Calvary'.[126] And, thirdly, he is led to a doctrine of revelation essentially focused on the interplay between the spiritual and the civil: hence, he affirms Christian *Sittlichkeit* in its most shaken form – willingly receptive to the perennial critical disturbance of philosophy but, at the same time, no less alert to the potential novelty of the demands properly made on religious tradition in unprecedented political circumstances.

In his day the immediate revelatory *novum* was the French Revolutionary Terror, considered as an eruption of barbarism laying bare the spiritual frailty of the *ancien régime*, its lack of real binding roots, even in a country like

France where the Catholic church was outwardly so powerful. Here was a religious and political culture which had manifestly failed to adapt in any adequate manner to the legitimate aspirations of the age; with horrific consequences plain for all to see. In a sense, the whole of Hegel's mature theology may be seen as a response to this shock. It is an extended meditation on the requirements of a form of Christian faith that would genuinely help to bolster civilization, in the strongest possible way, against such catastrophes: how, to this end, the church would ideally have to refashion its whole sense of history, and of its own traditional identity.

And this is very much the context in which his Neo-Platonism also belongs. For it represents his envisioning of a faith which might, after all, have the intellectual integrity to respond with far greater openness to the critique of the 'enlightened' than had hitherto been the rule – thereby, hopefully, helping to overcome that widespread fracturing of tradition which the more militant forms of Enlightenment had, in general, tended to bring about.

Transcendent Generosity (Levinas)

'Free-spiritedness' and 'flair for tradition': Hegel's thought – I have been arguing – combines these two virtues in an exemplary way.

But what about the third virtue, a transcendent *'generosity'* of spirit? I would immediately concede that from this point of view (equiprimordial to the others as it is) Hegel does indeed seem a little less reliable.

Thus the basic difference, here, is that the first two are the virtues of the citizen, in relation to other citizens: one being the virtue which responds to one's responsibility with regard to one's ownmost vocation as a citizen; the other being the virtue which responds to one's responsibility with regard to one's cultural inheritance as a citizen. This third however – which transcends them – consists, on the contrary, of a generous readiness, if need be, to *surrender* the privilege bound up with citizenship. Here, finally, we have to do with a response to one's responsibility with regard to the sheer otherness of the Other; the Other as one's 'neighbour' – whether fellow-citizen or not.

The Hegelian term for an ethics of pure 'neighbourliness' – as distinct from the community-related phenomenon of *Sittlichkeit* – is *Moralität*. For his part, of course, Hegel consistently subordinates *Moralität* to *Sittlichkeit*.[127] He sees *Moralität* always as something that needs to be built into some overarching *Sittlichkeit*, to give it coherence; as the moment of abstract Reason which, in *Sittlichkeit*, is to be reconciled with self-expressive Nature (that is, the 'nature' of the particular community); never as something which might, even in the best of times, also validly point beyond *Sittlichkeit*.

But this is, surely, just because he considers *Moralität* only as it appears in one specific, limited form of philosophical expression. Namely: *the 'moral law' doctrine of Kant and Fichte.*

One may, I think, distinguish two basic problems with the Kantian/Fichtean doctrine. The first we have already touched on: in the thinking of Kant and Fichte the universal demands of the abstract moral law are affirmed very much in the context of their attack on the particularity of revealed religious tradition. They thus pit what Hegel calls *Moralität* decisively against what he calls *Sittlichkeit* – at any rate in that revealed-religious mode, which for him is the highest.

And the second problem has to do with the nature of the moral law as a form of *law*. For, in so far as this indicates its direct availability as a basis also for political legislation, again it is brought into irreconcilable conflict with *Sittlichkeit*: in that it implies a positive devaluation of the stability which *Sittlichkeit* embodies, as a basis for law; an apparent legitimation, on the contrary, of – *perpetual revolution.*

Nothing indeed could better illustrate this danger than Fichte's philosophy of history, in particular. Fichte certainly saw his own doctrine as a direct development of Kant's – and yet 'Fichtianity' is in its own way a clear precursor of twentieth-century totalitarian ideology.[128] This is not just because of the high-flown German nationalism of his *Addresses to the German Nation*. True, much of that is very silly, in particular the way in which every element of corruption in contemporary German culture is immediately designated here as an outcome of 'foreign' influence. But Fichte is at any rate not a racist; unlike other leading German nationalists of his day (such as J.F. Fries, whom Hegel savages in the Preface to his *Philosophy of Right*) he has no interest in playing on people's prejudices against the Jews for instance. Rather, his is a nationalism conceived strictly in instrumental terms, as a providentially available means of popularizing, and helping to stir up enthusiasm for, the universal truths of a purified moral Reason; and therefore, whilst the Germans are called upon to act as pioneers, their cause as Fichte presents it is identical with that of humanity in the abstract. In principle it excludes no one: 'whoever believes in spirituality and in the freedom of this spirituality, and who wills the eternal development of this spirituality by freedom, wherever he may have been born and whatever language he speaks, is of our blood; he is one of us, and will come over to our side'.[129] No, what is sinister in Fichte, and heavy with latent disaster, is just his view of the ideal state as providing a systematic *schooling* in morality – the whole enterprise which his nationalism is designed to serve.[130]

The main item of concrete historical evidence which Fichte brings forward to justify his idealization of German-ness is the Reformation: the Germans, the people who were able to initiate the Reformation, remain the people most deeply marked by it. Fichte seeks to mobilize the memory of that upheaval, and all the pride associated with it, to inspire his people to an even greater undertaking, which will in effect be a second, Kantian Reformation. And just as Luther's Reformation depended on the active support of the German princes, so too will this – but to a much greater extent, and with alarming implications. So, in his *Characteristics of the Present Age* he divides world history into five 'epochs', the first three of which follow a steady trajectory of decline.[131] Human history, for Fichte, issues out of a prehistory of 'innocence'; this is the first epoch. There follows the epoch of 'progressive sinfulness' which covers the bulk of the recorded past, and then the epoch of 'completed sinfulness'. That is how he thinks of his own age. The enhanced sickness of this age, which is closely identified with the Enlightenment, lies in the widespread calling into question of traditional values, and a pervasive tendency to subordinate ethics to utilitarian calculation. The moral traditions of the second epoch may always, in so far as they rested on a belief in religious revelation, have been irrational and distorted, but at least they had real moral force. Fichte laments the loss of that moral force in his own day. He also however sees this loss creating, as never before, the opportunity to make a complete fresh start; to replace the old traditions with a new, more rational set of ruling values, of Kantian purity. This is the basic task of the fourth epoch which, he declares, is now dawning.[132] How, though, is it to be accomplished? Above all, through a new system of schooling; one aiming at the most rigorous 'moral' indoctrination of the young. Fichte is one of the first advocates of compulsory universal education; its central purpose however, as he sees it, is the breaking of refractory wills, the radical extirpation of the pupils' egoism:

> The existing education has at most only exhorted to good order and morality, but these exhortations have been unfruitful in real life, which has been moulded on principles that are quite different and completely beyond the influence of that education; in contrast to this, the new education must be able surely and infallibly to mould and determine according to rules the real, vital impulses and actions of its pupils . . . [It] must consist essentially in this, that it completely destroys freedom of

will in the soil which it undertakes to cultivate, and produces on the contrary strict necessity in the decisions of the will, the opposite being impossible.[133]

Altogether, the Fichtean *Notstaat* of the fourth epoch looks ominously like a high-minded pre-socialist precursor of the Marxian 'dictatorship of the proletariat'. Just as the dictatorship of the proletariat is supposed to usher in a withering away of the state, so too in the fifth epoch, when the educational process is complete and human nature has been transformed, the need for coercive government will clearly have disappeared: the basic goal of the Fichtean enterprise is after all the realization of freedom, in the sense of spontaneous moral rectitude. And yet in the meantime that idyllic goal requires the imposition of an iron pedagogic regime.

In short, one cannot help but be disturbed by the ease with which morality, having been defined by Kant in terms of an infinitely transcendent moral 'law', immediately begins to mutate here into the menacing ideology of a revolutionary 'moral' elite – a modern equivalent to Plato's philosopher-rulers – whose domination would be legitimated by their supposed role as enlightened representatives of that 'law'; with the insatiable absoluteness of true *Moralität* apparently transferring over into a justification for the absolute intransigence of their demands.

But what is the *real* moral of this cautionary tale? Is it just (as Isaiah Berlin for instance argues[134]) that we need to set strict negative-libertarian limits on the rhetoric of moral duty, in public life?

Or is Hegel right? Is the only way to preserve the element of truth in pure *Moralität* systematically to subordinate it, as he urges, to the natural gradualism of a rooted, and roots-preserving, concrete *Sittlichkeit* – to keep it tame?

Are there no alternative strategies to avoid the danger; strategies better calculated to preserve an *authentically* sharp critical edge to the demands of generosity?

Another thinker who actually differs from Kant and Fichte on both counts referred to above, but in an emphatically un-Hegelian way, is Emmanuel Levinas.

Thus, Levinas is in the first place by no means to be numbered among the advocates of 'religion within the limits of Reason alone': he writes as a Jewish believer. But this is a Jewish philosophy from the age of the Holocaust, a meditation on transcommunal moral generosity, beyond *Sittlichkeit*, in a world which had experienced its general eclipse, where it was most urgently needed; an attempt at the philosophical reaffirmation of the eclipsed, so far as possible commensurate – in its intensity – to the original absoluteness of that trauma.

Levinas himself is not on the whole a systematic critic of other thinkers. He argues against them only by implication or passing allusion – as he struggles, over and over again, to find his own distinctive way of saying that which is the most unsayable. Nevertheless, his critique of Kantian *Moralität* runs roughly as follows.

(a)   He locates the basic threat to generosity elsewhere. For him this threat does not just belong to one particular mode of thinking, the dogmatically religious. But, instead, he radicalizes the more general Rousseauian critique of inflamed *amour propre*: locating the problem in the very nature of language itself. It cannot therefore simply be escaped by the Kantian device of theological reductionism – from the Levinasian perspective that is much too easy a solution. Kant's thought is still not restless enough, still not *self*-critical enough. For Levinas what has to be overcome is far rather: 'the hold the *said* has over the *saying*'[135]

By 'the saying' is meant communication as the action of the Other, my neighbour, laying claim on me. By 'the said' is meant the message of any communication, considered in itself, as an object of interpretation – where, on the contrary, *I* the interpreter am the active one. To be sure, all language is simultaneously, and inextricably, both a 'saying' and a 'said', but the source of the true ethical relation, Levinas insists, is strictly the experience of language as saying. The problem lies not just in what religion tends to do to this. What is problematic, rather, is the way in which, in so far as the saying of any sort of language is 'thematized' into something said, the relationship with the Other is already, thereby, laid open to my interpretative and judgemental control. For that is where the operation of unneighbourly self-interest primordially begins. *Every* interpretation, at every level, is already also part of a strategy of exculpation.

Hence, as Levinas practises it, philosophy becomes in the first instance an infinitely restless play of language; a consistent strategy designed, so far as possible, to pick out and to highlight the ever-elusive trace of the saying within and behind whatever is said. Philosophy is language subverting itself, the text circling around its *own* problematic nature as something said; staying with the awkward truth of its own inevitable untruth.

(b)   This also leads to quite a different notion of the 'subjectivity' corresponding to true generosity. Thus, whereas for Kant authentic moral agency is constituted by a certain very specific manner of knowing one's duty – namely, that knowledge which comes from strictly autonomous reflection, as opposed to the mere acceptance of what one knows to be customary or required by revealed religion – Levinas, by contrast, goes further. He denies 'knowledge' any role at all.

'Subjectivity' in this sense is not a process of knowing, *actively* delineating a field of knowledge within which the Other is objectively immanent. It is, rather, a mode of *passive* 'responsibility'; an immediate response to the Other, experienced in this case as pure transcendence. The subjectivity with which Levinas is concerned is 'traceable back to the vulnerability of the ego, to the incommunicable, non-conceptualizable, sensibility':[136] the sensuous experience of the sheer 'proximity' of the Other, completely prior to any sharing of language or culture, completely prior therefore to any actual knowledge of the Other's identity. This is a level of responsibility which originates prior to any positive act of will on the part of the subject; we may choose how we respond to what is said but, by definition, in so far as we encounter the element of saying which lies behind the said we find ourselves left with no choice. 'The responsibility for the Other cannot have begun in my commitment, my decision.' The 'responsible subject', at this level, is 'more passive than any passivity': than any passivity, namely, which might be chosen, or which holds open other possibilities.[137]

(c) In opposition to both Kant and Heidegger, Levinas presents his thought as a form of constructive 'metaphysics': grounding the true passivity of 'the responsible subject' in the metaphysically prior passivity of human 'creatureliness'.

Given that this is a 'metaphysics' which consistently dissolves knowledge, it is not however the sort that falls under Kant's critique. And neither is it metaphysics in the broader sense, in which Heidegger claims finally to have 'overcome' metaphysics; for of course Heidegger's critique of metaphysics' 'forgetfulness of Being' is also directed at an illusion of knowledge. But Levinas adopts the term precisely in order to mark the radicality of the difference between his thought and theirs. The Platonic idea of 'the Good beyond Being' is crucial here; although, as Levinas emphasizes, not in the Plotinian sense – he charges Plotinus with compromising the otherness of the Good again, by supposing Being to 'emanate' from it. Unlike Plotinus, he has no interest in affirming the latent divinity within human being; for his concern is not so much with the vindication of free-spiritedness.[138] But in Levinas's text 'the Good beyond Being' becomes a formula for the reaffirmation of generosity, over against the one-sided free-spiritedness of

Heideggerian *Entschlossenheit*. The shakenness of the Heideggerian 'thinking of Being' is here preserved, but transformed; and the actual significance of the term 'Being' is also entirely reversed in consequence. So it is not forgetfulness of Being, but forgetfulness of the Good beyond Being, that Levinas's thought seeks to highlight and to remedy. And the term 'Being' – no longer designating that which has been overlaid and forgotten – becomes on the contrary precisely another name for that which overlays the forgotten: everything which remains within 'the said'. Not self-sufficient metaphysics, therefore, but self-sufficient 'ontology' is what has to be overcome; for, as the thinking of the Good beyond Being – 'metaphysics precedes ontology'.[139]

Fundamentally, by virtue of the theological primacy he also accords to ethical transcendence, Kant *is* an advocate of 'the Good beyond Being'. Indeed, Levinas remarks,

> If one had the right to retain one trait from a philosophical system and neglect all the details of its architecture (even though there are no details in architecture, according to Valéry's profound dictum, which is eminently valid for philosophical construction, where the details alone prevent collapse), we would think here of Kantism, which finds a meaning to the human without measuring it by ontology . . .[140]

At that basic level he is certainly quite happy to acknowledge his closeness to Kant. And yet, when it comes to 'the details', what troubles him is just what is lacking in Kant's interpretation of infinity:

> The Kantian notion of infinity figures as an ideal of reason, the projection of its exigencies in a beyond, the ideal completion of what is given incomplete – but without the incomplete being confronted with a privileged *experience* of infinity, without it drawing the limits of its finitude from such a confrontation.[141]

For Kant, in fact, the infinity of God or of the noumenal self is essentially a *theoretical* proposition: a setting of limits to metaphysical language. Its whole meaning is bound up with the double agnosticism of his insistence, against 'metaphysics', that the existence of God, the freedom of the will and human immortality are nothing more than 'postulates'; and, against revealed religion, that nothing other than these postulates, and whatever else may be shown to be in some way necessary as a logical grounding for morality (in his sense), is required. Thus, beyond this, in the Kantian scheme of things, it is enough just to say that what is infinite is intrinsically unknowable, and to leave it at that. But for Levinas, on the contrary, 'infinity' is the name for what, in the urgency and anguish of properly ethical encounter, is encountered; a dimension of encounter which, it is true, can scarcely be articulated or 'known'; an insight which needs all the potential resources of language, operating at full stretch, to force its way through – but which nevertheless *cries out* to be expressed. And, as a result, the taboo which Kant would lay on the philosopher's own personal adherence to a particular, given tradition of revealed religion is lifted.

Where Kant is a philosophical legislator, Levinas is content to leave law to religion. He writes as a philosophical poet. His basic insight is perhaps translatable into more than one metaphysical language. (Besides his own Jewish version, one can well imagine it being applied to the interpretation of the Mahayana Buddhist *Bodhissatva* ideal, for instance.[142]) But, in general, it issues in a much freer relationship to religious thought than Kant will allow. He goes beyond Kant not in the way that Kierkegaard goes beyond Kant, with his intensification of 'subjectivity' in 'the leap of faith'; nor in the way that Schleiermacher does so, by invoking a special 'religious' domain of experience; nor 'even' in the way that the dialectical theology of Barth does so, by insisting on the radical otherness of the God of revelation.[143] But he poses the question: whether there is not some form of rational theology which might go beyond both ontology *and* faith – in the sense that each of these, in their various ways, identifies salvation with faith; beyond 'the formal opposition, established by Yehouda Halevy and taken up by Pascal, between the God of Abraham, Isaac and Jacob, invoked in faith without philosophy, and the god of philosophers'?[144] For the faith defined by this opposition is simply what an anti-fideist philosophy scorns as 'opinion', invested with the sort of 'thematized' interpretative ultimacy which that philosophy would reserve for its own conclusions. And both, for Levinas – in so far as the debate continues at that level – therefore remain equally trapped within 'the language of Being'; whilst the summons of the Good beyond Being can, in principle, be made equally audible in *either* medium.

No doubt Kant is quite right in denying the name of 'knowledge' to anything that is formulated in the language of metaphysics or of revealed religion. Yet, even so, all sorts of elements from those traditions can still continue to help disturb us, provoke us out of complacency, undermine our defences against the transcendent – and that is what really matters.

(d)   Moreover, the whole logic of the Levinasian doctrine, therefore, is such as to render it immune also from secular ideologization. The secular Fichtean ideology builds on the abstractness of Kantian ethics, but that abstractness is just what Levinas has swept away. And so, whereas in Kantian theory, with its quest for universally valid maxims, the *dramatis personae* are (i) the self, and (ii) the whole of the rest of the human species considered together, *all* my neighbours at once, for Levinas it is always the self and the immediate Other, here and now.

In *Totality and Infinity* he speaks of two basic categories of encounter with the reality of the Other, in which my egoism may be transcended: on the one hand, encounter 'face to face'; on the other hand, encounter which goes 'beyond the face'. Much of the book consists of an elaborately suggestive phenomenological analysis and comparison of these two. In the first case, he is talking about the Other encountered as my neighbour. In the second case he is talking about the Other encountered within relationships of erotic or familial intimacy: the Other who, as he puts it, is at the same time both other and not other to me.[145] But in both cases he is concerned with that which essentially eludes any ideology of domination. The claim which the Other, one's neighbour, makes upon one is, from this perspective, certainly of infinite authority; evoking in principle an infinite vulnerability. Yet that authority is exclusively identified with his or her *own* vulnerability: present in everyone since no one is invulnerable, it is nevertheless most clearly apparent in the 'destitution' of, to use the biblical terminology, 'the stranger, the orphan and the widow'. Nothing therefore could be further from the sort of power which builds or organizes political society; for, of course, to exercise that kind of power almost by definition means to set one's vulnerability, at least so far as appearances go, aside. And so too with the allure of the beloved. What Levinas is concerned to celebrate is not 'family values' as a political theme. But, on the contrary, it is a quality of relationship tending to relativize and subdue political passion in general – by virtue of providing an alternative, and potentially far deeper, source of meaning in life. 'The family', he remarks, 'does not only result from a rational arrangement of animality; it does not simply mark a step toward the anonymous universality of the state. It identifies itself outside of the state, even if the state reserves a framework for it.'[146] Outside of the state, its goodness for him lies very much in its function as an alternative centre of moral gravity.

In both cases alike, the response is to the unique particularity of the Other, not to the Other as presented to us in the universal terms of a 'moral law'. To be sure, no sooner has a 'third party' appeared on the scene than one finds oneself compelled to start thinking in terms of moral law, or objective public justice, as well. And it is also obvious that the requirements of justice in this sense must entail a certain suspension, at least, of the 'asymmetry' which Levinas insists on, in one's self-abnegating relationship to the Other. In the first place, before the moral law we are all equal, just as we should be before the laws of the state. And, moreover, the claims of justice sometimes oblige a person – precisely in the name of morality – to assume the role of one who 'commands' others: the role of the prophet. But it is a question of priorities. In Levinas's presentation the political good of justice is always placed in strict subordination to the good which transcends politics.[147] However necessary the requirements of public justice may be, in other words, the primary task both of philosophy and of religion is always, for Levinas, so far as possible to get beyond them: to awaken our sensibility for that which would go further.

Over against the Kantian concern with moral law, ethics in the Levinasian sense therefore originates in 'the absolutely *anarchical* passion of obsession'.[148] It is 'obsessive', in that it entails the abandonment of control, the pure antithesis to that traditional philosophic serenity which is still such a vital ingredient in Kantian rationality. What is demanded is that one put oneself in the Other's place – quite unconditionally. In this surrender, 'The self is through and through a hostage . . . The self, a hostage, is already substituted for the others.'[149] We find here, in fact, with this talk of 'substitution', the traditional language of Christian soteriology, which of course partly derives from the 'suffering servant' texts in the prophecy of Isaiah. Levinas is a sharp critic of mainstream Christianity, for the element of self-preoccupation in its disciplines of care for the soul. But, whether consciously or not, like Hegel – although in quite an opposite way – his thinking thus echoes key aspects of this tradition, transposed into a philosophical context: what is there affirmed of the suffering servant (or of Christ) in particular, is applied here to the calling of each one of us. So it is, he suggests, above all in the suffering of *persecution* that the true, absolute unconditionality of the ethical may be revealed: 'The face of the neighbour in its persecuting hatred can by this very malice obsess as something pitiful'; to experience that 'is to pass from the outrage undergone to the responsibility for the persecutor, and, in this sense, from suffering to expiation for the other . . . The uniqueness of the self is the very fact of bearing the fault of another . . .'[150]

What all language betrays is just this quality of 'anarchy'. By its very nature language organizes experience, reduces it to formulas, subordinates it to the needs of the active ego, imposes the rule of law upon it; an ordering process which ends up alloting to each precisely what Heidegger terms their '*own-*

most' authentic vocation, with a burden of guilt which is merely their *own* – precluding substitution.

Religious language about God is just one example, albeit the most momentously ambivalent. The contrast enshrined in the title of Levinas's book *Totality and Infinity* is, on the one hand, a contrast between two modes of relatedness to God; in the sense that the religious idea of divine 'infinity' may function either 'anarchically', to liberate the ethical from the ideological, or else as the mere equivalent to 'totality', with God 'thematized' as the ordering principle for a coherently ordered view of the world – and worshipped in some abstraction from the claims of the Other. (To mark the distinction here, he also circles away from talk of 'God', to escape the falsifying familiarity of the name, and speaks instead of '*illeity*', or third-person-hood; the third who floods the I/thou encounter with cosmic significance, in its anarchic 'infinition'.[151]) But, on the other hand, his argument is about 'infinity' in general, not just about the infinity that figures explicitly in the language of theology: 'infinity' as the invalidity of all purported 'knowledge' regarding the 'totality' of things, inasmuch as such knowledge derives its aura of certitude from its role as the doctrinal justification of our egoism; as that which upholds us in waging war with a clear conscience against those who stand in our way.

And so, then, is such an argument ultimately reconcilable in any way with the Hegelian one – which is grounded in the other virtues of free-spiritedness and flair for tradition?

Somehow, I think it must be; even though they pull in diametrically opposite directions: Hegel towards an 'absolute knowing' beyond the fideistic surrender of the alienated, Levinas towards an absolute unknowing.

Levinas himself simply continues to insist on the radicality of the opposition.[152] We have already seen Deleuze's critique of the 'master–slave' dialectic in Hegel's *Phenomenology of Spirit*. Levinas's difference from Hegel begins even further back: the asymmetry with which he is preoccupied, between my claims on the Other and the Other's claims on me, is obviously by no means the same as the asymmetry of master and slave – but is nevertheless in stark contrast to the carefully balanced reciprocity of equality-in-difference towards which the Hegelian argument is pointing as the most liberating of relationships.

Hegel's *Phenomenology* is a study of the education of a subject who, as Levinas puts it, is 'posited on the basis of the for-itself'.[153] At the beginning this subject is abstractly conceived as being on his or her own, feeling his or her way around in the midst of a world of objects. And when the Other first emerges into view it is as an essentially hostile figure, setting limits to the subject's self-assertion. What interests Levinas, on the other hand, is the *prior* possibility of relationships altogether free of what he calls the fundamental 'allergy' to the Other, which Hegel here, notwithstanding his aspiration to do without presuppositions, in fact simply presupposes. He is interested in how (as the saying of language is betrayed in the said) that possibility – the 'inspiration' inherent in ethical encounter, before which there is no true *Geist* – is *then* disguised and covered over.[154] The Levinasian subject, unlike the Hegelian, is therefore thought of in terms of his or her relationship to the Other right from the outset; as having no autonomous existence logically prior to relationships. 'The Other', in the Levinasian scheme of things, 'is not initially a *fact*, is not an *obstacle*, does not threaten me with death; he is desired in my shame'.[155] Conflict only arises later on.

Surely, though, *both* approaches are valid. The sequence of the Hegelian analysis derives quite naturally from his primary concern with political justice. Given that human relationships at the social level are as a matter of empirical fact marked by the conflict of egos, he wants to enquire how such conflict is best – that is, most justly – to be negotiated. Hence, he envisages 'freedom' as both the product and the source of justice in that sense; and he sets himself the political challenge of writing a history of the truth of freedom, so defined. The master–slave relationship is the first and crudest stage of negotiated settlement between egos (the victor in war allows the vanquished to survive, at this price). The history of freedom is the history of the negotiations which supersede it: a history of the State, in that light. It is a story of the religious and philosophical overcoming of unhappy consciousness, as the necessary spiritual background to the patient achievement of political justice in the State, that is, the ideal social context for conflict resolution. Notwithstanding its essential shakenness, 'absolute knowing', the goal of such thinking, is called a 'knowing' rather than an 'un-knowing' simply in order to give positive emphasis to its legitimacy as a wisdom in adjudicating between competing interests.

The 'freedom' Levinas has in mind, by contrast, is what one is 'invested' with by the Other – by virtue of the 'abdication' of one's egoism, the sheer abandonment of conflict, love even for one's enemies.[156] Indeed, in redefining freedom this way, it is not just Hegel whom Levinas seeks to call in question, it is the whole Western tradition of political theory. The freedom he means is freedom beyond ontology, where 'ontology' signifies the study of what conceivably might be, from a political point of view; he means the aspiration to an impossible perfection of non-violence: an ethics altogether beyond that art of the possible which is politics. And what history is there to tell of freedom at such a level?

The Other, revealing itself by its face, is the first intelligible, before cultures and their alluvions and allusions. This is to affirm the independence of ethics in relation to history. Showing that the first significance arises in morality, in the quasi-abstract epiphany of the face, which is stripped of every quality – absolute – absolving itself of cultures, means tracing a limit to the comprehension of the real by history and rediscovering Platonism.[157]

Encounter with the Other, face to face, is always prior to historical interpretation.

In the end the problem here is just the same as with the absolutism of Simone Weil.[158]

But these two modes of freedom thus belong in different contexts – and so why, after all, should either exclude the other? Is it not rather the case that there is one sort of truth belonging to ontology and another sort of truth which, in its fulness, belongs beyond ontology: diagnoses differing, not absolutely, but in just the same way that the requirements of prophylaxis (effective structures of justice, inhibiting the operations of malign ideology) differ from those of therapy (the call of conscience not to succumb, even when such ideology comes to prevail in the world).[159] Granted, the virtues do not live easily at peace with one another: out of self-defence, human frailty continually sets one virtue against another. Each has to be defended against such manoeuvring – and yes, better a radical one-sidedness than any too easy compromise in this conflict! Yet that can scarcely be the final word on the matter. (There can be no *final* word.)

Hegel aspires to do philosophy without presuppositions. So his thought is intended as a systematic explication of the ambitions implicit in the very venture of thinking itself. In the *Logic* he therefore sets out to explore all the various different possible *a priori* frameworks for thought, in order to ensure that it does not get trapped in any metaphysically dogmatic absolutization of one of these, to the exclusion of others. And in the *Phenomenology* he sets out to explore all the various different existential levels of thought, in order to highlight and criticize the possible blockages that arise at each level. Yet, as Levinas's critique highlights, the Hegelian system still does presuppose a certain set of *practical priorities*, the exclusive claims of which certainly do remain quite questionable.

A truly presuppositionless thinking must indeed involve some explicit consideration of this practical dimension as well: in other words, very much the sort of approach I have been sketching out in this chapter, a systematic exploration of the nature of intellectual *virtue* in general. Levinas's own morally therapeutic thought may be seen as a brilliant but nevertheless one-sided beginning. Given the complementary need for prophylaxis, on the other hand, its completion will surely also bring us back into Hegelian territory, in the end.

And this, I think, is what the practical discipline of civil theology has, in its own way, first and foremost to attempt. It has essentially to be judged in terms of its binding together of all three of the virtues discussed here: free-spiritedness, flair for tradition, and the sort of generosity which transcends both those. Its task is to mediate between the competing demands of each, upholding each to the very utmost.[160]

5 'Antipolitics'

Let us finally consider three, I think very alluring and closely related, visions of the ideal political future.

At the conclusion of his influential essay, 'The Power of the Powerless', completed in October 1978 – that is, in the second year of the Charter 77 movement – Václav Havel turns to consider what the long-term aims of the movement might be.[1] Mistrustful as he is of the potential for Utopian thinking to be infected with delusions of grandeur, he does so only hesitantly; but nevertheless justifies his speculation on the grounds that the counter-culture or 'parallel polis' of 'dissent', embodied by organizations like Charter 77, in a sense already constitutes an actually existing anticipation of the sort of ideal he has in mind. Havel is not content merely to play the Cold War game: Western liberal democracy may be preferable to communist 'post-totalitarianism', but that does not, for him, make it the ultimate ideal – and what he opposes to the one-party state is not just a system in which several parties compete. Instead, it is one in which political parties as such would have effectively ceased to exist. The conduct of politics would be determined in such a system, not primarily by considerations of 'technical' efficiency, but more by the need to keep alive the most vigorous possible ethical debate:

> There can and must be structures that are open, dynamic and small; beyond a certain point, human ties like personal trust and personal responsibility cannot work . . . Their authority certainly cannot be based on long-empty traditions, like the tradition of mass political parties, but rather on how, in concrete terms, they enter into a given situation. Rather than a strategic agglomeration of formalized organiza-

tions, it is better to have organizations springing up *ad hoc*, infused with enthusiasm for a particular purpose and disappearing when that purpose has been achieved. The leaders' authority ought to derive from their personalities and be personally tested in their particular surroundings, and not from their position in any *nomenklatura*. They should enjoy great personal confidence and even great lawmaking powers based on that confidence.[2]

Nowhere, however, would there be any great institutional accumulation of power. In other words, it would be just as if the communist government had disappeared and the 'dissident' movement had come to power, but – in stark contrast to what then did happen eleven years later – *without in any way changing its organizational character in the process.*

Hannah Arendt outlines a rather similar ideal in the closing pages of her book *On Revolution* (1963). This comes in the context of the comparison she develops between what she sees as the two major political inventions of the modern period: the 'party system' (of which liberal democracy and totalitarianism are two variants) and the 'council system'. The former is the dominant model with which we are all familiar; the latter is that splendid recrudescence of isonomy which one glimpses in the opening moments of the great revolutions. 'Councils', in this sense, are gatherings or assemblies whose members, whilst they may divide themselves into informal factions, are nevertheless essentially independent of any strict party discipline. 'The conflict between the two systems', she argues, 'has come to the fore in all twentieth-century revolutions' – as indeed it did again, in new ways, in 1989.

> The issue at stake was representation versus action and participation. The councils were organs of action, the revolutionary parties were organs of representation, and although the revolutionary parties half-heartedly recognized the councils as instruments of 'revolutionary struggle', they tried even in the midst of revolution to rule them from within'.[3]

Political parties are designed as instruments for efficient and legitimated ruling, councils by contrast are designed to maximize the scope for free debate. And when Thomas Jefferson, at the end of his life, was moved to advocate the proliferation of such 'elementary republics' as the one means of truly safeguarding the moral health of the American republic as a whole, this had nothing to do with reinforcing the apparatus of rule: on the contrary,

'Jefferson knew well enough that what he proposed as the "salvation of the republic" actually was the salvation of the revolutionary spirit through the republic.'[4]

One of the historic achievements of the party system has been to open up the possibility of a political career to members of the less-privileged classes. But in maintaining politics as an affair, primarily, for professional careerists, parties at the same time merely help perpetuate the old division between the ruling few and many ruled (the exact opposite of democracy in its original sense) in 'democratic' form. The council system, on the other hand, would be both a means towards the 'no-rule' of isonomy for its direct participants and, in relation to the wider community, an authentic aristocracy. That is to say, quite literally, a system of 'rule by the best': not the best, of course, in the conventional sense of 'aristocracy', as consisting of those born into the ranks of the 'noble' and the wealthy; but in the sense of being among those most actively concerned with public affairs – 'those few from every walk of life who have a taste for public freedom and cannot be "happy" without it'.[5] In such a system decision-making power would belong to those who were concerned enough to turn up to meetings. It would not depend upon the ability to persuade the mass of more or less apathetic voters to support some given programme; the masses, *as such*, would on the contrary be altogether excluded from the process. There would be no general elections.

> However, this exclusion from politics should not be derogatory, since a political elite is by no means identical with a social or cultural or professional elite. The exclusion, moreover, would not depend on an outside body; if those who belong are self-chosen, those who do not belong are self-excluded.[6]

In place of general elections, the self-selected members of the lowest level of councils would select from among themselves delegates to the next level up, and likewise at each level after that. And this, she remarks, would obviously solve 'one of the most serious problems of modern politics, which is not how to reconcile freedom and equality but *how to reconcile equality and authority*'.[7] For, whilst the system would have the pyramidal shape of an authoritarian regime, it would operate in a quite opposite way from such regimes, with authority not originating from the top and being filtered down, but instead being generated by the agreement, on each different layer, of peer-groups.

Simone Weil, meanwhile, puts things even more vigorously than either Havel or Arendt: writing as an exile in London in 1943, and looking forward to the liberation of France and the establishment of a new constitution, she proposes that the first step should be the positive suppression by law of all political parties.[8]

She bases her argument on Rousseau's notion of the 'general will'. Decisive here is her deep mistrust, which she shares with Rousseau, of any sort of collective passion (bound up with the inflammation of corporate *amour propre*). How, then, are just political decisions most likely to be made? With Rousseau she argues: by the *dispassionate* consideration of what is in the common interest – that is what gives us the general will, the source of all true legitimacy. Since it is a matter of the common interest, it follows that all should be consulted; but the general will is by no means necessarily the same as 'the will of all', as expressed by a majority vote. For that majority may well have been swayed by some collective passion. And the issues must also be properly presented: that is to say, case by case; not in terms of any prepackaged choice between the representatives of competing collective passions, and their programmes.

The party system is fundamentally corrupt, for Weil, on three counts:

> A political party is a machine for fabricating collective passion.
>
> A political party is an organization designed to exercise collective pressure on the thinking of each of the human beings who belong to it.
>
> The highest good, and in the final analysis the only good, for any political party is its own growth, and this without any limit.
>
> By virtue of that threefold character every party is, in germ and in aspiration, totalitarian.[9]

Parties, of course, seek to grow and so to gain power for the professed purpose of contributing to the public good. But it is so much easier to be thoughtlessly partisan than to be, in a truly open way, thoughtful about the good that is thereby being served. It is so much easier to say, 'As a conservative – I think so and so', or, 'As a socialist – I think such and such'; in other words (no matter how glib, or clued up one may be) not to think at all. And so the means becomes the end: the party programme, far from representing a purely disinterested collective perception of the wider public good, tends inevitably to degenerate into a mere instrument in the service of growth. That the party's own well-being thereby becomes its highest good is indeed the very essence of idolatry – 'for to be the highest good for oneself is only legitimate for God'.[10] In so far as this is the case, parties are 'organisms publicly and officially dedicated to killing off all sense of truth and justice in people's souls'.[11] She finds here an all too direct analogy to what she most deplores in institutionalized Christianity: the rigidly authoritarian demarcation of orthodoxy from heresy 'first introduced into history by the Catholic Church'.[12] But, unlike the church, political parties have no redeeming features – and, whatever the practical difficulties, should therefore, she concludes, be outlawed.

It has to be conceded that there are serious problems with these various proposals. In the first place, Arendt's claim that those who show most concern for public affairs are *ipso facto* 'the best' for the purpose of conducting them is certainly very debatable. Like Nietzsche, she appears to be oblivious here to the potential problems posed in particular by gangsterism: at all events it is not at all clear what safeguards, if any, there would be to protect the council system as she envisages it from the manipulative tactics of politically motivated gangs. Whatever its other failings, a properly organized pluralistic system of universal suffrage does at least have the merit of inhibiting such behaviour; for, however much gang-like coteries may form themselves within political parties, it still requires a far more overt exercise of violence to intimidate a whole electorate than to pack and control a series of small councils. It is true that a council system would no doubt help to generate public-spiritedness – but it would surely also presuppose a very high degree of public-spiritedness, and resultant civil courage in the community at large, if it were to be kept safe from such corruption.

Weil, on the other hand, seems to envisage the retention of a form of universal suffrage; perhaps (although she does not spell this out) in the shape of continual non-partisan referenda. In that case, though, one cannot help wondering about the sheer political stamina it would require from the general public to sustain the system. Nor is it by any means clear how fair her polemical description of political parties actually is: she herself draws an explicit distinction between the political parties of continental Europe, which are what she has in mind, and the parties of the Anglo-Saxon world; these latter she admits to finding a good deal less objectionable, thanks to, as she puts it, 'the playful, sportive element' in them, deriving she thinks from their more aristocratic origins.[13] But, whatever the validity of this comparison (with reference of course to the world of the 1920s and 1930s), it is left hanging very much in the air; dismissed with the brusque statement that the Anglo-Saxon model is not transplantable.

And besides, as was remarked above, the argument she derives from Rousseau, if taken in isolation, would clearly tend to discredit a good deal more than just political parties. Like all the other agencies of civil society, trade unions for instance necessarily tend to elicit, and to thrive upon, collective passions. Yet Weil remained an enthusiastic champion of non-party-affiliated trade unionism. Aware of the difficulty, in *The Need for Roots* she therefore proposes a sharp distinction between 'interest groups', such as trade unions, and 'idea groups'. It is the *ideologization* of collective passion that she really seeks to prohibit. That is the real obstacle to the creation of an atmosphere in which people would be properly encouraged to think for themselves. 'For liberty of thought to be protected requires that it should be forbidden by law for any group to express an opinion'[14] – an *ideological* 'opinion', that is, as opposed to a straightforward, immediate expression of solidarity. Solidarity in defence of corporate interests she argues is legitimate, just so long as it is expressed in strictly non-ideological terms. The obvious problem with this argument, however, is that, in order for her proposal to be workable, one would actually have to be able to draw the line here – to determine the exact point where the legitimate expression of solidarity may be deemed to end, and the illegitimate expression of opinion to begin – with absolute, lawyer-proof precision. Which is surely quite impossible in practice.

Nevertheless, all the signs are that the great age of political parties' ideological self-definition is well and truly over. They are no longer the sort of institution from which one expects gripping new ideas, capable of winning the passionate allegiance of intellectuals; in Hegelian terms they have ceased to be, in any real sense, effective carriers of *Geist*.

For the foreseeable future they will, no doubt, continue to be the natural agencies for the political management of states: notwithstanding the immense personal prestige of Havel as the new president of Czechoslovakia in 1990, and all his protests, the disintegration of the ex-dissident movement there, following its victory, into a conventional range of competing parties was clearly quite inevitable.[15]

And yet the basic question is still as pressing as ever: how to maximize the space in our culture – even if it has to be alongside the activity of the parties – for an alternative type of politics which, by contrast, would be altogether free of propaganda? Inasmuch as we have now come to such a pass that the very word 'politics', for most people, has in effect been reduced to little more than a mere synonym for the propaganda game, Havel defines his ideal as an embodiment of '*anti-political*' politics'.[16] And this is also what George Konrad meant by the title of his book: *Antipolitics*. Written in the early 1980s (it first appeared in 1982), Konrad's work represents a Hungarian 'dissident' perspective on the Cold War, and the imminent apparent threat of its escalation into all-out hostilities. By 'antipolitics', then, he means the most radical sort of opposition to the whole system that renders such a threat possible. He links it to civil society:

Antipolitics strives to put politics in its place and make sure it stays there, never overstepping its proper office of defending and refining the rules of the game of civil society. Antipolitics is the ethos of civil society, and civil society is the antithesis of military society.[17]

Unlike Arendt, Konrad takes 'politics' to signify the struggle for power, in the sense of the capacity to rule (in whatever domain): a 'politician for whom the exercise of power is not an end in itself is a contradiction in terms'.[18] But by contrast,

Antipolitics is the political activity of those who don't want to be politicians and who refuse to share in power.

Or, rather, it has to do with another species of power, independently organized:

It is a counter-power that cannot take power and does not wish to. Power it has already, here and now, by reason of its moral and cultural weight . . . Antipolitics and government work in two different dimensions, two separate spheres.[19]

Antipolitics springs from 'the rejection of the power monopoly of the political class'; the frank self-affirmation of an intellectual class which proudly insists on retaining its moral independence, at all costs.

Liberated from the tactical constraints imposed by the quest for the power to rule, the practitioners of antipolitics need no longer be governed by dictates of calculating shrewdness, but are free to cultivate the true virtues of discernment, without distraction. This would be the practical, public expression of the solidarity of the shaken; the most direct possible contribution to a general raising of both the moral and the intellectual level of public debate.

Without going as far as Arendt or Weil, I would therefore like to make the following modest proposal. Given the inevitability of political parties, it may well be that democratic public debate would be considerably enhanced by a system of state funding for parties, in order to reduce their dependence on their financial sponsors. But still more valuable, it seems to me, would be a generous programme of state funding for what I would term non-party 'ethical lobbies'.

In Britain today charities are favoured with tax concessions, but the privilege is conditional on their staying out of the political arena. Agencies with an active commitment to improving the quality of public awareness of ethical issues receive no such recognition at all. My suggestion is that they should be given not just tax concessions – but substantial support out of tax revenue.

By 'ethical lobbies' I mean licensed agencies of antipolitics. They would, therefore, have to remain entirely independent of the government. What I am advocating would not be direct government funding. A major part of their proper role would be to operate as licensed gadflies to the government, a permanent non-partisan opposition. But funds would be allocated to them by an independent commission – maybe consisting of elected representatives of the various religious and philosophical communities within the state, and the charities.

In order to qualify for such support an organization would have to show that it was not deliberately fomenting, or playing upon, collective passions in the manner of propaganda; that its work was educationally provocative, but quite without any admixture of propaganda methods; that it was genuinely independent of, and separate from, any political party, any religious denomination, any big financial interest; that it was an exploration open to new insights, new ideas, new questions; perhaps that it helped to draw attention to longer-term issues, of the sort that party politics' imprisonment within the horizon of the next elections tends to obscure; perhaps, too, that it helped give a public hearing to voices which would otherwise tend not to be heard: the voices of the poor, the discriminated against, the excluded, the inarticulate – voices from abroad, voices representing the interests of future generations. It would also be desirable that, in relation to any particular contentious issue, the widest possible range of different points of view should be aired in this way. One can well imagine that the application of these criteria would give rise to heated dissent and much complaining; all the more so if substantial sums were involved. But that in itself would be very much one of the benefits of the system: for as a result there would emerge a whole new mode of public debate – alongside that of party politics; debate focusing, far more, on questions of fundamental principle regarding the nature of ethical rationality. The aim, in the long run, would be to transform the whole context of the democratic process, and thereby to help create a state of affairs significantly enhancing the chances of just and appropriate decision-making.

And so – why not?

It might no doubt be objected that this is not what people pay their taxes for. Why, though, do we pay taxes? There are of course those, like Robert Nozick, who consider that we already, in every modern state, pay for far too much. This is an argument based on the defence of a supposed set of elementary, inviolable rights. 'Individuals have rights' – so Nozick begins – 'and there are things no person or group may do to them (without violating their rights). So strong and far-reaching are these rights that they raise the question of what, if anything, the state and its officials may do . . .'[20] A state, he insists, is justified only as a device for protecting its members' rights, that is to say, defending their lives, their health and their property from the aggressive impulses of their neighbours. And, yes – if one starts out from this principle it is certainly hard to see how one could ever get further than justifying the most minimal of states. As Nozick argues, on this basis there can be no real justification for redistributive taxation at all.

I do not want to go into the details of Nozick's elegant presentation of this case, or the academic debate around it. But it does at least force us to reconsider what the proper starting point for political theory should be. For my quarrel is just with the first premiss of the argument: the supposition that one may legitimately try to base a comprehensive theory of political justice on an unargued-for intuition as to the nature of rights; that it is unnecessary first to ask where these rights themselves have come from.[21]

Where should one logically begin, in thinking about politics? Surely, the political question of justice is a derivative one – deriving from the prior question of the intrinsic nature of truth itself, or the ethics of communication.

In terms of the argument developed above, I would essentially define 'justice' as *the institutionalization of the virtues of discernment.* 'Justice' in this sense would be that which constitutes the most favourable social environment for the emergence of truth; the ideal framework for good dialogue, writ large. Or rather, all other things being equal – setting aside any consideration of the participants' native intelligence, expertise or state of mind – the question of 'justice' is the question of those basic procedural rules which are most likely to contribute to our learning from one another, in a fruitful way; rules which we cannot, in the end, thoughtfully reject – without at the same time rejecting the good of thoughtfulness, as such.

Now, from this point of view there can certainly be no questioning the fundamental importance of rights, here redefined as those consensually accepted guarantees which are required to give people a sufficient sense of security for them to participate freely in the dialogue of society; on their own terms, when and where they choose, and without any pressing need to conceal what they truly think. In default of which any dialogue will be falsified from the outset by ill-will. It seems to me, in fact, that the right to free speech (or the choice of silence) is the primary right, from which all others follow – as universal rules designed, so far as possible, to deprive those who would seek to suppress free speech from having the means of doing so. Unlike Nozick's, it should be noted, such an understanding of the nature of rights would be quite compatible with a defence of the welfare state. For the welfare state can also be seen as a strategy to help guarantee people's sense of security – essentially, by defusing the threat represented by revolutionary mobs, the reckless destructive rage of the destitute. There is, after all, no greater danger to free speech than the panic fear of a ruling elite, and its supporters, at the prospect of unchannelled insurrectionary mob violence; their fear of anything that might ignite such violence, or inhibit their repression of it. And the welfare state is, in practice, primarily intended to do away with the sort of economic conditions in which that threat is greatest.

But good dialogue does not only depend on freedom of participation. It also depends on one's actually being stimulated to throw one's whole self into it, in a spirit of real openness. And that is where the work of ethical lobbies comes in; it being their role to provide this stimulus.

In short, what I am suggesting is that a truly just society would be one characterized by the liveliest and most open-minded continual public mulling over of what justice truly is. Even if it could escape from the endemic condition of civil war between rich and poor which is its most probable fate, a minimal state of the kind advocated by Nozick would still be quite unlikely to provide this since, in so far as it had the effect of removing most of the (potential) significance of citizenship, the result would surely also be to reinforce, as people's means of defining their corporate identity, the narrowest sort of introverted communalism or sectarianism. In existing states, on the other hand, the quality of public ethical debate seems to be at its best wherever civil society in general happens to be strongest. And the conclusion therefore appears inescapable, that the state ought deliberately to cultivate this aspect of the life of civil society – as a most urgent matter of policy.

But how then (to take up, and adapt, a question I posed above with particular regard to Kierkegaard) is the necessary moral energy to be found, to begin to shift us in this direction?

This whole book has been about trying to locate that energy – in theological or meta-theological terms.

In the modern world, every justification for a system of rule – that is, every ideology – rests on a certain interpretation of history; the more violent the system, and hence the greater its need for such justification, the more crudely reductionist generally the interpretation. At the beginning of his novel, *The Book of Laughter and Forgetting*, Milan Kundera refers for instance to the photograph which records that historic moment in February 1948 when the

Czech communist leader Klement Gottwald, standing on a balcony above the Old Town Square in Prague, officially announced his party's seizure of power. It was a cold day and he was wearing a fur hat, a hat he had in fact just borrowed from his foreign minister Clementis, who stood at his side. In the photograph, however, Clementis is no longer to be seen. Four years later, charged with high treason, he was hanged, and since from the point of view of the party a traitor has no proper place in this historic scene he has been airbrushed out, so that now nothing is left of him except his hat – poignantly perched on the head of the man who was to order his death. 'The struggle of man against power', one of Kundera's characters remarks, 'is the struggle of memory against forgetting.'[22]

Of course, the capitalist free market system, more efficient than communism in every useful respect, also produces more sophisticated modes of propaganda. But *any* move towards setting greater limits on the power of our rulers must to a very large extent depend on challenging their self-serving ideological over-simplifications of the past. It requires us, not least, to work towards a culture of, so to speak, proper 'remembrancing' (well beyond the capitalist efforts of the 'heritage industry'). And the specifically theological contribution to such a culture might be termed *civil faith*. 'Faith' is a Christian term, but civil faith in this sense does not depend upon Christian faith as its propaedeutic, neither does it have to be in any way in competition with Christian faith. It is simply of another order: the theistic expression of the solidarity of the shaken; a faith in God mediated through faith in the city, at its most open.

What Kierkegaard affirmed of confessional Christian faith is true, I think, of faith in general – including civil faith: its validity lies in its potential quality as an *intensification* of what truth demands. That is, the demand that we should truly *think*. True faith intensifies this demand by dramatizing it, contextualizing it within the drama of a liturgy, representative of the cosmic drama of truth's emergence. It dramatizes the demand in order to intensify it. By contrast, propaganda may also dramatize elements of truth – and yet propaganda-ideology can never make truth more demanding; it may serve to disseminate truth, but only by dramatically simplifying it. Propaganda-ideology may also make great demands, but never the demand that we truly think. And where faith is converted into something communicable by propaganda means, that surely is the great betrayal: idolatry.

Faith versus propaganda-ideology: these are two great opposing modes in which community-building ideas may be dramatized. In this respect the new possibilities opened up by the modern technology of mass-communication simply serve to clarify an age-old opposition. And herein, I think, lies the great advantage of civil theology: that it is able to address that primary conflict in the most *direct* manner; more directly than any confessional thinking, as such, can – since in confessional thinking this underlying issue is always overlaid by *other*, more or less distracting issues of faith versus unbelief.

The faith which a de-ideologized civil theology seeks to articulate represents an unqualified exposure to *all* that is unmastered, but still living, in our history.

It is a faith in the rationality of history, that is, reason's ever-present need for an intensified historical consciousness; yet it transcends reason in the sense that this exposure is prior to, and remains undiminished by, any specific rationalization, ideological or otherwise, of the data. It is not a matter of approaching history with some given notion of its reasons, or lessons, for which one is seeking confirmation or illustration. One cannot help having such presuppositions and it is obviously right that they should be rationally tested – but faith is something else. In relation to the historical data, the leap of faith is a leap of the imagination; a movement of imaginative sympathy with past generations – which can establish nothing, but only disturb. It is a thirst for discernment; a hearkening to the voice of God, as that voice relentlessly calls one back to the difficulty of difficult reality; a placing of oneself in the age-old drama of this God's wrestling with humankind; the trust, prayerfully cultivated, that allows one in principle to drop one's defences against unwelcome historic memories. Over against the intended pure attractiveness of propaganda, which one has to school oneself to resist, here we have the authentically numinous, a consistent attraction-in-repulsion; the repulsion of which – the intransigence, the wrath, the judgment of God, in this calling – one has to school oneself to endure.

Christian faith is a response to revelation in an event of the ancient world, dramatizing in the most violent manner inner freedom in conflict with a system of ruthless domination. The potential there for revelatory drama lay partly in the sheer extremity of the political background. Civil faith, by contrast, is a response to revelation in other memories: those, namely, which provide the main reference points for understanding what it means to be a citizen *today*, rather than at any other time. But for this purpose too, I have argued, the most important memories surely refer to much the same basic kind of dramatic conflict as one sees in the gospel. In many ways, most thought-provoking of all must still be the stories of Nazi and Soviet totalitarian genocide – mass-crucifixion in the modern style, at its most horrific; and the stories of resistance to those regimes, and to their heirs, from within. Those who have lived in a police state have already had a taste of the day of judgment. Those of us who have not must ask ourselves, with the most sceptical humility, how we ourselves would have fared in similar circumstances. And it is that embarrassing enquiry – indeed, precisely the embarrassment of it – which unlocks the moment of revelation in the memory.

My claim has been that there is a revelatory quality about this aspect of twentieth-century experience, to which only a certain form of civil theology can do justice. The element of revelation, for those of us who are inheritors of the culture of Christendom, lies partly in the fact that these horrors erupted in Christian Europe itself. Some church people collaborated. Others resisted. Some were inspired to resist by a strictly confessional theology. And, to that extent, it is clear that there is much to be said in favour of traditionalist confessional loyalties – also from the point of view of the critical civil theologian. But in other situations – and most notably when it came to the need to show solidarity with the Jews under the Third Reich – the ecclesiocentric bias of the stricter forms of confessionalism seems to have been very much a hindrance. At all events, the particular brand of civil theology I have been trying to open up differs from confessional theology, of any sort, first and foremost by virtue of its being a discipline of reflection *exclusively* based on just such criteria.

Among the stories of resistance there is, clearly, an especial civil-theological interest attaching to those cases where a whole church, or other religious community, has by force of circumstance been drawn into the political arena on behalf of the wider public. Take, for example, the case of the Evangelische Kirche in East Germany.

In the German Democratic Republic the churches were the only organizations allowed any independence at all from the state. Church–State relations were grounded in a fundamental compromise: in 1969 the Evangelische Kirche, by far the largest church in the country, had formally split away from its West German counterpart, and soon afterwards adopted the formula, 'We want to be neither indifferent nor hostile, but rather to be a church *within* socialism'; in exchange for which the state authorities had also informally agreed to refrain from any further outright hostilities. It may be that only a minority of pastors and church people were eager, or prepared, to make full use of the opportunities this situation provided for 'constructive' criticism of state policy; and since 1989 it has also been disclosed just how energetically the state security police worked to infiltrate church activities, at every level.[23] But, even so, in East Germany the church did offer a significant shelter for organized non-partisan dissent. It struggled in the first place to resist the creeping militarization of society: active from the early 1960s in supporting conscientious objectors to military service (a notable departure from earlier Lutheran or Reformed tradition), it protested vigorously against the introduction of new 'military instruction' classes – that is to say, yet further propaganda sessions – into the school curriculum in 1978; and was then, in the early 1980s, caught up into a major protest movement against nuclear weapons – which from the state's point of view got seriously out of hand.[24] At the same time it provided a home for civil rights campaigners. I remember, for instance, meeting a group of gay activists in Berlin in 1984; in reaction to the treatment of gay people in the Nazi period the GDR did in fact have admirable legislation prohibiting discrimination on grounds of sexual orientation, but laws alone cannot abolish prejudice; and so here they were as well – paradoxically enough, in view of the church's general moral conservatism in such matters – organizing for self-defence under its official auspices. Other church-sponsored groups, again, took up controversial ecological issues which no other sort of agency could tackle; it was a security police raid on the environmentalist library at the Zion church in Berlin, in November 1987, which precipitated the final phase of open conflict between the state and opposition groups. And then in 1989 church people played a major role in helping to initiate the revolution, steering it, keeping it peaceful. The first great demonstrations were church-organized torch-lit processions through the streets of Leipzig, an offshoot from the weekly vigil services at the Nikolai church; and this pattern was subsequently reproduced throughout the country. The original centre for the revolutionary New Forum was the Gethsemane church in Berlin. And with the collapse of Party authority at the local government level it was to a large extent church people who stepped in to help run things, through the so-called 'round-table process'; not surprisingly – since for over 40 years the only way anybody had had any actual training or practice in genuine democratic procedures had been through the church. Here then was at least one experience of a major religious institution committed, in quite dramatic fashion, to a comprehensively conceived 'antipolitical' vocation; pure antipolitics, spanning a range of different issues.

It is true that this transformation of the church into an agency of antipolitics happened only by accident, due to peculiar circumstances which more or less imposed it, without its being rooted in any very theologically thought-through civil faith – and hence its transience (on the whole).

But still – such memories do give at least a glimpse of what might, in other circumstances, be altogether more deliberately cultivated.

Notes

Introduction

1 George Mosse, *Fallen Soldiers* (London: Oxford University Press, 1990). There was, on the other hand, a more strongly civilian element in the original observance of Armistice Day than there is in that of Remembrance Sunday, since its falling on a weekday militated against the formal participation of ex-servicemen's organizations. And clearly, this did somewhat dampen down the 'Myth'. See Adrian Gregory, *The Silence of Memory: Armistice Day, 1919–46* (Oxford: Berg, 1994).

2 Robert Bellah, 'Civil religion in America', in Russell E. Richey and Donald G. Jones (eds), *American Civil Religion* (New York: Harper & Row, 1974). Bellah in fact originally presented the paper to a conference in Boston in 1965. As Martin Marty remarks, 'the date is significant because his essay reflects the liberal academicians' briefly held positive views of the American process. These were inspired by identification with the New Frontier and the Great Society of the Kennedy and early Johnson years. By the time the essay appeared, the climate had already changed, but the category remained' (*A Nation of Behavers*, Chicago, Ill.: University of Chicago Press, 1976), p. 183.

3 Bellah, 'Religion and the legitimation of the American Republic', in Robert N. Bellah and Phillip Hammond (eds), *Varieties of Civil Religion* (San Francisco, Cal.: Harper & Row, 1980), p. 15.

4 Ibid., pp. 8–10.

5 Lloyd Warner, 'An American sacred ceremony', in Richey and Jones (eds), *American Civil Religion*. And see also his *The Family of God: A Symbolic Study of Christian Life in America* (New Haven, Conn.: Yale University Press, 1961). The portrait is of the town of Newburyport, and much of Warner's actual research dates back to the 1930s.

6 'Out of the first and second times of trial have come . . . the major symbols of American civil religion. There seems little doubt that a successful negotiation of the third time of trial – the attainment of some kind of viable and coherent world order – would precipitate a major new set of symbolic forms . . . It would

necessitate the incorporation of vital international symbolism into our civil religion, or, perhaps a better way of putting it, it would result in American civil religion becoming simply one part of a new civil religion of the world . . . Indeed, such an outcome has been the eschatological hope of American civil religion from the beginning. To deny such an outcome would be to deny the meaning of America itself' (Richey and Jones (eds), *American Civil Religion*, p. 40).

7 Bellah, *The Broken Covenant: American Civil Religion in Time of Trial* (New York: Seabury Press, 1975). The immediate context for this passage is Vietnam and Watergate. See also 'American Civil Religion in the 1970s', in Richey and Jones (eds), *American Civil Religion*.

8 See Bellah's discussion of this in *The Broken Covenant*, ch. 2.

9 See Nathan O. Hatch, *The Sacred Cause of Liberty* (New Haven, Conn.: Yale University Press, 1977), ch. 1. But cf. George Armstrong Kelly, *Politics and Religious Consciousness in America* (New Brunswick: Transaction Books, 1984), pp. 215–19. Kelly's thesis by contrast is that, strictly speaking, American civil religion should be seen as a phenomenon of the late nineteenth century, coming into its own in the aftermath of the Civil War and starting to fade away around the turn of the century, with Woodrow Wilson 'perhaps [its] last genuine articulator'. But this is because he measures the prevalence of civil religion exclusively in terms of the degree of integrative consensus obtaining: thus, the period he has in mind was a period when the mainstream Protestant denominations in America had, in a competitive way, converged, to form the various sub-divisions of a single dominant culture, such as had not existed before; and which could not altogether survive the influx of new immigrants. The same interpretative slant also emerges, for instance, in his incidental characterisation of Calvin's Geneva as a classic centre of Christian civil religion (p. 220). Certainly, this was an example of integrative consensus, doing away with the old boundaries between the church and the world; but I would not therefore call it 'civil religious'. It was an attempt to create a confessional theocracy. Kelly's usage, in short, seems to me both too narrow and too broad to be helpful. Not only is civil religion potentially more than just social cement; at the same time not all that binds a state together religiously is civil.

10 Agnes Heller proposes an alternative way of drawing the necessary distinctions here: describing what obtained in Fascist Italy, the USSR before Stalin and the Soviet bloc after Stalin as 'totalitarianism', simply, but the Hitler and Stalin regimes (or Pol Pot's Cambodia) as 'terroristic totalitarianism': in F. Feher, A. Heller and G. Markus, *Dictatorship over Needs: An Analysis of Soviet Societies* (Oxford: Basil Blackwell, 1983). At any rate, some such distinction clearly is needed, if the word is to be more than just a loosely ideological expression.

11 One early example of the new usage is the article by the émigré Czech writer Jacques Rupnik, 'Dissent in Poland, 1968–78: the end of revisionism and the rebirth of civil society in Poland', in Rudolf Tökes (ed.), *Opposition in Eastern Europe* (London: Macmillan, 1979). Polish thinkers especially, such as Adam Michnik, also began to speak in similar terms. See Z.A. Pelczynski, 'Solidarity and "The Rebirth of Civil Society" in Poland, 1976–81', in John Keane (ed.), *Civil Society and the State* (London: Verso, 1988); Václav Havel et al., *The Power*

of the Powerless: Citizens against the State in Central-Eastern Europe (London: Hutchinson, 1985); V. Benda et al., 'Parallel Polis', in *Social Research*, 55 (1988), 211–46.

For what follows see also the other articles in *Civil Society and the State*: in particular John Keane, 'Despotism and democracy'; Norberto Bobbio, 'Gramsci and the concept of civil society'.

Keith Tester, in his book *Civil Society* (London: Routledge, 1992), has sought to argue that the concept is intrinsically incoherent. His argument, however, seems to me to be vitiated by a failure to recognize just how different the new usage is from earlier ones. Thus, in particular, he assimilates it to earlier liberal arguments for 'democracy'; yet is this not exactly what Havel for instance rejects, in counterposing to 'post-totalitarianism' an altogether more radical ideal of '*post*-democracy'? (See below, pp. 200–1.)

12 Ferdinand Tönnies, *Gemeinschaft und Gesellschaft* (1887); English trans. published as *Community and Association* (London: Routledge & Kegan Paul, 1955) p. 251 (translation adapted); although cf. pp. 38–9.

13 Keane (*Civil Society and the State*, p. 67) finds the earliest formulation in the opening paragraph of Paine's *Common Sense* (Philadelphia, 1776), where the contrast is grounded in two different functions: 'Society is produced by our wants, and government by our wickedness; the former promotes our happiness *positively* by uniting our affections, the latter *negatively* by restraining our vices. The one encourages intercourse, the other creates distinctions. The first is a patron, the last a punisher'. But the chief problem he seeks to address is the tendency of the state to seek to over-reach its properly negative role.

14 See E.P. Thompson, *Double Exposure* (London: Merlin, 1985). And cf. also Thompson's other splendid writings of this period: *Protest and Survive* (Harmondsworth, Middx: Penguin, 1980); *Zero Option* (London: Merlin, 1982); *The Heavy Dancers* (London: Merlin, 1984).

15 Václav Havel, *Letters to Olga: June 1979–September 1982*, English trans. Paul Wilson (London: Faber & Faber, 1988), p. 288.

16 Havel, *Living in Truth*, English trans. ed. Jan Vladislav (London: Faber & Faber, 1987), p. 167.

17 Ibid., p. 168.

18 Ibid., p. 182.

19 G.W.F. Hegel, *Philosophy of Right*, Preface, English trans. T.M. Knox (London: Oxford University Press, 1952), p. 13.

20 Dorothee Sölle, *Political Theology*, English trans. J. Shelley (Philadelphia: Fortress Press, 1974), p. 89.

21 The official propaganda of the German Democratic Republic is the classic case. But compare, also, the way in which the commemoration of the Holocaust in Israel has become infused with nationalistic sentiment.

22 Einstein's famous remark, quoted in Jonathan Schell, *The Fate of the Earth* (London: Picador, 1982), p. 188.

23 *The Challenge of Peace: God's Promise and Our Response: The US Bishops' Pastoral Letter on War and Peace in the Nuclear Age* (London: Catholic Truth Society, 1983); *The Church and the Bomb* (London: Hodder & Stoughton, 1982): report of a working party under the chairmanship of the Bishop of Salisbury, for the Church of England's General Synod Board of Social Responsibility.

24 Bellah, 'Civil religion in America', p. 33. For a (later) example of what he is criticizing, see J. Moltmann, 'Christian theology and political religion', in L.S. Rouner, *Civil Religion and Political Theology* (Notre Dame, Ind.: University of Indiana Press, 1986), pp. 41–58.

25 F. Nietzsche, *The Anti-Christ*, §533; trans. R.J. Hollingdale, *The Twilight of the Idols/The Anti-Christ* (Harmondsworth, Middx: Penguin, 1968), p. 170.

26 Following Erik Peterson, he takes this as classic evidence for the true political rationale of orthodox trinitarianism: see, for instance, *The Crucified God* (London: SCM Press, 1974), pp. 325–6.

27 Andrew Shanks, *Hegel's Political Theology* (Cambridge: Cambridge University Press, 1991), pp. 4–13.

Chapter 1 Negative Revelation

1 Emil Fackenheim, *God's Presence in History* (New York: Harper Torchbooks, 1972), *The Jewish Return into History: Reflections in the Age of Auschwitz and a New Jerusalem* (New York: Schocken Books, 1978), *To Mend the World* (New York: Schocken Books, 1982).

2 Hannah Arendt refers to two of Weil's works in the footnotes to *The Human Condition* (Chicago, Ill.: Chicago University Press, 1958): *La condition ouvrière* and an article, 'Réflexions à propos de la théorie des quanta', in *Cahiers du Sud*, December 1942. Of the former she remarks that it is perhaps 'the only book in the huge literature on the labour question which deals with the problem without prejudice and sentimentality'.

3 See in particular Arendt's contribution to 'Religion and the intellectuals', *Partisan Review*, 17 (Feb. 1950). The editors had invited a number of prominent figures to comment on what was perceived as a general revival of interest in religion among English-speaking intellectuals at the time. Among the questions they asked were: 'Can culture exist without a positive religion?' and: 'Is a return to religion necessary in order to counter the new means of social discipline that we all fear: totalitarianism?' Arendt replied that it is really quite comical to suppose institutional religion might be justified by such spin-offs: 'The idea of somebody making up his mind to believe in God, follow His Commandments, praying to Him and going regularly to Church, so that poets again may have some inspiration and culture be "integrated", is simply exhilarating ... The same is true, of course, with respect to the use of religion as a weapon against totalitarianism or "a safeguard for civilized tradition" ' (p. 115). The actual record of religious institutions under totalitarianism hardly suggests that this is likely to be a very successful strategy; and, besides, true faith cannot be instrumentalized in this sort of way.

   Taking religious faith as a fixed datum, however, and then seeking to use it as a 'weapon' against totalitarianism is one thing, and opening oneself up to the possibility that there might be something theologically 'revelatory' in such experiences as that of totalitarianism is another thing altogether. And who can tell whether it might not make at least some difference to the quality of the resistance if the latter attitude were to prevail, in actual practice?

For an earlier theological discussion of Arendt's thought, see James Bernauer, 'The faith of Hannah Arendt: Amor Mundi and its critique – assimilation of religious experience', in the volume also edited by him, *Amor Mundi: Explorations in the Faith and Thought of Hannah Arendt* (Boston, Mass., Dordrecht and Lancaster: Martinus Nijhoff, 1987).

4 On this latter point, see F.-W. Marquardt, *Theologie und Sozialismus: das Beispiel Karl Barths* (Munich: Kaiser Grünewald, 1972).

5 Václav Havel, 'Politics and conscience', in his *Living in Truth*, English trans. ed. Jan Vladislav (London: Faber & Faber, 1987), p. 146. And cf., for instance, Z. Bauman, *Modernity and the Holocaust* (Cambridge: Polity Press, 1989).

6 Arendt, *The Human Condition*, p. 40.

7 Ibid., p. 46. On the place of Arendt's critical meditation on Marxism in the general evolution of her thinking, see Margaret Canovan, *Hannah Arendt: A Reinterpretation of her Political Thought* (Cambridge: Cambridge University Press, 1992), ch. 3. It is what links *The Origins of Totalitarianism* (London: George Allen & Unwin, 1967) to *The Human Condition*. Arendt initially meant to follow up the former book, lop-sided as it is in its concentration on Nazism, with a second, separate book on 'Totalitarian Elements in Marxism'. (The two do, after all, have quite different sorts of pre-history, in her view: Nazism as a form of totalitarianism arising out of 'subterranean currents' essentially alien to the mainstream Western intellectual tradition; Marxism as a form of totalitarianism arising directly out of that mainstream.) This second book, however, was never written; its argument was absorbed instead into *The Human Condition*. Canovan is surely right, however, to emphasize the essential underlying continuity of Arendt's concerns through all her writing, even where the ostensible subject matter seems to shift.

8 Arendt, *The Human Condition*, p. 43.

9 Ibid., p. 33.

10 Ibid., p. 29.

11 Ibid., p. 43.

12 For what follows, see especially ibid., pp. 38–9, and *Between Past and Future* (London: Faber, 1961), pp. 199–200.

13 Arendt, *Between Past and Future*, p. 199.

14 Hannah Arendt, *On Revolution* (Harmondsworth, Middx: Penguin, 1973), p. 105.

15 This is the main theme of Chapter 2 of ibid.

16 Arendt, *The Human Condition*, pp. 215–20.

17 See Canovan, *Hannah Arendt*, p. 120: 'We can best understand the conjunction of the two by recalling that within the vocabulary of the European intelligentsia from which Arendt came, "bourgeois" was a term of opprobrium referring both to capitalist economics and to social philistinism . . . [T]hat traditional prejudice against the bourgeoisie was conspicuous in *Totalitarianism*, but what is perhaps more important is that it was complemented there by the distinction between "bourgeois" and "citoyen". In criticizing "society", Arendt was not issuing an unqualified condemnation of modernity. . . .'

18 Michael Oakeshott, 'Dr Leo Strauss on Hobbes', in *Hobbes on Civil Association* (Oxford: Basil Blackwell, 1975), pp. 147–8.

19 See below, pp. 96–100, 108–14, for a fuller discussion of both Hobbes and Hegel as 'civil theologians'.

20 Arendt, *The Human Condition*, p. 31.
21 It is true that considered in abstraction from the polemic it does seem somewhat arbitrary – as Bhikhu Parekh, for instance, argues, in *Hannah Arendt and the Search for a New Political Philosophy* (London: Macmillan, 1981), pp. 108–10. But I cannot see that that invalidates it, as he perhaps somewhat pedantically suggests.
22 Thomas Hobbes, *Leviathan*, Introduction; and see Arendt, *The Human Condition*, pp. 299–301.
23 On the complexities of Arendt's notion of 'action', see Canovan, *Hannah Arendt*, pp. 136–43. Drawing on the unpublished manuscripts of lecture notes, both pre-dating and post-dating *Human Condition*, Canovan is able to show the unsettled shifting back and forth of her thinking on the subject. Whereas in *The Human Condition* the ancient *polis* appears as the primary model of a culture properly appreciative of the potentiality of action, elsewhere she associates action far more with what Homer portrays in a figure like Achilles: the violent enterprises of the heroic warrior. In this context, the *polis*, with its relatively peaceable internal order, may appear as a culture which has successfully tamed that earlier ethos – to some extent at least subordinating the glory of heroic violence to the glory of noble speech. Here it is the destructive potential of action which is to the forefront of her mind. And, notwithstanding her apparent idealization of ancient Athens in *The Human Condition*, she can also speak very critically of the 'intense and uninterrupted contest of all against all' which it continued to glorify in this way: as a spirit which 'poisoned the domestic life of the citizens with envy and mutual hatred', a 'reckless individualism' which 'eventually brought the *polis* to its doom'.
24 See Paul Franco, *The Political Philosophy of Michael Oakeshott* (New Haven, Conn.: Yale University Press, 1990), pp. 222ff.
25 Arendt, *On Revolution*, p. 30. She refers here to two sources in particular: Herodotus, Book III, 80–2, and Thucydides, Book III, 82.8. The notion of isonomy as 'no-rule' comes out most clearly in the passage from Herodotus. The context is the *coup d'état* in which the government of Smerdis the Magus has been overthrown in Persia. The seven conspirators are debating the future form of government. One of them, their leader Otanes, advocates isonomy. He also calls it 'the rule of the people'; but when he loses the debate, and the others decide for a system of kingship instead, he declines to stand as a candidate for the throne, declaring, 'I want neither to rule nor to be ruled'.

Thucydides, on the other hand, deplores what he sees as the dishonesty of factional politicians: with those who really favour democracy dressing it up in the fairer sounding name of isonomy, just as those who really favour oligarchy prefer to speak of 'moderate aristocracy'.

For a detailed discussion, see Gregory Vlastos, 'Isonomia', in *American Journal of Philology*, LXXIV (1953), 337–66. Vlastos argues that *demokratia* was a later word, not yet known to Herodotus.

'Isonomy' evidently did have very positive connotations: so much so that even Plato, paradoxically, wants to call his ideal 'a just and isonomous constitution' (*Seventh Letter* 326d) – although one should also note the hostile references to isonomy in *The Republic* (561e and 563b). And cf. Thucydides (III, 62.3), where reference is made to the possibility of 'isonomous oligarchy': 'oligarchic' because restricting citizenship to a minority of the native born.

(Aristotle also uses 'democracy' as a derogatory term; but he speaks of it as the corrupt version of 'polity', *politeia*.)

26 For Arendt's revaluation of opinion, see especially *On Revolution*, pp. 226–9; and the essay on Lessing in *Men in Dark Times* (London: Jonathan Cape, 1970). This clearly also relates to her argument about 'truth' and 'meaning' in *The Life of the Mind*, vol. 1: *Thinking* (London: Secker & Warburg, 1978).

27 Plato, *The Republic*, 420; and see Arendt, *The Human Condition*, pp. 220–7.

28 See the discussion of Aristotle in *Between Past and Future*, pp. 115–120.

29 Aristotle, *Metaphysics*, 1025b25 ff, 1064a17 ff; Arendt, *The Human Condition*, pp. 301–2.

30 *Aristotle*, Politics, 1332b12, 1332b36.

31 Arendt, *Between Past and Future*, p. 106.

32 See below, pp. 126–36, 189–99.

33 See Hannah Arendt, *The Life of the Mind*, vol. 2: *Willing* (London: Secker & Warburg, 1978), Part II; and the essay, 'What is freedom?', in *Between Past and Future*.

34 She refers to Aristotle, for example: *Nicomachaean Ethics*, 1166b5–25.

35 Arendt, *Between Past and Future*, pp. 128–35.

36 Arendt, *The Human Condition*, pp. 18–19; and see also pp. 55–6.

37 Hannah Arendt, *The Jew as Pariah: Jewish Identity and Politics in the Modern Age*, ed. R.H. Feldman (New York: Grove Books, 1978), p. 76. Her *Rahel Varnhagen* (New York: Harcourt Brace Jovanovich, 1974) is the study of a parvenu who nevertheless managed to 'salvage her pariah qualities'.

38 Arendt, *Men in Dark Times*, pp. 31–8.

39 Hannah Arendt, *On Violence* (New York: Harcourt, Brace & World, 1970), p. 28. Arendt was at the same time quite critical of the student movement, insofar as it turned its attack onto the university system, not only for selling out to the military-industrial establishment as a major funder of research – a criticism she wholeheartedly endorsed – but, more generally, for its 'elitism'. (For when is the cause of academic excellence not 'elitist'?) See Elizabeth Young-Bruehl's biography, *Hannah Arendt: For Love of the World* (New Haven: Yale University Press, 1982), pp. 416–19.

40 Arendt, *Between Past and Future*, p. 100.

41 Ibid. p. 91.

42 Ibid., pp. 101–3 (my emphasis). Another example she cites is 'the widespread conviction in the free world today that communism is a new "religion", notwithstanding its avowed atheism, because it fulfills socially, psychologically, and "emotionally" the same function traditional religion fulfilled and still fulfills in the free world'. To which she adds: 'It is as though I had the right to call the heel of my shoe a hammer because I, like most women, use it to drive nails into the wall.'

43 Ibid., p. 99 (my emphasis).

44 Ibid., p. 100.

45 Ibid., p. 122 (Cicero, *De Legibus* 3. 12. 38).

46 Ibid., pp. 121–2.

47 Ibid., p. 125.

48 See the account of the furore in Elizabeth Young-Bruehl, *Hannah Arendt: For Love of the World* (New Haven, Conn.: Yale University Press, 1982), Chapter 8.

49 Arendt, *The Life of the Mind*, vol. 1: *Thinking*, p. 4.

50 See Young-Bruehl, *Hannah Arendt*, p. 369. She refers here partly to Arendt's notes for an unpublished lecture delivered in 1964; and partly to *The Life of the Mind*, vol. 1, pp. 3–5.

51 See, for example, Carole E. Adams, 'Hannah Arendt and the historian: Nazism and the New Order', in Gisela T. Kaplan and Clive S. Kessler (eds), *Hannah Arendt: Thinking, Judging, Freedom* (Sydney: Allen & Unwin, 1989).

52 Young-Bruehl, *Hannah Arendt*, p. 369.

53 The full correspondence is to be found in *Encounter*, January 1964, pp. 51–6.

54 Martin Heidegger, *What Is Called Thinking?*, English trans. J. Glenn Gray (New York: Harper & Row, 1968), p. 159.

55 Arendt, *Thinking*, pp. 62–3.

56 Ibid., p. 15.

57 Ibid., p. 123.

58 Cicero, *De Republica*, I. 17.

59 Plato, *Theaetetus*, 155d; Arendt, *Thinking*, pp. 141–3.

60 Arendt, *Thinking*, pp. 40–5. (This is of course the exact opposite of Schopenhauer's view, that we encounter the noumenal in our experience of pre-calculative, impulsive inner restlessness.)

61 Of course it does require *some* moral input – as Agnes Heller objects in her essay 'Hannah Arendt on the "Vita Contemplativa" ', in Kaplan and Kessler, *Hannah Arendt*, pp. 154–7. But this hardly seems to me a crushing objection.

62 Arendt, *Thinking*, p. 188. Cf. Plato, *Gorgias*, 474b, 482c.

63 Kaplan and Kessler, *Hannah Arendt*, pp. 144–5.

64 See George L. Mosse, *The Crisis of German Ideology: Intellectual Origins of the Third Reich* (London: Weidenfeld & Nicolson, 1966).

65 Simone Weil, *The Need for Roots*, English trans. A.F. Wills (London: Routledge & Kegan Paul, 1952), p. 42.

66 See, in particular, her article 'Reflections on the origins of Hitlerism', in *Selected Essays, 1934–1943*, English trans. R. Rhees (London: Oxford University Press, 1962), p. 101: 'The analogy between the systems of Hitler and of Ancient Rome is so striking that one might believe that Hitler alone, after two thousand years, has understood directly how to copy the Romans.'

67 Weil, *The Need for Roots*, p. 45.

68 Simone Weil, *Oppression and Liberty* (London: Routledge & Kegan Paul, 1958), p. 101.

69 Ibid., p. 106.

70 On her 'determination to live like a man', see Simone Pétrement's monumental biography, *Simone Weil*, English trans. (London: Mowbrays, 1976), pp. 27–8.

71 Weil, *Oppression and Liberty*, p. 104.

72 Ibid.: 'It is not a question of anything comparable to the religion of production which reigned in America during the period of prosperity, and has reigned in Russia since the Five Year Plan [this was written in 1934]; for the true object of that religion is the product of work and not the worker, material objects and not man.'

73 Ibid., p. 106.

74 Ibid., p. 107.

75 Ibid., p. 105.

76　Ibid., p. 107; Weil, *The Need for Roots*, p. 91. In the latter passage she also refers, for instance, to the papal encyclicals of Leo XIII.

77　Weil, *Oppression and Liberty*, p. 19.

78　Weil still remains perhaps the most eloquent exponent of this point of view. See David McLellan, *Simone Weil: Utopian Pessimist* (London: Macmillan, 1989), Ch. 4. Her most systematic discussion of Marxism is in *Oppression and Liberty*, pp. 39–56, 147–55, 169–95.

79　Weil, *The Need for Roots*, p. 164.

80　Ibid., p. 140.

81　Ibid., p. 126.

82　Simone Weil, *Gravity and Grace* (London: Routledge, 1952), pp. 144–5.

83　On this eccentrically Christianizing view of Plato, see McLellan, *Simone Weil*, pp. 202–11: 'Her *Notebooks* show us a Plato who is just as much a disciple of Weil as Weil is of Plato.'

84　My emphasis. *Simone Weil, Cahiers* 3, p.120. The best systematic study of this whole aspect of Weil's thought remains that of Miklos Vetö, *La métaphysique religieuse de Simone Weil* (Paris: Vrin, 1971).

85　Arendt, *Willing*, ch. 15.

86　Weil, *Gravity and Grace*, p. 105.

87　Ibid., pp. 12–13.

88　Ibid., p. 29.

89　*Weil, Cahiers*, vol. 3, p. 230. Revelation 13: 8. The similarity of this understanding of creation to the Cabbalistic concept of 'tzimtzum', as developed by Isaac Luria and his followers – or to the related speculations of Schelling, for instance – appears to be quite coincidental.

90　Simone Weil, *Waiting for God*, trans. Emma Craufurd (New York: Harper & Row, 1951), p. 111.

91　Weil, *Gravity and Grace*, p. 34. My emphasis.

92　Ibid., p. 152.

93　Ibid. p. 151.

94　Arendt, *The Human Condition*, p.73.

95　Ibid., p. 74.

96　Matthew 6: 3–4.

97　Arendt, *The Human Condition*, p. 74.

98　Ibid., p. 75.

99　Luke 18: 19.

100　Arendt, *The Human Condition*, p. 76. She contrasts the loneliness of the lover of goodness with the solitude of the lover of wisdom, the philosopher.

101　Weil, *Gravity and Grace*, p. 146. Her most committed involvement in politics was in the three years 1931–4, when she was a very active trade unionist. But already in March 1934 she writes, 'I have decided to withdraw entirely from any kind of political activity, except for theoretical work' (Simone Pétrement, *Simone Weil* (London: Mowbrays, 1976), p. 198). Her religious conversion dates from 1938.

　　Cf. Conor Cruise O'Brien's critique of her 'antipolitics', from the perspective of a professional politician: 'Patriotism and *The Need for Roots*: the antipolitics of Simone Weil', in George Abbott White (ed.), *Simone Weil: Interpretations of a Life* (Amherst, Mass.: University of Massachusetts Press, 1981).

102 Arendt, *The Human Condition* pp. 51–2. Arendt's doctoral thesis was on *Der Liebesbegriff bei Augustin* (Berlin: J. Springer, 1929). See Patrick Boyle, 'Elusive neighbourliness: Hannah Arendt's interpretation of Saint Augustine', in Bernauer (ed.), *Amor Mundi*.

103 Ibid., p. 53.

104 Ibid., p. 54; and see also p. 314.

105 See Arendt, *On Revolution*, p. 280, where she describes 'freedom from politics' as 'one of the most important negative liberties we have enjoyed since the end of the ancient world . . . unknown to Rome or Athens and . . . politically perhaps the most relevant part of our Christian heritage'.

106 Matthew 5: 41.

107 Luke 6: 37; Matthew 7: 1.

108 Matthew 6: 34.

109 Arendt, *The Human Condition*, pp. 238–43, 246–7.

110 Machiavelli, *The Prince*, ch. 15; Arendt, *The Human Condition*, p. 77; Arendt, *Between Past and Future*, p. 137.

111 *The Letters of Machiavelli*, ed. Allan Gilbert (New York: Capricorn Books, 1981) no. 225. Arendt, *On Revolution*, p. 286: 'We, who no longer take for granted the immortality of the soul, are apt to overlook the poignancy of Machiavelli's credo. At the time he wrote, the expression was no cliché but meant literally one was prepared to forfeit an everlasting life or to risk the punishments of hell for the sake of one's city. The question, as Machiavelli saw it, was not whether one loved God more than the world, but whether one was capable of loving the world more than one's own self. And this decision indeed has always been the crucial decision for all who devoted their lives to politics.'

112 Arendt, *On Revolution*, pp. 82–8.

113 Ibid., p. 89.

114 Ibid., p. 88.

115 This is more or less the argument George Kateb develops, in his study, *Hannah Arendt: Politics, Conscience, Evil* (Oxford: Martin Robertson, 1984), esp. ch. 3.

116 *Early Christian Writings*, trans. Maxwell Staniforth (Harmondsworth, Middx: Penguin, 1968), p. 230.

117 Cf. Chancellor Helmut Schmidt's response, in 1981, to those who invoked the Sermon on the Mount against the NATO deployment of nuclear weapons in Germany: 'I consider it quite wrong to take the Sermon on the Mount as a canon for affairs of state. It wasn't meant that way; it was addressed to another community, in another context, in another age' (in Wolfgang Brinkel, Burckhardt Scheffler and Martin Wächter (eds), *Christen im Streit um den Frieden*, Freiburg: Dreisam-Verlag, 1982, p. 57).

Chapter 2   Religion, Civility, Faith

1 The title of perhaps the most notable of Kierkegaard's *Edifying Addresses*, written in 1846.

2 Søren Kierkegaard, *The Concept of Anxiety*, English trans. R. Thomte and A.B. Andersen (Prnceton, N.J.: Princeton University Press, 1980), p. 42.

3 Søren Kierkegaard, *Journals and Papers*, English trans. H.V. Hong and E.H. Hong (Bloomington, Ind.: Indiana University Press, 1967–78), vol. I, §699.

4 Søren Kierkegaard, *Philosophical Fragments*, English trans. D.F. Swenson, 2nd edn, rev. H. Hong (Princeton, N.J.: Princeton University Press, 1962), p. 130.

5 Kierkegaard, *Journals and Papers*, vol. I, §323.

6 Hence the importance Kierkegaard attaches in particular to Lessing's statement of principle, discussed at length in *Concluding Unscientific Postscript:* 'Accidental truths of history can never become the *proof* of necessary truths of reason.'

7 Søren Kierkegaard, *The Sickness Unto Death*, English trans. A. Hannay (Harmondsworth, Middx: Penguin, 1989), pp. 121–2.

8 Alasdair MacIntyre, *After Virtue* (London: Duckworth, 1981), pp. 39–45.

9 Karl Barth, *The Epistle to the Romans*, English trans. Edwyn C. Hoskins (London: Oxford University Press, 1933), p. 269.

10 See, for example, E.P. Sanders, *Paul and Palestinian Judaism* (London: SCM Press, 1977).

11 Kierkegaard, *Journals and Papers*, vol. III, §2548.

12 Barth, *The Epistle to the Romans*, p. 240.

13 Ibid., p. 258.

14 Ibid., pp. 252–3.

15 Ibid., p. 268.

16 Karl Barth, *Church Dogmatics*, vol. I, part 2, English trans. G.T. Thomson and H. Knight (Edinburgh: T. & T. Clark, 1956), p. 280.

17 Ibid., pp. 299 ff.

18 Ibid., p. 325.

19 Barth, *The Epistle to the Romans*, p. 269.

20 An English version of the Declaration appears in Clifford Green (ed.), *Karl Barth: Theologian of Freedom* (London: Collins, 1989), pp. 148–51.

21 Quoted in Richard Gutteridge, *Open Thy Mouth for the Dumb* (Oxford: Basil Blackwell, 1976), pp. 303–4.

22 Eberhard Busch, *Karl Barth*, English trans. John Bowden (London: SCM Press, 1976), p. 248. More generally, cf. his 'confession' in 1945, addressed 'to German theologians in prisoner-of-war camps': 'I . . . confess that, if I reproach myself for anything when I look back on the years I spent in Germany [1921–35], it is that, out of sheer concentration on my churchly and theological task . . . I failed . . . to give a warning, not just implicitly, but explicitly, not merely privately but also publicly . . . against the tendencies in the Church and the world about me' (quoted in Eberhard Bethge, *Dietrich Bonhoeffer*, English trans. London: Collins, 1970, p. 92).

23 First of all by Barth himself: see his remarks in his 'Letter to Superintendent Herrenbrück', in Ronald Gregor Smith (ed.), *World Come of Age: A Symposium on Dietrich Bonhoeffer* (London: Collins, 1967). The same is true, for instance, of the other articles in the same collection; or of Heinrich Ott's substantial study, *Reality and Faith: The Theological Legacy of Dietrich Bonhoeffer*, English trans. (Philadelphia: Fortress Press, 1972).

On Bonhoeffer's very early understanding of the necessity for solidarity with the Jews, see Bethge, *Dietrich Bonhoeffer*, pp. 206–10, 234 ff.

So pervasive was theological anti-Semitism in that culture, it has also to be conceded that even his thinking still shows residual traces of it: as in *No Rusty*

Swords, English trans. (London: Collins, 1970), p. 222. But the basic thrust is in the opposite direction. See, for instance, the discussion in Emil Fackenheim's two books: *The Jewish Return to History* (New York: Schocken Books, 1978), pp. 35–6, 74–5; and *The Jewish Bible after the Holocaust* (Manchester: Manchester University Press, 1990).

24 Dietrich Bonhoeffer, *Letters and Papers from Prison*, ed. Eberhard Bethge, English trans., enlarged edn (London: SCM Press, 1971), p. 286; and cf. also pp. 280, 382.

25 Immanuel Kant, 'An answer to the question: What is Enlightenment?', in *Kant's Political Writings*, ed. H. Reiss (Cambridge: Cambridge University Press, 1970), p. 54.

26 Bonhoeffer, *Letters and Papers from Prison*, pp. 285–6. My emphases.

27 Ibid., p. 380.

28 Friedrich Schleiermacher, *On Religion: Speeches to its Cultured Despisers*, trans. Richard Crouter (Cambridge: Cambridge University Press, 1988), vol. IV, pp. 165–7.

29 Ibid., p. 177.

30 This is also, for instance, what Stanley Hauerwas eloquently advocates: see his books *A Community of Character* (Notre Dame, Ind.: University of Notre Dame Press, 1981) and *The Peaceable Kingdom* (London: SCM Press, 1984).

31 For an eavesdropping portrait of a Latin American basic community at work, see Ernesto Cardenal, *Love in Practice: The Gospel in Solentiname*, English trans. (London: Search Press, 1977). On the Hungarian phenomenon, and especially the struggle of the pacifist followers of Father Bulanyi against both the state and the church authorities, see Steven Polgar, 'A summary of the situation of the Hungarian Catholic Church', *Religion in Communist Lands*, 12(1984), 11–38; also the documentation, ibid., 38–44, 215–26; 11 (1983), 95–108; 15 (1987), 346–50.

32 Bonhoeffer, *Letters and Papers from Prison*, p. 382.

33 A central theme of Michel Foucault's lecture course for 1977–8 at the Collège de France: see the *Annuaire du Collège de France*, 78.

34 Psalms 23; 28: 9; 77: 20; 78: 52; 79: 13; 80: 1; 95: 7; Isaiah 40: 10–11; 49: 9–10; Jeremiah 31: 10; Ezekiel 34: 11–31; Micah 4: 8; 7: 14.

35 Jeremiah 10: 21; 23: 1–4; 25: 34; 50: 6; Ezekiel 34: 2–10; Zechariah 10: 2; 11: 4–17.

36 Ezekiel 34: 23. See also Zechariah 12: 10 and 13: 7.

37 John 10: 1–30. See also Matthew 9: 36; 10: 6; 15: 24; 26: 31; Mark 6: 34; 14: 27; Hebrews 13: 20; 1 Peter 2: 25; Revelation 7: 17.

38 John 21: 15–17.

39 1 Peter 5: 1–4. See also Acts 20: 28–9; Ephesians 4: 11.

40 The argument is known to us chiefly from Augustine's attack upon it in *The City of God*, especially Books 6 and 7. The tradition Varro is developing actually distinguishes between (a) 'natural theology', which is the concern of philosophy, dealing with the universal underlying truth of religion; (b) 'mythical theology', which is the work of poets, dealing with sacred narratives; and (c) 'civil theology' (*theologia civilis*), as the empirical study of actual religious practices, dealing with their *usefulness*, in general. But, being a Roman, he naturally conceives of this usefulness above all in terms of the prosperity of the city, as such. The secret of Rome's greatness, he argues, lies in the piety of the people, which therefore needs to be fostered.

41 Niccoló Machiavelli, *The Discourses*, English trans. Leslie J. Walker SJ (Harmondsworth, Middx: Penguin, 1970), Book I, p. 11.

42 Ibid., Book I, p. 12.

43 Ibid., Book II, p. 2.

44 Michael Oakeshott, Hobbes on *Civil Association* (Oxford: Basil Blackwell, 1975), p. 71.

45 Thomas Hobbes, *Leviathan*, ch. 31. And there is perhaps some justice in F.C. Hood's remark that this is 'one of the weakest chapters in the book', and that in general 'the kingdom of God by nature was of minor interest to Hobbes . . . [He] never gave to this part of his argument the deep and recurrent thought which he devoted to other parts' (*The Divine Politics of Thomas Hobbes*, London: Oxford University Press, 1964, p. 226).

46 Leo Strauss actually stresses Hobbes's evident indifference to the political dangers that might be inherent in the spread of unbelief as one of the most pioneering aspects of his thought; a lamentable modern departure, in Strauss's view, from the wiser caution of the secretly unbelieving ancients. See, in particular, his discussion of Hobbes in *Natural Right and History* (Chicago, Ill.: University of Chicago Press, 1953) and *The Political Philosophy of Hobbes* (Chicago, Ill.: University of Chicago Press, 1952).

For a summary of the recent debate, see A. P. Martinich, *The Two Gods of Leviathan: Thomas Hobbes on Religion and Politics* (Cambridge: Cambridge University Press, 1992). Martinich attempts a systematic refutation of the prevailing 'secularist' reading of Hobbes. (I think he somewhat overstates his case, though, when he calls Hobbes a 'Calvinist': surely, not everyone who like Hobbes is anti-scholastic and anti-Arminian is *ipso facto* a positive Calvinist. Hobbes's presbyterian opponents were Calvinists – but his theology, by contrast, was much too original for such a label to fit).

47 Thomas Hobbes, *Opera*, ed. Sir William Molesworth (London, 1839–45), vol. III, pp. 561–2.

48 Hobbes, *Leviathan* (Cambridge: Cambridge University Press edition, 1991), ch. XLV; and cf. ch. XII.

49 Ibid., ch. XLVII, pp. 475–6; and cf. pp. 427–8.

50 Ibid., ch. XLI.

51 Ibid., ch. XLII, pp. 375–7.

52 Ibid., ch. XLVII, pp. 479–80.

53 Ibid., ch. XLII, p. 341.

54 Ibid., ch. XXXVI, p. 299.

55 Ibid., ch. XXXIX, p. 322.

56 Ibid., ch. XXXII, p. 259, and cf. ch. XXXVII.

57 Ibid., ch. XXXVI, pp. 294 ff.

58 Ibid., ch. XL, p. 324.

59 Ibid., ch. XLII, p. 374.

60 Ibid., ch. XLII, pp. 342 ff, 399–400; ch. XLIII, pp. 413–4.

61 Ibid., ch. XLII, p. 389.

62 Schmitt's *magnum opus* is available in English translation: *Political Theology* (Cambridge, Mass.: MIT, Press, 1985). For a later statement of his view of Hobbes, however, see his article in *Der Staat*, 4 (1965), 51–69.

63 Benedict de Spinoza, *Tractatus Theologico-Politicus*, ch. 14; English trans. R.H.M. Elwes as *The Chief Works of Benedict de Spinoza* (New York: Dover, 1951), vol. I, pp. 186–7.

64 Such was the scandal, even in the relatively liberal atmosphere of the Netherlands, that Spinoza had the work published anonymously, in Latin, and tried to prevent its publication in a Dutch translation. Four years after publication, it was banned by the States-General.

   Not that Spinoza was altogether alone in holding such ideas at the time. There existed in particular the community of the Collegiants – effectively, the Dutch equivalent to the Quakers – whom he never joined, but amongst whom he lived for some years following his expulsion from the Jewish community.

65 Spinoza, *Tractatus Theologico-Politicus*, ch. 14, Elwes, trans., p. 189.

66 On Spinoza's tactical mobilization of Christian anti-Semitic prejudice here, in his struggle against prejudice in general, see Leo Strauss's preface to the English version of his *Spinoza's Critique of Religion* (New York: Schocken Books, 1965).

67 Jean-Jacques Rousseau, *The Social Contract*, English trans. Maurice Cranston (Harmondsworth, Middx: Penguin, 1968), p. 180.

68 Rousseau refers in passing to Spinoza as an 'atheist': 'Lettre à M. de Beaumont' (1763), in *Religious Writings*, ed. R. Grimsley (London: Oxford University Press, 1970), p. 234.

69 Ibid., p. 270.

70 Rousseau, *The Social Contract*, pp. 182–4.

71 Ibid., p. 182. In this sense, Rousseau did claim to be a good Christian himself: 'Lettre à M. de Beaumont', p. 264.

72 The Savoyard Vicar is a Catholic priest, and aspires to be a good one; but his protégé was born a Calvinist. Like the adolescent Rousseau himself, this young man has run away South from his native Geneva, and allowed himself to be converted to Catholicism in exchange for food and shelter in an almshouse for proselytes. The good Vicar urges him to go back home and return to the religion of his fathers. For the original autobiographical basis for this story, see Jean-Jacques Rousseau, *The Confessions*, English trans. (Harmondsworth, Middx: Penguin, 1953), Book 2, pp. 92–3 and 118.

   Immediately after its publication in 1762 *Emile* was condemned and publicly burnt both in Catholic Paris, from which its author was forced to flee, and in Calvinist Geneva; chiefly because of the theological views which Rousseau expresses through the Vicar. But even then he continued to attend the Calvinist church at Motiers, where he was in exile; until the further scandal provoked by his *Lettres de la Montagne*, openly criticizing the Genevans, finally rendered it impossible. Rousseau was certainly quite serious about this adherence to the externals of one's people's religion.

73 'I foresee', Rousseau writes, 'how many readers will be surprised at seeing me trace the whole first age of my pupil without speaking to him of religion. At fifteen he did not yet know whether he had a soul. And perhaps at eighteen it is not yet time for him to learn it; for if he learns it sooner than he ought, he runs the risk of never knowing it': *Emile*, English trans. Allan Bloom (New York: Basic Books, 1979), p. 257.

74 Again: 'All my researchers have been sincere – I take as my witness that God
of peace Whom I adore and Whom I proclaim to you. But when I saw that
these researchers [into philosophical and dogmatic theology] were and always would be unsuccessful, and that I was being swallowed by in an ocean
without shores, I retraced my steps and restricted my faith to my primary
notions. I have never believed that God commanded me, under penalty of
going to hell, to be so learned. I therefore closed all the books. There is one
open to all eyes: it is the book of nature . . . Let us assume that I was born
on a desert island, that I have not seen any man other than myself, that I
have never learned what took place in olden times in some corner of the
world; nonetheless . . . if I make good use of my God-given faculties which
require no intermediary, I would learn of myself to know Him' (ibid.,
pp. 306–7).

75 J. Hoffmeister (ed.), *Dokumente zu Hegels Entwicklung* (Stuttgart, 1936), p. 430:
'I do not know whether, or to what extent, Hegel changed during his final year,
after I had left. But at any rate during the four years when I was in close contact
with him, metaphysics was not exactly Hegel's speciality. His hero was Rousseau, whose "Emile", "Contrat Social" and "Confessions" he was constantly
reading. He believed himself to be liberated by these writings from, as he put it,
the shackles of common prejudices and the tacit assumptions of the world.' At
this stage, Leutwein remarks, he still remained outside the circle of enthusiastic
Kantians at the Stift.

76 H.S. Harris, *Hegel's Development*, vol. I: *Towards the Sunlight (1770–1801)* (Lon-
don: Oxford University Press, 1972), p. 499. The full text is in H. Nohl, *Hegels
Theologische Jugendschriften* (Tübingen, 1907), as one of the 'Fragmente über
Volksreligion und Christentum'.

77 G.W.F. Hegel, 'The positivity of the Christian religion', Part II, §1, in *Early
Theological Writings*, trans. T. M. Knox (Philadelphia: University of Pennsylvania
Press, 1971), pp. 146–7.

78 G.W.F. Hegel, *Philosophy of Right*, trans. T. M. Knox (London: Oxford University Press, 1952), §270, p. 174.

79 'Isonomous freedom' is, of course, my phrase not Hegel's. But for a more
extended discussion of the following argument, see my *Hegel's Political Theology*
(Cambridge: Cambridge University Press, 1991).

80 G.W.F. Hegel, *The Phenomenology of Spirit*, trans. A.V. Miller (London: Oxford
University Press, 1977), pp. 126–38.

81 Ibid., ch. 8; cf. *Lectures on the Philosophy of Religion*, English trans. ed. Peter C.
Hodgson (Berkeley, Cal.: University of California Press, 1984) vol. I, pp. 153,
446.

82 Ibid., pp. 445–6.

83 Hegel, *The Phenomenology of Spirit*, pp. 131–2.

84 Ibid., pp. 132–5.

85 Ibid., pp. 135–8.

86 Richard Rothe, *Theologische Ethik* (Heidelberg, 1848), vol. III, §477. Rothe was
one of those who sought to reconcile the ideas of Hegel and Schleiermacher;
but he was something of a theological maverick, and his thinking has a supra-
naturalistic and apocalyptic quality which distances him in the end quite considerably from Hegel.

Chapter 3 'The Solidarity of the Shaken'

1 For a detailed account of the early years of the movement, see Gordon Skilling, *Charter 77 and Human Rights in Czechoslovakia* (London: George Allen & Unwin, 1981); which also includes a collection of Chartist documents, among them a number of tributes to Patočka.

2 Jan Patočka, 'What Charter 77 is and what it is not', in ibid., p. 217. The question of how 'political' the movement should become was naturally much debated within the Chartist community (cf. pp. 181–3). Patočka's particular vision was carried forward perhaps especially by Havel and by the (Bonhoefferian) Protestant philosopher Ladislav Hejdanek.

3 See Erazim Kohák, *Jan Patočka* (Chiacago, Ill.: University of Chicago Press, 1989): the only systematic discussion of Patočka's thought in English; also containing an English translation of a number of his essays.

4 'In short, one might say that Czech-speaking Bohemia possessed greatness just so long as it found a chance to put its particularity to the service of a universal mission as it did in the case of the eastward thrust of occidental Europe at the end of the Middle Ages. That is: It was great just so long as its specifically Czech qualities remained incidentally: that is the 'greatness' he would have his people seek to revive. See 'Qu'est-ce que les Tchèques?', in *L'Idée de l'Europe en Bohême* (Grenoble: J. Millon, 1991), pp. 19–20.

5 This work, also completed in 1975, has been translated into French, German, Italian, Spanish, Norwegian, but alas – apart from the final chapter, published in *Telos*, 30 (1976–7) – not yet into English. The French translation by Erika Abrams is published as *Essais hérétiques sur la philosophie de l'histoire* (Lagrasse: Editions Verdier, 1981); the German, *Ketzerische Essais zur Philosophie der Geschichte*, ed. Klaus Nellen and Jiři Němec (Stuttgart: Klett-Cotta Verlag, 1988); both of these include an Introduction by Paul Ricoeur. And cf. also two other works of Patočka's: *Platon et l'Europe* (Lagrasse: Editions Verdier, 1983); *Liberté et sacrifice* (Grenoble: J. Millon, 1990).

6 Patočka, *Essais hérétiques*, pp. 43 ff.

7 See the collection of Jan Patočka's essays, *Le Monde naturel et le mouvement de l'existence humaine* (Dordrecht: Kluwer Academic Publishers, 1988), which begins with the 1965 article.

8 Patočka, *Essais hérétiques*, pp. 29–31, 38, 51–4.

9 The following account is drawn from the three articles brought together in Part I of Patočka, *Le monde naturel et le mouvement de l'existence humaine*: 'Notes sur la préhistoire de la science du mouvement', 'Le monde naturel et la phénoménologie', 'Méditation sur "Le monde naturel comme problème philosophique" '; and from the concluding article of Part II, 'Le tout du monde et le monde de l'homme'.

10 Patočka, *Essais hérétiques*, p. 111. The whole passage from p. 108 onwards is concerned with the contrast between the categories sacred/profane and the categories authentic/inauthentic.

11 Cf. the discussion of Babylonian mythology in ibid., pp. 32–6.

12 Patočka, *Le Monde naturel et le mouvement de l'existence humaine*, p. 10.

13 Ibid.; and cf. Patočka, *Essais hérétiques*, pp. 111–12.

14 Patočka, *Le Monde naturel et le mouvement de l'existence humaine*, p. 11.

15 Ibid., pp. 43–4.

16 Patočka, *Essais hérétiques*, pp. 46–7.

17 Patočka, *Le Monde naturel et le mouvement de l'existence humaine*, pp. 120–2.

18 Patočka, *Essais hérétiques*, pp. 42–3, 48–50.

19 Ibid., pp. 52–4, 74–5.

20 Heraclitus, Fragment 114, in G.S. Kirk, *Heraclitus: The Cosmic Fragments* (Cambridge: Cambridge University Press, 1962), p. 48.

21 Fragment 80, ibid., p. 238. Heraclitus is also said to have criticized Homer, or rather Achilles as portrayed by Homer in the Iliad (xviii, 107), for expressing a desire that all strife, both among men and among the gods, should come to an end: on the grounds that this would mean the end of all existence. See Kirk, *Heraclitus*, pp. 242–4.

22 Patočka, *Essais hérétiques*, p. 56.

23 In the concluding passage of the *Essais hérétiques* (p. 146) Patočka also cites fragment no. 53, in which Heraclitus attributes to Polemos the traditional titles of Zeus: 'Polemos is the father of all and king of all, and some he shows as gods, others as men; some he makes slaves and others free' (Kirk, *Heraclitus*, p. 245). Somewhat speculatively, he (Patočka) takes the phrase 'some he shows as gods' as a statement about those who attain to this sort of perspective, from above.

24 Patočka, *Essais hérétiques*, p. 76.

25 Ibid., pp. 90–3.

26 Ibid., pp. 77–80.

27 Ibid., pp. 83–4.

28 Ibid., p. 134; Pierre Teilhard de Chardin, *Ecrits du temps de la guerre* (Paris: Grasset, 1965), p. 210.

29 Patočka, *Essais hérétiques*, p. 146; Ernst Jünger, 'Der Kampf als inneres Erlebnis' (1922), in *Werke* (Stuttgart: Ernst Klett Verlag), vol. 5, p. 101.

30 Patočka, *Essais hérétiques*, p. 141.

31 Cf. Kohák, *Jan Patočka*, pp. 16–17: 'In the 1950s, the period of his closest association with J.B. Souček, [Patočka] is said to have come close to joining the Czech Brethren Protestant church – and it was Souček, the theologian, who dissuaded him from it. Again, in the 1970s, perhaps under the influence of the grand Catholic theologian Josef Zvěrina, Patočka is said to have come close to a formal conversion to Catholicism . . . And yet [he] never took the formal step of a conversion, and, in a private lecture he gave in 1974, "Christianity and the 'Natural' World", he lets the hearer know why: his pre-reflective life-world, the 'natural' world of his life, simply did not include the experience of God.'

32 See the concluding pages of Patočka, 'Méditation sur "Le monde naturel comme problème philosophique" ', in *Le Monde naturel et le mouvement de l'existence humaine*, pp. 122–3. Also, on 'sacrifice': 'The dangers of technicization in science according to E. Husserl and the essence of technology as danger according to M. Heidegger', in Kohák, *Jan Patočka*, pp. 335–9.

33 Patočka, *Essais hérétiques*, pp. 116–17.

34 Patočka, 'The dangers of technicization in science', p. 339.

35 Patočka, *Essais hérétiques*, pp. 71, 102–3.

36 See especially Patočka, 'Méditation sur "Le monde naturel comme problème philosophique" ', pp. 91–101.

37 *Nietzsche*, English trans. ed. David Farrell Krell (San Francisco, Cal.: Harper & Row, 1982), vol. 4; *Nihilism*, p. 3.

38 Cf. Alan White's rather different three-fold classification, into 'completed', 'radical', and 'religious' nihilism: *Within Nietzsche's Labyrinth* (London: Routledge, 1990), ch. 2.

39 Nietzsche, *The Will To Power*, ed. Walter Kaufmann (New York: Vintage Books, 1968) §1.

40 See, for example, *The Antichrist*, §20.

41 Ibid., §153–6, 401, 461, 703.

42 Ibid., §114.

43 See also §§4, 55; and §437 on Pyrrho. But then note how it actually seems to be excluded in §1.

44 Mark Warren, *Nietzsche and Political Thought* (Cambridge, Mass.: MIT Press, 1991), pp. 242–6.

45 *Nietzsche*, vol. 4, pp. 205, 211.

46 Ibid., p. 201.

47 Martin Heidegger, 'The word of Nietzsche: "God is dead" ', in *The Question Concerning Technology and Other Essays*, trans. William Lovett (New York: Harper & Row, 1977), pp. 62–3.

48 On anti-metaphysical Scepticism as 'the last form' or 'the extreme form' of nihilism, see Nietzsche, *The Will to Power*, §§12, 15.

49 Ibid., §579. And compare Bonhoeffer's notion of a post-'metaphysical' Christianity, discussed above (pp. 85–7): Bonhoeffer, too, is deeply mistrustful of any evangelistic strategy appealing to such desires.

50 Ibid., §§401, 461. And cf. *The Twilight of the Idols*, English trans. R.J. Hollingdale (Harmondsworth, Middx: Penguin, 1968), chs 3 and 4. For a systematic discussion of Nietzsche's view of 'metaphysics', see, for instance, Richard Schacht, *Nietzsche* (London: Routledge & Kegan Paul, 1983), ch. 3.

51 The logic of this notion of 'nihilism' as being universally present, yet only in certain circumstances – partly thanks to its (Christian) intensification, partly thanks to the (post-Christian) breakdown of its self-concealment – becoming apparent, is closely parallel to Kierkegaard's analysis of 'despair' in *The Sickness Unto Death* (English trans. A. Hannay, Harmondsworth, Middx: Penguin, 1989). It is just that the evaluation of Christianity is reversed.

52 Mark Warren, for instance, in *Nietzsche and Political Thought*, seeks to defend Nietzsche from Heidegger's critique of his 'metaphysics', arguing that Heidegger has misinterpreted the Nietzschean doctrine – rendering it more arbitrarily dogmatic than it really is. But, however valid Warren's counter-argument may be, it hardly affects Heidegger's main point.

53 Nietzsche, *The Will to Power*, §1067.

54 Martin Heidegger *Gelassenheit* (Pfullingen, 1959), p. 33; English version trans. John M. Anderson and E. Hans Freund as *Discourse on Thinking* (New York: Harper & Row, 1966), p. 60. Cf. Hannah Arendt's discussion, in *The life of the Mind*, vol. 2: *Willing* (London: Secker & Warburg, 1978), ch. 15.

One should note Heidegger's historical situating of this dialogue between 'a scientist, a scholar, and a teacher' in the winter of 1944–5. This appears to be Heidegger's ultimate response to the genocidal catastrophe of the Third Reich – and positively invites critical assessment in that context!

55 F. Nietzsche, *Thus Spoke Zarathustra*, English trans. R.J. Hollingdale (Harmondsworth, Middx: Penguin, 1969), III: 'Of old and new law tables', §16.

On Nietzsche's affinity to Epictetus, see again Arendt, *Willing*, p. 170. As she remarks, however, in this concern for the perfect creativity of the *übermensch* he also obviously goes a long way beyond Epictetus – who is, besides, still essentially concerned with *prudential* arguments, addressed to everyman. As is Spinoza, too; the other philosophical predecessor to whom Nietzsche is most closely akin. (Hence, Spinoza remains a 'metaphysician'.)

56 F. Nietzsche, *The Gay Science*, English trans. Walter Kaufmann (New York: Vintage Books, 1974) §127.

57 F. Nietzsche, *The Twilight of the Idols*, English trans. (with *The Antichrist*) by R.J. Hollingdale (Harmondsworth, Middx: Penguin, 1969), III, §5.

58 Ibid., VI, §3.

59 On 'the will': Nietzsche, *The Will to Power*, §§46, 671, 692, 751. On 'the soul': ibid., §§480, 631. On 'the subject': ibid., §§390, 481, 488. On 'the ego': ibid., §370, *The Twilight of the Idols*, IV, §3.

60 When he speaks of this as the 'solution' to all the world's 'riddles', it is certainly the most paradoxical of solutions!

61 Nietzsche, *The Will to Power*, §§84, 95. 'Schopenhauer spoke of "will"; but nothing is more characteristic of his philosophy than the absence of all genuine willing.'

62 Ibid., §84.

63 F. Nietzsche, *The Gay Science*, English trans. W. Kaufmann (New York: Vintage, 1974), §357.

64 Cf. Martin Heidegger, *The Question Concerning Technology*, English trans. W. Lovitt (New York: Harper & Row), p. 90.

65 Martin Heidegger, *Letter on Humanism*, English trans. Frank A. Capuzzi with J. Glenn Gray in *Heidegger: Basic Writings*, ed. David Farrell Krell (London: Routledge & Kegan Paul, 1978): see esp. pp. 229–30.

66 So Hitler declared in *Mein Kampf* (Munich, 1933), p. 379: 'The movement entirely declines to take up any position on questions which lie outside the scope of its political work, or which lack any fundamental significance for it. Its task is not a religious reformation, but a political reorganization of our people.'

67 For a survey of the now rather large literature on Heidegger's politics – including the furious debate in France triggered by Victor Farias's prosecutorial *Heidegger et le Nazisme* (Lagrasse: Editions Verdier, 1987) – see Tom Rockmore, *On Heidegger's Nazism and Philosophy* (Hemel Hempsted, Herts.: Harvester Wheatsheaf, 1992). Rockmore identifies a three-fold 'turn' in Heidegger's political thinking: first a turn to Nazism, then a turn back away from Nazism as it actually existed – but only to an 'ideal form of Nazism'. To what extent, though, is that 'ideal form' still in any meaningful sense 'Nazi'? It is after all a thinking radically withdrawn into contemplative mode. Perhaps it is not exactly Nazi – but the basic point is that it nevertheless still does exclude any critique of Nazism from an alternative *political* standpoint: a quite arbitrary closure!

On the *völkisch* background to Heidegger, see Pierre Bourdieu, *L'Ontologie politique de Martin Heidegger* (Paris: Editions de Minuit, 1988). Richard Wolin's book, *The Politics of Being* (New York: Columbia University Press, 1990) is intended as 'a philosophical complement' to Bourdieu's essentially sociological study.

68 The interview appears in *Der Spiegel*, 31 May 1976. It had been conducted nearly ten years earlier, in September 1966, but was always intended for posthumous publication, largely as Heidegger's own attempt to put his side of the story about the events of 1933–4. The relevant passage, in full, runs as follows. He has been asked about the potential role of philosophy as an inspiration for political action now, in relation to what he himself has spoken of as the fateful rise of technocracy in our world. He replies: 'There is no prospect of philosophy's making any direct impact on the present state of the world. That goes not only for philosophy, but for any merely human enterprise. Only a God can save us. The only possibility left us is to prepare a readiness, through thought and poetry, for the appearance of the God, or for the absence of the God, as we go under: that we should go under, gazing upon the absent God.' Then, however, in response to the question whether this means that we may, by our thinking, draw this God close to us, he says no – 'the most we can do is awaken the readiness for expectancy'.

69 'The divine God': *Identity and Difference*, English trans. Joan Stambaugh (New York: Harper & Row, 1969), p. 72. 'The last God' appears in the (not yet translated) 1936 *Beiträge zur Philosophie (Vom Ereignis)*, ed. Friedrich-Wilhelm von Herrmann (Frankfurt a. M.: Vittorio Klostermann, 1989): especially in Part VII, but also in a pervasive way throughout the latter part of the work. And cf. also the discussion of *das Geviert*, 'the foursome': earth, sky, gods and mortals – in the essays, 'The Origin of the Work of Art', 'Building Dwelling Thinking', and 'The Thing'; English trans. Albert Hofstadter, in *Poetry, Language, Thought* (New York: Harper & Row, 1971). These gods, Leo Strauss remarks, occupy the space in Heidegger's thought where a proper political philosophy might be expected; excluding it: *Studies in Platonic Political Philosophy* (Chicago, Ill.: University of Chicago Press, 1983), p. 30.

70 For a biographical account of Heidegger's shifting relationship to his Catholic religious roots, see especially Hugo Ott, *Martin Heidegger: A Political Life* (London: Harper Collins, 1993).

71 This is not to deny the truth which is also expressed by Kathleen Raine, for instance, in *The Inner Journey of the Poet* (London: George Allen & Unwin, 1982), p. 64: 'The poets and painters of the Renaissance did not, surely, turn to the Pagan gods and their myths because these seemed more true, or even more beautiful than the Christian, but because, being freed from cult, the old gods had, paradoxically, become more valid as symbols of the primordial images; the archetypal figures of Apollo and Venus and the rest once more plastic in the imaginations of Botticelli, Spenser and Shakespeare; freed from cult, they moved once more towards their source.'

But one can scarcely base a whole *political* ethic solely on the requirements of *poetic* freedom, as Heidegger seems to want to do. The cultic communities remain a political reality, which cannot simply be by passed.

Chapter 4   The Virtues of Discernment

1 This is, admittedly, not how Heidegger himself uses the term 'reality'. Instead, he is preoccupied with its usage in metaphysics: the way in which metaphysics always understands itself as a study of the question of what is, or is not, ultimately 'real'. And so he presents his move beyond metaphysics as a wholesale dethroning of that question. Cf. Martin Heidegger, *Being and Time*, English trans. John Macquarrie and Edward Robinson (Oxford: Basil Blackwell, 1962) §43.
   But what other word is there for what discernment discerns as the revelatory truth of historical actuality?

2 Cf. Heidegger on truth as *a-létheia*. He certainly does not want to use the term 'subjectivity', with all its old metaphysical connotations. But his notion of *a-létheia* as *Erschlossenheit*, 'disclosedness' – 'the most primordial phenomenon of truth' (*Being and Time*, p. H220), 'truth' as a condition of one's being, 'being in the truth' – clearly does come very close to the Kierkegaardian concept. Just as his account of the reduction of 'truth' to the 'present- at-head' nature of an 'assertion' corresponds to Kierkegaard's concept of 'objectivity' (ibid., §44, esp. pp. H223–5: the metaphor of 'the present-at-hand' and 'the ready-to-hand' helps bring out the way in which ideas here are, as it were, reduced to commodities – with their *adaequatio intellectus et rei* functioning in effect as their cash value – in the Marxist phrase, a sort of 'commodity fetishism').

3 In what follows I leave it in the German, so as to advert to the intimate link with *Erschlossenheit* (see preceding note).

4 Heidegger, *Being and Time*, p. H305; and cf. p. H297.

5 Ibid., p. H186.

6 Ibid., p. H189.

7 Søren Kierkegaard, *The Concept of Anxiety*, English trans. Reidar Thomte and Albert Anderson (Princeton, N.J.: Princeton University Press, 1980).

8 Heidegger, *Being and Time*, pp. H283–6. Macquarrie and Robinson, in their concern to preserve something of the colloquial flavour of the German, translate *Nichtigkeit* as 'nullity'. But this also seems rather inappropriately contemptuous.

9 'The expression *Gerede* is not to be used here in a "disparaging" signification', Heidegger remarks (ibid., p. H167). It is a necessity of life, serving many genuinely useful purposes: only, not the articulation of philosophical truth.

10 Ibid., p. H266.

11 Ibid., p. H263.

12 Ibid.

13 See above, p. 45.

14 Thus what is really gained by his sweeping identification of 'completed metaphysics' with 'technology', in *Überwindung der Metaphysik*, x; English trans. *The End of Philosophy* (New York: Harper & Row, 1973)? Of course, one can always draw connections betwen metaphysical theory and technological practice – but that is quite another matter.

15 G.W.F. Hegel, *Lectures on the Philosophy of History*, English trans. J. Sibree (New York: Dover, 1956), p. 19.

16 For a more extended discussion of this, see my *Hegel's Political Theology* (Cambridge: Cambridge University Press, 1991), ch. 1.

17 G.W.F. Hegel, *The Phenomenology of Spirit*, English trans. A.V. Miller (London: Oxford University Press, 1977), para. 199 (my emphasis).

18 Ibid., para. 197.

19 Ibid., para. 200.

20 Ibid., para. 199.

21 Ibid., para. 200.

22 Ibid., para. 202.

23 Ibid., para. 204.

24 Ibid., para. 205.

25 F. Nietzsche, Fragment dated 1882–4, in the Kröner edition of Nietzsche's *Werke* (Leipzig: Kröner, 1919), vol. XII, part II, §274. See the discussion by Henri Birault, 'Beatitude in Nietzsche', English trans. in David Allison (ed.), *The New Nietzsche: Contemporary Styles of Interpretation* (London and Cambridge, Mass.: MIT Press, 1985).

26 F. Nietzsche, *Ecce Homo*, English trans. W. Kaufmann (New York: Vintage, 1969), p. 273.

27 Cf. Paul Ricoeur, *Freud and Philosophy: An Essay on Interpretation*, English trans. (New Haven, Conn.: Yale University Press, 1970), Bk III, ch. 3.

28 F. Nietzsche, *On the Genealogy of Morals*, II, §16; English trans. W. Kaufmann (New York: Vintage, 1969), p. 84.

29 Ibid., II, §17, p. 86.

30 Ibid., II, §14, pp. 81–2; and cf. §10.

31 Ibid., III, §§24, 27.

32 The imagery operates at various levels: in the religion of the original Zarathustra, the eagle represented the light-principle Ormuzd, the snake represents Ahriman, the principle of darkness. Their reconciliation takes us 'beyond good and evil'.

33 F. Nietzsche, *Thus Spoke Zarathustra*, English trans. R.J. Hollingdale (Harmondsworth, Middx: Penguin, 1969), p. 115.

34 F. Nietzsche, *The Will to Power*, ed. Walter Kaufmann (New York: Vintage Books, 1968), §404.

35 Nietzsche, *On the Genealogy of Morals*, III, §16, p. 128.

36 Ibid., III, §15, p. 126.

37 Ibid., pp. 126–7.

38 Nietzsche, *Ecce Homo*, p. 327.

39 Cf., for example, F. Nietzsche, *Beyond Good and Evil*, English trans. R.J. Hollingdale (Harmondsworth, Middx: Penguin, 1973), §4, p. 17. Here Nietzsche claims this as an important aspect of his originality, his having been liberated from the prevailing 'prejudices of the philosophers': 'The falseness of a judgement is to us not necessarily an objection to a judgement: it is here that our new language perhaps appears strangest. The question is to what extent it is life-advancing, life-preserving, species-preserving, perhaps even species-breeding; and our fundamental tendency is to assert that the falsest judgements (to which synthetic judgements *a priori* belong) are the most indispensable to us, that without granting as true the fictions of logic, without measuring reality against the purely invented world of the unconditional and self-identical, without a continual falsification of the world by means of numbers, mankind could not live – that to renounce false judgements would be to renounce life, would be to deny life.'

However, it all depends on what exactly is meant by 'falseness' here. If the examples he gives are indeed necessarily 'false', this would only be in a relatively pedantic sense. No doubt there is good reason to be suspicious of the perennial temptation to pedantry which afflicts philosophers. The falsehood which prevents us from taking to heart those aspects of reality that are *emotionally* most difficult, on the other hand, is quite another matter.

40 Nietzsche, *On the Genealogy of Morals*, III, §18, p. 136.

41 Ibid., i, §10, p. 37. The full text runs: 'When the noble mode of valuation blunders and sins against reality, it does so in respect of the sphere with which it is *not* sufficiently familiar, against a real knowledge of which it has indeed inflexibly guarded itself: in some circumstances it misunderstands the sphere it despises, that of the common man, of the lower orders; on the other hand, one should remember that, even supposing that the affect of contempt, of looking down from a superior height, *falsifies* the image of that which it despises, it will at any rate be a much less serious falsification than that perpetrated on its opponent – *in effigie* of course – by the submerged hatred, the vengefulness of the impotent. There is indeed too much carelessness, too much taking lightly, too much looking away and impatience involved in contempt, even too much joyfulness, for it to be able to transform its object into a real caricature and monster.'

My question is simply whether there is not in this text perhaps a bit 'too much carelessness, too much taking lightly' of the actual problems potentially involved in such light-mindedness.

42 Ryszard Kapuscinski, *The Emperor*, English trans. (London: Picador, 1984).

43 Nietzsche, *Beyond Good and Evil*, §294, p. 199.

44 See Donald N. Levine, *Wax and Gold: Tradition and Innovation in Ethiopian Culture* (Chicago, Ill.: University of Chicago Press, 1965), pp. 183–7.

45 Ibid., pp. 167–77.

46 Levine, *Wax and Gold*, pp. 11 and 155, suggests an interesting comparison with the culture of imperial Japan; as perhaps an even more extreme example of the same.

Haile Selassie was indeed a great exponent of the art of numinous self-presentation. And, of course, in the cult of Rastafari he has become God incarnate: the ultimate legendary symbol of aristocratic values, to a people seeking emancipation from their heritage of slavery. Nor did he reject the worship of the Rastafarians. The story is perhaps apocryphal; but I can think of nothing more beautifully ironical than the remark he is supposed to have made, on the occasion of his state visit to Jamaica, to those who urged him to disillusion the Rastas and, as a good son of the Church, to make it clear that he was, after all, only a man: 'Who am I to disturb their faith?' Who indeed?

47 Kapuscinski, *The Emperor*, p. 45.

48 Alasdair MacIntyre, *After Virtue* (London: Duckworth, 1985), p. 223. He sharply differentiates his notion of tradition from that of 'conservative political theorists': 'Characteristically such theorists have followed Burke in contrasting tradition with reason and the stability of tradition with conflict. Both contrasts obfuscate. For all reasoning takes place within the context of some traditional mode of thought, transcending through criticism and invention the limitations of what had hitherto been reasoned in that tradition: this is as true of modern

physics as of medieval logic. Moreover when a tradition is in good order it is always partially constituted by an argument about the goods the pursuit of which gives to that tradition its particular point and purpose . . . Indeed when a tradition becomes Burkean, it is always dying or dead' (pp. 220–1).

49 This point is also closely related to Walter Benjamin's critique of modernity as an age rich in information yet deeply impoverished in 'experience' (*Erfahrung*, by which he means precisely experience incorporated into a depth-giving context of tradition – as opposed to *Erlebnis*, experience outside such a context); an age therefore largely unable, for instance, to sustain the popular craft of story-telling, in the manner of the folk tale or other orally transmitted forms. See his essay, 'The storyteller: reflections on the work of Nikolai Leskov', in *Illuminations*, ed. Hannah Arendt (London: Fontana/Collins, 1973).

50 John Milbank, *Theology and Social Theory* (Oxford: Basil Blackwell, 1990), p. 5.

51 Ibid., ch. 11.

52 Ibid., p. 9.

53 Ibid., ch. 12. (I have already referred to Arendt's discussion of Augustine: above, pp. 34–5, 37, 63).

54 Ibid., p. 419.

55 Ibid., p. 416.

56 Ibid., p. 403; and cf. pp. 364–9.

57 Ibid., pp. 417–22. Hence, he completely rejects traditional 'political Augustinianism' – of the sort which came to its purest practical embodiment in the empire of Charlemagne.

58 G.W.F. Hegel, *Faith and Knowledge*, English trans. Walter Cerf and H.S. Harris (Albany, N.T.: SUNY Press, 1977), pp. 150–2.

59 G.W.F. Hegel, *Philosophy of Right*, English trans. T.M. Knox (London: Oxford University Press, 1952), Preface, p. 10; and, in this layout, *Encyclopaedia Logic*, English trans. William Wallace (London: Oxford University Press, 1975), Preface, p. 9.

60 *Encyclopaedia Logic*, §142, p. 200.

61 Hegel's critique of Lutheran tradition is more often implicit than explicit. But cf., for example, his formula in the *Lectures on the Philosophy of History*, English trans. J. Sibree (New York: Dover, 1956), p. 438: 'Protestantism had introduced the *principle* of Subjectivity [i.e. free-spiritedness] importing religious emancipation and inward harmony, but accompanying this with the *belief* in Subjectivity as Evil, and in a power [adverse to man's highest interests] whose embodiment is "the World".' For him, it is that persistent 'belief' that has to be transcended, for the sake of the 'principle' which it inhibits.

62 Milbank, *Theology and Social Theory*, pp. 153–7.

63 Ibid., pp. 148–53. What Hamann and Herder represent is 'a different, "counter" modernity, a phantom Christian modernity which has never been . . . a Christianization of the Renaissance' – in that sense 'a continuation of the Baroque' – by-passing the Enlightenment. Both of them developed what they themselves called a 'metacritique' of Kant's *Critique of Pure Reason*. And as Milbank puts it, ' "Metacritique" does not imply a further critique founded on Kant's initial effort, but rather a *denial* of the possibility of Kant's critical endeavour, from a critical point of view that is a more genuine and secure one. This point of view is that of language. If it is true that we only think in language, then it is simply

not possible to investigate our thinking instrument – to say what it can or cannot think in advance of its deployment.' Against the universalism of Kantian Reason, they pitted the vocation of each distinct linguistic culture to express its own particular corporate vision of reality.

64 Ibid., pp. 157–73.

65 See above, pp. 108–14.

66 Nietzsche's most explicit statement to this effect is perhaps *Human, All Too Human*, English trans. Helen Zimmern (New York: Gordon Press, 1974), §438. But it is a judgement which is implicit throughout his work.

67 Gilles Deleuze, *Nietzsche and Philosophy* (London: Athlone Press, 1983), p. 195. For another critique of Deleuze, see S. Houlgate, *Hegel, Nietzsche and the Criticism of Metaphysics* (Cambridge: Cambridge University Press), pp. 5–8, 24–5.

68 Ibid., p. 8.

69 Ibid., p. 162.

70 On Alexandre Kojève, see Stanley Rosen, *Hermeneutics as Politics* (London: Oxford University Press, 1987), ch. 3. Deleuze's book was originally published in France in 1962.

71 F. Nietzsche, *The Twilight of the Idols*, trans. R.J. Hollingdale, with *The Antichrist* (Harmondsworth, Middx: Penguin, 1968), 'The Problem of Socrates', §5, p. 31.

72 Cf. Hugh Tomlinson, 'Nietzsche on the edge of town: Deleuze and reflexivity', in D.F. Krell and D. Wood (eds), *Exceedingly Nietzsche* (London: Routledge, 1988).

73 Hegel, *Phenomenology of Spirit*, pp. 111–19.

74 Deleuze, *Nietzsche and Philosophy*, pp. 9–10, 80–2.

75 The actual phrase, 'religion of humanity' occurs for instance in G.W.F. Hegel, *Lectures on the Philosophy of Religion*, English trans. ed. Peter C. Hodgson (Berkeley, Cal.: University of California Press, 1984–87) vol. II, pp. 457, 642. He also speaks of this religion as the religion of beauty, or of freedom.

76 Ibid., pp. 464–7, 644–6, 650, 753.

77 Hegel, *Lectures on the Philosophy of History*, p. 239 (translation adapted).

78 See Hegel, *Lectures on the Philosophy of Religion*, vol. II, pp. 531–2.

79 Ibid., p. 664.

80 F. Nietzsche, 'The Greek State: preface to an unwritten book' (1871), English trans. in *Complete Works*, ed. Oscar Levy (London and Edinburgh: T.N. Foulis, 1911) vol. II.

81 Ibid., p. 7.

82 Ibid., p. 13.

83 Ibid., p. 9.

84 Hegel, *Lectures on the Philosophy of History*, p. 457; and cf. p. 15.

85 F. Nietzsche, 'On the Use and Disadvantage of History for Life', §8, English trans. R.J. Hollingdale, in *Untimely Meditations* (Cambridge: Cambridge University Press, 1983).

86 Ibid., Preface.

87 Ibid., §8.

88 Nietzsche, *Thus Spoke Zarathustra*, Part IV, 'The Awakening' and 'The Ass Festival', pp. 319–26. And cf. also Part III, 'The Spirit of Gravity', p. 212; where the ass appears alongside that other symbolic beast of burden, the camel of the first section of Part I, 'Of the Three Metamorphoses', pp. 54–6.

89 Deleuze, *Nietzsche and Philosophy*, pp. 180–6.

90 Nietzsche, *The Will to Power*, §95. Hegel and Goethe were of course friends.

91 Mircea Eliade, *Cosmos and History: The Myth of the Eternal Return*, English trans. (New York: Harper & Row, 1959), p. 152. And cf. the conclusion to his essay on the popular culture of his own native Romania, relating the trans-historical quality of Romanian folk-Christianity to the experience of a people situated 'at the very crossroads of invasions': 'The Clairvoyant Lamb', in *Zalmoxis: The Vanishing God*, English trans. (Chicago, Ill.: University of Chicago Press, 1972), pp. 254–5. The basic point is common to a large number of critics – including, not least, Hannah Arendt. But it is good to hear it for once from a Romanian.

92 Eliade's main critical discussion of Marxism is in *Mephistopheles and Androgyne: Studies in Religious Myth and Symbol*, English trans. (New York: Sheed & Ward, 1965).

93 Eliade, *Cosmos and History*, p. 159.

94 Mircea Eliade, *The Sacred and the Profane* (New York: Harcourt Brace Jovanovich, 1959), p. 164; see also *Cosmos and History*, p. 142.

95 Eliade, *Cosmos and History*, p. 162. On the 'fallen-ness' of modernity, cf. especially *The Sacred and the Profane*, pp. 212–3.

96 Mircea Eliade, *Images and Symbols*, English trans. (New York: Sheed & Ward, 1969), p. 120; and cf. *Patterns in Comparative Religion*, English trans. (New York: World Publishing Co., Meridian Books, 1963), p. 454.

97 Mircea Eliade, *Yoga: Immortality and Freedom*, English trans. (New York: Pantheon Books, 1958), p. xiii.

98 This definition is originally Judith Shklar's. Richard Rorty, *Contingency, Irony and Solidarity* (Cambridge: Cambridge University Press, 1989), p. xv.

99 Ibid., p. 78.

100 Ibid., p. 102.

101 *Platons Lehre von der Wahrheit* (Bern: Francke, 1954), p. 42; English trans. in W. Barrett and H.D. Aiken (eds), *Philosophy in the Twentieth Century* (New York and London: Harper & Row, 1962), vol. III.

102 Plato, *Republic*, 509b.

103 Plotinus, *The Enneads*, trans. S. MacKenna (London: Faber & Faber, 1969): on the Good beyond Being, V, 3.17.12–14; on the Good beyond the Idea of the Good, VI, 9.6.55–7.

104 Ibid., IV, 9; pp. 364–8.

105 Ibid., V, 3:13; p. 395.

106 Ibid., p. 63: ' "Let us flee then to the beloved Fatherland": this is the soundest counsel. But what is this flight? How are we to gain the open sea? For Odysseus is surely a parable to us when he commands the flight from the sorceries of Circe or Calypso – not content to linger for all the pleasure offered to his eyes and all the delights of sense filling his days.

'The Fatherland to us is There whence we have come, and There is the Father.

'What then is our course, what the manner of our flight? This is not a journey for the feet; the feet bring us only from land to land; nor need you think of coach or ship to carry you away; all this order of things you must set aside and refuse to see: you must close the eyes and call instead upon another vision which is to be waked within you, a vision, the birth-right of all, which few turn to use.'

107 See, for instance, Wolfhart Pannenberg, 'The appropriation of the philosophical concept of God as a dogmatic problem of early Christian theology', in *Basic Questions in Theology*, vol. 2, English trans. (London: SCM Press, 1971).

108 Jewish 'Wisdom' literature is one source – which also obviously lies in the background to Philo: the Logos is readily identifiable with Sophia, the Wisdom of God. The actual term 'Logos' also plays a major role in Stoic theory, and is in general a commonplace of Hellenistic philosophical theology.

109 See Frank Tobin, *Meister Eckhart: Thought and Language* (Philadelphia: University of Pennsylvania Press, 1986), p. 70.

110 Sermon 5b, in *Meister Eckhart: The Essential Sermons, Commentaries, Treatises and Defense*, trans. E. Colledge and B. McGinn (New York: Paulist Press, 1981), p. 184 (insertions by Tobin).

111 Sermon 52, ibid., p. 202.

112 See Tobin, *Meister Eckhart*, pp. 35–43.

113 Sermon 5b, ibid., pp. 123–4.

114 Sermon 29, ibid., p. 102.

115 It is present in the work of the Pseudo-Dionysius, which is the most important seminal influence on the mysticism and 'negative theology' of the West. On the Eastern tradition, see V. Lossky, *The Vision of God* (London: Faith Press, 1963).

116 On the various issues raised here, see Tobin, *Meister Eckhart*, pp. 126–40.

117 Sermon 10, ibid., p. 136.

118 Ibid., pp. 90–4.

119 See Hugo Rahner, *Die Gottesgeburt. Die Lehre der Kirchenväter von der Geburt Christi aus dem Herzen der Kirche und der Gläubigen*, in *Symbole der Kirche* (Salzburg: O. Müller, 1964).

120 Sermon 6, Colledge and McGinn, *Meister Eckhart*, p. 187.

121 See Tobin, *Meister Eckhart*, p. 98, for various examples.

122 Sermon 75, ibid.

123 Sermon 39, Tobin, p. 99.

124 See Cyril O'Regan, 'Hegelian philosophy of religion and Eckhartian mysticism', in David Kolb (ed.), *New Perspectives on Hegel's Philosophy of Religion* (Albany, N.Y.: SUNY Press, 1992).

125 G.W.F. Hegel, *Lectures on the History of Philosophy*, English trans. (London: Kegan Paul, Trench, Trübner & Co., 1892), vol. II, p. 429. This use of imagery tends to disguise abstraction – still only *abstractly* loosened up by reference to the ineffable transcendence of the One: Hegel actually translates *nous* in this context as *Verstand*. Cf., for example, his general comments on 'mysticism' in the *Encyclopaedia Logic*, §82, p. 121.

126 Hegel, *Phenomenology of Spirit*, p. 493.

127 On the evolution of Hegel's critique of *Moralität*, see for instance Allen W. Wood, *Hegel's Ethical Thought* (Cambridge: Cambridge University Press, 1990), ch. 7. In the *Phenomenology of Spirit*, one does in fact find a certain revaluation upwards of *Moralität*: it is here viewed as a characteristic phenomenon of modernity, and as marking an advance over the naïveté (at least) of ancient *Sittlichkeit*. But he is still looking here for its overcoming in a higher restoration of *Sittlichkeit* – hence the immediate transition to his discussion of religion: as the domain in which, above all others, this has to be worked out.

128 George Armstrong Kelly – in his *Idealism, Politics and History* (Cambridge: Cambridge University press, 1969), pp. 187–8 – adopts the term 'Fichtianity' from a letter written by one of Fichte's contemporaries, the legal philosopher Erhard, in 1796: 'God forbid that Fichte should be persecuted, or else there might very well arise a Fichtianity a hundred times worse than Christianity.'

Kant himself, as an old man in 1799, formally declared that he considered Fichte's *Wissenschaftlehre* 'a wholly untenable system'. However, he never dealt with Fichte's claims in any detail; and, besides, Fichte's more prophetic writings are of a later date.

Hegel's main discussions of Fichte, in *The Difference Between the Systems of Fichte and Schelling* (1801) and *Faith and Knowledge* (1802), also pre-date these writings. In his *Lectures on the History of Philosophy*, on the other hand, he still focuses on Fichte's earlier work – casually dismissing the prophetic later writings as entirely lacking in philosophical interest.

129 J.G. Fichte, *Addresses to the German Nation*, English trans. (New York: Harper Torchbooks, 1968), p. 108. The fervour of this nationalism also, of course, needs to be understood against the background of the immediate historical circumstances. When Fichte first delivered these addresses, in 1807–8, it was in a Berlin occupied by the troops of Napoleon. Fichte's pride in German 'spirituality' is also a reaction to his people's actual humiliation, from a more worldly point of view.

130 Lectures delivered in 1804–5; translated in *The Popular Works of Johann Gottlob Fichte*, ed. W. Smith (London, 1889), vol II.

131 See also his letter to Jacobi, 31 March 1804: 'I believe that I have understood our age as that of the absolute corruption of all ideas. Nevertheless, I am of good cheer; for I know that new life can come only from complete decay.' And in 1807 we actually find him announcing that the corner has just been turned: 'Time', he declares at the beginning of his *Addresses*, 'is taking giant strides with us more than with any other age since the history of the world began. At some point within the three years that have gone by since my interpretation of the present age that epoch has come to an end . . .' (!)

132 Cf. the discussion in Kelly, *Idealism, Politics and History*, pp. 226–32.

133 Fichte, *Addresses to the German Nation*, pp. 16–17.

134 Isaiah Berlin, *Two Concepts of Liberty* (London: Oxford University Press, 1958). Berlin here of course lumps Hegel together with Fichte.

135 Emmanuel Levinas, *Otherwise than Being, or Beyond Essence*, English trans. (The Hague: Martinus Nijhoff, 1981), p. 5.

136 Ibid., p. 14.

137 Ibid., pp. 10, 14–15.

138 Ibid., p. 113 (my emphasis).

139 Ibid., pp. 117–18.

140 Ibid., pp. 111–12.

141 Levinas introduces the term in *En découvrant l'existence avec Husserl et Heidegger* (Paris: Vrin, 1967), pp. 187–203.

142 Emmanuel Levinas, *Totality and Infinity*, English trans. (The Hague: Martinus Nijhoff, 1979), p. 103. And cf. p. 292: 'The concept of a Good beyond Being and beyond the beatitude of the One announces a rigorous doctrine of creation, which would be neither a negation nor a limitation nor an emanation of the

One.' In the same way, for instance, he also rejects Plotinus's rhetorical longing for a return to the One, as to our 'fatherland' (as in the quotation given above, note 106): 'The metaphysical desire does not long to return, for it is desire for a land not of our birth, for a land foreign to every nature, which has not been our fatherland and to which we shall never betake ourselves' (ibid., pp. 33–4).

143 Ibid., pp. 42–8. The criticism of Heidegger runs right through Levinas's work. Cf., for example, ibid., pp. 46–7: 'The "egoism" of ontology is maintained even when, denouncing Socratic philosophy as already forgetful of Being and already on the way to the notion of the 'subject' and technological power, Heidegger finds in Presocratism thought as obedience to the truth of Being . . . Even though it opposes the technological passion issued forth from the forgetting of Being hidden by existents, Heideggerian ontology, which subordinates the relationship with the Other to the relation of Being in general, remains under obedience to the anonymous, and leads inevitably to another power, to imperialist domination, to tyranny. Tyranny is not the pure and simple extension of technology to reified men.'

   For a more detailed discussion of Levinas's relationship to Heidegger, see Adriaan Peperzak, 'Einige Thesen zur Heidegger-Kritik von Emmanuel Levinas', in A. Gethmann-Siefert and O. Pöggeler (eds), *Heidegger und die praktische Philosophie* (Frankfurt: Suhrkamp, 1988). Also, Jacques Derrida's essay, 'Violence and Metaphysics', in *Writing and Difference* (Chicago: University of Chicago Press, 1978); but Derrida's defence of Heidegger does seem to me to be vitiated by his largely ignoring what Levinas is ultimately reacting against, the only half-sublimated völkisch element in Heidegger's thought.

144 Levinas, *Otherwise than Being*, p. 129.

145 Levinas, *Totality and Infinity*, p. 196. (He subsequently recoils from appeal to 'experience'. See the closing lines of 'Signature', in *Difficult Freedom*, English trans. Sean Hand (London: Athlone Press, 1990), p. 295: 'The ontological language which *Totality and Infinity* still uses . . . is henceforth avoided. And the analyses themselves refer not to the *experience* in which a subject always thematizes what he equals, but to the *transcendence* in which he answers for that which his intentions have not encompassed.'

146 This is not, so far as I am aware, an affinity which Levinas himself remarks. And yet is not what Levinas describes as the 'active', or 'knowing' – and to that extent unethical – self ultimately identical with the 'unreal' self from which the *Bodhisattva* is released? Is not Levinas's move 'beyond Being' ultimately identical with the Buddhist transcendence of *samsara*, beyond the 'illusion' of a self which appears as one distinct being among others? The wisdom (*prajna*) of the *Bodhisattva*, too, is inextricably bound up with a consuming compassion (*karuna*) towards, or self-identification with, all sentient beings: for the *Bodhisattva* there can be no liberation, no final entry into *Nirvana*, until *all* are liberated.

147 Cf. Emmanuel Levinas, 'God and philosophy', in *Collected Philosophical Papers*, English trans. (Dordrecht: Martinus Nijhoff, 1987), pp. 158–9.

148 Ibid., p. 155.

149 The curious way in which he writes, in this particular connection, always only from an explicitly masculine point of view – of *l'Aimée*, of paternity, filiality,

fraternity – has naturally elicited considerable discussion: see, for example, the articles by Tina Chanter and Alison Ainley in *The Provocation of Levinas*, ed. Robert Bernasconi and David Wood (London: Routledge, 1988), and those by Luce Iragaray, Catherine Chalier and Tina Chanter in *Re-reading Levinas*, ed. Robert Bernasconi and Simon Critchley (London: Athlone Press, 1991).

150 Levinas, *Totality and Infinity*, p. 306.

151 See especially ibid., pp. 213–14.

152 For another discussion of Levinas on Hegel, see Robert Bernasconi, 'Levinas face to face – with Hegel', *Journal of the British Society for Phenomenology*, vol. 13, no. 3, October 1982; and cf. Levinas's essay 'Hegel and the Jews' in *Difficult Freedom*.

153 Levinas, *Otherwise than Being*, p. 103; and see also ibid., p. 79.

154 Levinas speaks of 'the allergy . . . on which the Hegelian dialectic rests' (*Totality and Infinity*, p. 203).

155 Ibid., p. 84.

156 Ibid., pp. 84 ff, 208.

157 Levinas, *Difficult Freedom*, p. 295.

158 See Levinas's essay 'Simone Weil against the Bible', in *Difficult Freedom*. What they have in common is their radical Platonism. Besides Weil's injustice to Judaism, however, there are also two other complicating factors. In the first place, Levinas chooses to take the term 'rootedness' only in its *völkisch*, 'pagan' sense – and so presents himself as a positive advocate of uprootedness. But, as we have seen, Weil is also quite capable of doing the same, on occasion.

   And secondly, he criticizes her paradoxical love of 'necessity' – the theologized Stoic (Epictetian) element in her thought, so to speak; (the *amor fati* she has in common with Nietzsche). 'God's supernatural love, in Simone Weil's Christianity', he writes, 'if it goes beyond a compassion for the creature's misery, can signify only love of evil itself. God loved evil; this perhaps – we can say it with infinite respect – is the most fearful vision of this Christianity and the whole metaphysics of Passion. But our respect is mingled with a strong sense of dread. Our path lies elsewhere.'

159 This is my response, for instance, to John Milbank's criticism of Levinas: *Theology and Social Theory*, p. 306 – which is interesting, since otherwise Milbank is so close to Levinas. Thus, like Levinas, he too is essentially intent on identifying a tradition that might serve as an effective carrier of radical generosity. And yet here he nevertheless clings on to 'ontology', for the sake of a more 'incarnational' vision, in rejection of Levinas.

160 Although the basic argument in this chapter has been pre-theological in character, and hence in principle quite independent of Christian faith, from a Christian point of view the question certainly arises whether it might not *also* be taken as an echo of the Trinity? (That is, with the virtue of transcendent generosity corresponding, primarily, to the first person of the Trinity; the virtue of free-spiritedness to the second; and the virtue of flair for tradition to the third?)

   In fact, it surely could.

Chapter 5 'Antipolitics'

1 Václav Havel, 'The power of the powerless', English trans. P. Wilson, in *Living in Truth*, ed. Jan Vladislav (London: Faber & Faber, 1987), pp. 117–22.
2 Ibid., p. 118.
3 Hannah Arendt, *On Revolution* (Harmondsworth, Middx: Penguin, 1973), p. 273.
4 Ibid., pp. 250–1. The Jeffersonian spirit also lives on today, for instance, in Benjamin Barber's work. See his *Strong Democracy: Participatory Politics for a New Age* (Berkeley: University of California Press, 1984). Barber is anxious to distance himself from what he calls Arendt's 'republican nostalgia' (p. 118); but in the end simply seems to represent a more populist version of the same.
5 Ibid., p. 279.
6 Ibid., p. 280.
7 Ibid., p. 278 (my emphasis).
8 Simone Weil, 'Note sur la suppression générale des partis politiques', in *Ecrits de Londres et dernières lettres* (Paris: Gallimard, 1957), pp. 126–48. The immediate occasion appears to have been the official reconstituting of the Socialist Party, and their request to de Gaulle that 'the representatives of the various political parties and trade union movements that had been in the Resistance since June 1940 be allowed to participate in clandestine political activities': see Simone Pétrement, *Simone Weil*, English trans. (London and Oxford: Mowbrays, 1976), p. 504.
9 Weil, *Ecrits de Londres*, p. 132.
10 Ibid., p. 133.
11 Ibid., p. 135.
12 Ibid., p. 141.
13 Ibid., p. 126.
14 Simone Weil, *The Need for Roots*, English trans. A.F. Wills (London: Routledge & Kegan Paul, 1952), p. 26.
15 Was Havel wrong not to put himself at the head of his own political party? The end-result was a dramatic loss of power: he was quite soon reduced to little more than a mere figurehead as president, contributing the lustre of his prestige to a regime many of whose decisions (e.g. with regard to the 'lustration' law, the maintenance of the Czech arms trade, the secession of Slovakia) he deplored.

  During its brief history as a state, Czechoslovakia produced two philosopher-rulers. And certainly by any conventional standards Masaryk was very much more successful in the role than Havel has been. The question remains, though, whether perhaps this merely serves to illustrate the ultimate vanity–*sub specie aeternitatis*–of conventional standards?
16 Havel, *Living in Truth*: 'Politics and conscience', pp. 155–7.
17 George Konrad, *Antipolitics*, English trans. Richard E. Allen (London: Quartet Books, 1984), p. 92.
18 Ibid., p. 95.
19 Ibid., pp. 230–1.
20 Robert Nozick, *Anarchy, State and Utopia* (Oxford: Basil Blackwell, 1974), p. ix.

21 Although cf. Nozick's later *Philosophical Explanations* (Cambridge, Mass.: Harvard University Press, 1981), pp. 498–504.

22 Milan Kundera, *The Book of Laughter and Forgetting*, English trans. Michael Henry Heim (Harmondsworth, Middx: Penguin, 1980), p. 3.

23 See, for instance, Gerhard Besier, *Der SED-Staat und die Kirche* (Munich: C. Bertelsmann, 1994).

24 For a comprehensive contemporary account, see Klaus Ehring and Martin Dallwitz, *Schwerter zu Pflugscharen: Friedensbewegung in der DDR* (Hamburg: Rowohlt, 1982).

Index